FROM SH!TSHOW TO AFTERGLOW

FROM SH!TSHOW TO AFTERGLOW

Putting Life Back Together When It All Falls Apart

ARIEL MEADOW STALLINGS

SEAL PRESS

New York

Seal Press
Hachette Book Group
1290 Avenue of the Americas, New York, NY 10104
sealpress.com @sealpress

Printed in the United States of America
First Edition: June 2020

Published by Seal Press, an imprint of Perseus Books, LLC, a subsidiary of Hachette Book
Group, Inc. The Seal Press name and logo is a trademark of the Hachette Book Group.

Some names and identifying details have been changed to protect the privacy of
individuals.

The Hachette Speakers Bureau provides a wide range of authors for speaking events.
To find out more, go to www.hachettespeakersbureau.com or call (866) 376-6591.

The publisher is not responsible for websites (or their content) that are not owned by
the publisher.

Print book interior design by Jeff Williams.

Library of Congress Cataloging-in-Publication Data
Names: Stallings, Ariel Meadow, author.
Title: From sh!tshow to afterglow : putting life back together when it all falls apart / by
    Ariel Meadow Stallings.
Other titles: From shitshow to afterglow
Description: First edition. | New York : Seal Press, 2020. | Includes bibliographical
    references.
Identifiers: LCCN 2019042541 | ISBN 9781580059633 (hardcover) | ISBN
    9781580059626 (ebook)
Subjects: LCSH: Adjustment (Psychology) | Change (Psychology) | Self-help techniques. |
    Life change events.
Classification: LCC BF335 .S663 2020 | DDC 155.2/4—dc23
LC record available at https://lccn.loc.gov/2019042541

ISBNs: 978-1-58005-963-3 (hardcover); 978-0-30687-432-1 (ebook)

LSC-C

10 9 8 7 6 5 4 3 2 1

To Octavian Orion.
I do it all for you,
even the weird stuff.
Especially the weird stuff.

CONTENTS

part three

SPIRIT: WE'RE ALL ONE, BUT IN A SECULAR WAY

part four

ONWARD: INTEGRATING THE AFTERGLOW

WELCOME TO YOUR SHITSHOW!

OH, HELLO. NICE TO SEE YOU HERE. I WISH WE WERE MEETING UNDER DIFFERENT CIRCUM-stances, but here we are.

If you're reading this, chances are that shit feels pretty messed up in your life. Things may have collapsed. A slap in the face painfully announced that who you *thought* you were just doesn't line up with your current life. Where you thought you were going is no longer on the map. There's disorientation in the atmosphere. There's probably a lot of crying, maybe not a lot of sleeping (or too much sleeping), and freaking out. Your life may have fallen apart last month or last year, or maybe it was a decade ago and the janky old Band-Aid just fell off and you realized that the injury never healed.

Regardless, this much is sure: something has shifted, drastically. You may not have seen it coming, but even if you maybe sorta did, you didn't think it would feel like THIS . . . like your skin's being peeled off and your mind is filled with screaming monkeys.

Like every bone in your body has cracked and yet somehow you're supposed to keep walking. Like you don't know who you are anymore. You thought you sorta had life figured out, but it suddenly became clear that you really super didn't.

Life may feel so off that your brain can't handle it. You find yourself bumping into walls, dropping things, missing the last step when you go down the stairs. Maybe you felt like you had your situation handled, but now you wake up each morning and as you remember your new reality, you think, *This is my life now? Who even am I?*

This kind of existential life-crisis shitshow is like a freeway: there are a lot of different on-ramps, but once you're on it, things move whether you want them to or not, and you can't really slow down. However you found yourself here, chances are decent it wasn't just one precipitating incident. For me, it was a triple punch.

MY SHITSHOW, YOUR SHITSHOW

It's a good setup for a bad joke—did you hear the one about the divorced wedding expert? Did you hear the one about that offbeat lady who wrote a book about her offbeat wedding and then spent a decade supporting other people planning their offbeat weddings, who believed in nothing more than offbeat love, who then had her offbeat marriage abruptly end in the most on-beat way possible? HA HA!

So yeah, hi. I'm Ariel, and I'm the butt of that joke. I'm also the ventricles and bile and tear ducts and open palms and broken eyelid capillaries of that joke. That joke was part of my crisis, but just one part.

I'm lots of other things besides that joke . . . but many of the other things also sound like punch lines. I'm the forest-raised child of hippies who grew up to be an urban-condo-dwelling entrepreneur. I'm the brainy honors student whose stoner college goal was how little effort I could expend to maintain my A- GPA. I'm the daughter of an herbalist midwife who spent five years failing to get pregnant before having IVF and a C-section. I'm oh-so-iconoclastic with decades of rainbow-colored hair and weird clothes living a totally typical middle-class American life: education, career, wedding, home, family, divorce, aging.

So yeah: I'm the offbeat lady who's exactly like everyone else.

I got married in 2004 and wrote a book about it called *Offbeat Bride* while working a corporate day job. In 2007, I launched offbeatbride.com to promote the book, but the site turned into my job so I went full-time with my tiny digital media company in 2009 while breastfeeding my newborn son.

I spent years building my business, jokingly named the Offbeat Empire. It's a publishing company for nontraditional people going through traditional life passages: committing to a partner, creating a home, starting a family. I first shared my story and then the stories of thousands of other people, weaving a web of personal narrative and relationships and online community and empowerment and support all focused around one core belief: being offbeat could save us all! I handled my logistics like a boss, did a li'l therapy when needed, cuddled with my family on the couch, gossiped with friends, balanced my company's books, traveled a bit. Life was good! I felt like I had things sorta figured out.

Then 2015 happened.

In January of that year, my left ovary exploded while I was on a cross-country business trip. I thought it was food poisoning, so I went ahead with cohosting a five-hundred-person wedding expo in a silver dress and a bouffant, gritting through the pain and sweating off my red lipstick. I made it back to Seattle and ended up in the ER for emergency surgery, sliced up the middle with an eight-inch incision and a drainage tube hanging out of the side of my abdomen. I spent a week in the hospital, another month refiguring how to walk, and then a few months after that I turned forty. The milestone birthday was a gentle slap in the face, your classic midlife mortality check.

Then in November of 2015, my partner of eighteen years sat me down on the living room floor and told me he didn't see a future for us. I felt blindsided.

The year that followed was the most excruciating experience of my life. Already disoriented from my mortality check, I was completely leveled. Nothing made sense. I walked into walls. I randomly threw up. I barely slept. I couldn't digest food. It was a complete shitshow. Then, because I couldn't figure out how to fix it, I wholeheartedly surrendered.

Here's what no one tells you about surrendering to a shitshow: when you're in the thick of it, naked onstage forgetting your lines (even worse, you're not even sure what show this is, or whether it's a comedy or a tragedy), spotlight burning your bare skin, you don't know that in the surrender, you're already starting to heal. In the middle of a clusterfuck, all you know is that it's awful and that it's probably getting worse.

And it *does* get worse . . . but then, somehow, if you stay with it and keep paying attention and staying awake even in the awfulness, things go around some "even worse" bend and the mind-bending disorientation shifts, and you start being able to eat again, and your sleep gets a bit more normalized, and at some point you start bitterly laughing and can't stop, and then you start crying again but it feels cathartic instead of bad and you realize that you're somehow still alive—and maybe it even feels GOOD?

Then, if you roll up your sleeves and really get into it, maybe it feels *more* than good. Maybe it even feels great sometimes. That's the emotional-catastrophe survivor's high, the post-traumatic transformation that no one tells you about, the afterglow you can bask in after life fucks you HARD.

That afterglow is when your new self looks into the gaping hole that used to be your life and realizes, I might be able to grow some amazing things down here if I really try.

And, oh, it felt like I tried *everything*. Once I got my sea legs back, I decided that every moment I wasn't working or parenting would be invested into learning and growing. I would roll up my sleeves and try my best: I would learn all the things, examine all the internal lies, read all the books, take all the classes, date all the people, push all the edges, do all the healing. I would try every therapy I could find, and a few that I made up. Therapy is everywhere!

A shitshow can become the best worst time of your life. The shock and pain can become fuel for growth. I'm here in these pages because I want to help you find your afterglow. I can't change what happened to you, but just maybe I can support you in making the most of it.

WHAT EVEN IS A SHITSHOW?

Let's get clear about what I mean by *shitshow*. It's a cheeky term, but refers to a very specific kind of life crisis with a few key ingredients:

- **Uncontrollable change in foundational life structures** like your career, relationship, family, home situation, or health. Somehow it's never just one at a time. It's shit dominos, a chain reaction that feels out of your control.

- **Intense identity shift** so acute that you feel like you really don't know yourself—your self-definitions are stripped and you lose your core concepts about who you are and where you're going. It's just identity death, but in the thick of it, sometimes it feels like *actual* death.

- **Confusion like whoa.** You feel disoriented and baffled AF. How do I human? Where the hell? How did I get here? Who is this person I've become? Everything feels in-between and liminal.

- **Physical symptoms** like your sleep being jacked (too much, too little), messed-up appetite (again: too much, too little). You might be extra clumsy, or prone to injury. If grief is part of your experience (and it often is), you may even hallucinate or feel like you're losing your grasp on reality. If shock or trauma are part of your personal disaster (and they often are), you may randomly puke, sweat through your clothes for no reason, or have debilitating panic attacks.

While a shitshow is messy and feels devastating, it's not usually life-threatening. It might include a major illness or the death of a loved one, but it's not typically your own terminal diagnosis. This isn't a book about genocides or mass shootings or surviving an assault—to refer to a life-threatening situation as "a shitshow" would be insulting.

It's one of the things that's awkward about this kind of crisis: it *feels* like your life is ending, but when you're able to pull yourself back and get some perspective, you know your life isn't in danger. There's often a measure of shame; you know this isn't the end of the world—it just feels like it.

It's embarrassing to feel like you're overreacting, but here's the deal: your nervous system doesn't care if your life isn't actually being threatened. Once trauma reflexes kick in, you and your smarty-pants brain can try to rationalize all you want—you can't outthink your reaction.

Only you know whether your life is a shitshow. It's not cool for anyone to tell you whether or not you qualify. If you feel like you do, then you probably do. If you're still holding things together and you've got a sense of control, then it's probably not a shitshow. A shitshow makes it clear that control is an illusion.

If it's a shitshow, you can no longer hold your shit together. Access to shit-holding has been denied.

WTF CAN THIS BOOK DO FOR YOU?

This book is for people who want to make the best of a messy disaster. It's for folks who want to actively invest in their own healing, who want to funnel their suffering into change, transmute their misery into growth. We all have different styles of learning, and this book will probably feel the most useful for those who learn like me: through experiences and effort, through seeing how others do things, from contemplation and self-inquiry and a strong desire to be proactive. You need to *want* to get balls-deep in this— I'm not here to twist your arm.

This book is not here to be super prescriptive, telling you exactly what to do. One of the humbling lessons I've learned is that I don't have any of the answers. Before my life fell down, I really thought I had things figured out and loved to tell people what to do. But—surprise!—I wrote wedding and relationship advice for a living, *and then my marriage abruptly ended!* HA HA, JOKE'S ON ME! Now I understand how little I know.

I don't even have the answers to all *my* questions, so I can't pretend to have all the answers to yours. That said, I do love questions, and so this book wants to support you in digging to find answers that are already inside of you right now. This book isn't here to tell you exactly what your recovery should look like—I just want to support you in finding your afterglow.

The material is broken into four parts that loosely translate to mind, body, spirit, and integration. In each chapter, first I'll tell you my story as a sacrificial offering (because I don't think you should ever follow the guidance of someone who isn't willing to be vulnerable about their own struggles), and then I'll weave in bigger-picture context—stuff like research about why the methods work, and quotes from folks who are way smarter than I am.

Then, each chapter will wrap up with prompts to help you find what *your* afterglow might look like. It likely won't look like mine, because even though experiences of loss are remarkably similar, each of us will find recovery in our own way.

I strongly suggest you grab a notebook and journal through the questions at the end of each chapter, or dance through them, or draw through them, or sing through them in the car! Take the process seriously, and treat your healing like your art, or a sport, or like you're starring in the pilot for an inspiring Netflix series. Find ways to express your progress through writing, movement, assembling little piles of rocks in the park, or whatever mediums help you get out of your body and mind and out into the world. Better yet, find a shitshow buddy and share your progress.

I'm going to do my best to share my experiences responsibly and offer the research-backed guidance to help you peel back the layers of your emotional onion . . . but it's important to me that everyone reading this book be safe out there and get *real* advice from *real* people who *really* know your real-life situation.

This book wants to be your friend, but it is no substitute for folks who know you and can help you recognize if you need in-person support or treatment. I am not a doctor, a counselor, a coach, or a spiritual guide. I'm not an academic—I'm just an autodidactic writer in Seattle with a BA in sociology from a state school! I offer my story up for your entertainment, and I'm stoked to offer resources so you can learn about where to go next . . . but I am unqualified to tell you what to do with your mental, physical, or spiritual health.

In these pages, I hope that you find comfort—but if my story at times becomes the butt of the joke, I'm okay with that. If you're in pain, you probably need a few laughs and I'm down with you having a few at my expense. Like all of us, I'm a deeply flawed human, and this book shares a profoundly messy time in my life. This story is about falling down, trying to recover, failing, trying again, failing again, and trying something else. ONWARD, I shouted over and over again, face-planting in a steaming pile of my own ignorance and failures and blind spots and self-sabotage and bad choices.

I offer up my story not because I think it's especially unique (*Eat Pray Love*, *Portlandia*-style, anyone?) but as a sacrificial consolation, reassurance that as long as you're grieving forward, you're probably doing the best you can. Even if it feels awful, as long as there's movement, chances are good you're doing it right.

If you're in the thick of your shitshow right now, my heart (and one remaining ovary!) go out to you. This book is me in the middle of the night, sitting in a chair next to your bed, holding your hand while you wail, my bodily fluids leaking all over the upholstery in sympathy with your suffering.

This book is me in the dark with you, encouraging you to feel all the feels, because only then can you make the space for the new ones to come in. This book is me trying to help you carry the load.

Thank you for allowing me to share this awful wonderful time with you. It's an honor to get to be with you as you find your afterglow.

Let's do this.

part one

MIND

WHY YOU CAN'T OUTTHINK A SHITSHOW

chapter 1

SHOCK

AN UNWANTED INVITATION TO THE WAILING LODGE

I KNEW I HAD ENTERED MY SHITSHOW WHEN TIME AND SPACE BENT AND I STARTED tripping balls.

A shitshow has a way of doing that—one minute you're living through the pleasant tedium of the life you've known, the one that you've crafted, the one that might not be perfect but you've got it sorta figured out . . . and then the next thing you know, it's a Tuesday afternoon and you're sitting on the living room floor being informed that your marriage is over.

In that moment, I vortexed. Time slowed down. My vision got strangely sparkly. It was like I'd taken acid, except it was a heroic dose of abrupt life-changing news that challenged my core sense of identity. I didn't understand it at the time, but I was in a hallucinogenic state of shock, my mind bent by emotional disaster.

I mean, it had been a tough year, but that moment was the official shitshow on-ramp. When you experience that trippy, sparkly, time-warped feeling? That's your brain struggling to comprehend that life as you've known it is over. There's no going back.

On the third night after my shitshow officially began, I called my father in tears at 3:30 a.m. (I never called people in tears. I was not a crier. I took care of myself. On this side of the fissure in my life, though, I didn't know what else to do.)

My father picked up on the second ring because he'd had the phone next to his bed, waiting.

"I've never known this level of pain," I sobbed. "I had no idea how physically excruciating something like this could be."

"I know," my father said on the other end of the line, and he does know because he and my mother split up and went through their own shitshows when I was in college. "It's awful. But I'm also excited for you, in a way. If you can work through this, I mean, *really* work through it—this'll be a breakthrough."

"*Excited* for me?" I whined. "Fuck, Dad! That's brutal."

"Daughter, this stuff's the meat of life," my father said. "You're right on schedule to break through a ceiling and step up to the next level. You can do this."

A few hours later, I got out of my bed having not slept, but at least having spent some time horizontal. My son, Tavi, was with his father. I'd now be spending 50 percent of my time without my five-year-old.

I was alone.

I opened my drawers to get dressed and everything smelled of heartbreak and disbelief and panic. I wobbled through the empty house to the bathroom to find a sunken-cheeked, red-eyed, snot-crusted wraith staring from the mirror.

"What should I do?" I whispered to the reflection in the mirror, a haunted woman living in some other metaverse where there was no joy. Here in this new universe, this new woman? Things were the darkest gray and would always be gray. There was no meaning. There was no momentum. I had no idea what to do. I was alone. Panicked. Crushed. Broken. And confused—so, so confused. The screaming inside my head was so loud that I couldn't think or function. Functionality had always been my jam, but now I couldn't even figure out how to brush my hair.

How was it possible to have done so much in life and yet find myself completely demolished? All my various career defeats, interpersonal rejections, the five years of infertility, the various surgeries and medical emergencies—none of these felt as difficult as this moment. How was my oh-so-special offbeat life going off the rails in such a stereotypically pathetic way?

I shook my head and tried to focus my eyes on where I was. What's next? My manager brain desperately tried to step up. Surely there was a checklist or a schedule to lean on. Through the dense gray fog, I remembered that my friend Ellen was coming over to help me get myself together, to take me out to my mother's house.

I didn't trust myself to drive. I didn't trust myself to do anything, really.

Clearly, my brain wasn't functioning normally. During a shitshow, shock and loss aren't just mental and emotional experiences—they can come with physical symptoms that add extra confusion to the disorientation. Here are a few physical expressions you may encounter:

- ◆ Fatigue and feeling physically wobbly and weak

- ◆ Physical aches and pains, especially headaches

- ◆ Chest tightness and shortness of breath

- ◆ Digestive problems and lack of appetite

- ◆ Immune system suppression

- ◆ Rapid heartbeat

- ◆ Insomnia (or sleeping for days)

- ◆ Sexual function weirdness (zero sex drive or amped-up horniness)

- ◆ Hypervigilance, where your body is on high alert, looking out for warnings of potential danger

Of course, knowing these symptoms are normal won't make them go away (sorry 'bout that), but hopefully it's reassuring to know that, nope, *you're not losing your mind or actually dying*— both things I wondered for myself during various dark moments.

The physical symptoms associated with shock and profound loss can last for days or weeks (or even longer) and totally exacerbate any emotional and mental symptoms. In the early phase of a shitshow, you must truly take things one day at a time.

Just know that in your darkest, most painful moments, you're never *ever* alone—I've been there with you. So many of us have. Please hear this and feel it in your belly: *you are not alone right now*. That isolated feeling is your mind playing tricks on you, trying to tell you you're separate when the gallows-humor joke of life is that what unites us most as humans is our experience of suffering. Basically, when you feel your most alone and miserable? That's when you're the most like everyone else, because we've all wrestled those beasts. We're all together in this isolated misery.

That truth feels so backassward, and it's damn near impossible to wrap your brain around it when you're feeling alone and broken and panic-stricken. The truth that things *will* feel different someday is damn near impossible to understand when you're mid-shitshow.

I certainly didn't feel like things would ever get better. Staring into the mirror, all I knew was that I was the most broken I'd ever been, and that life as I'd known it was over. Both these things were in fact true, but what I didn't know was that both those painful truths could lead to a new existence that felt expansive and filled with so much more meaning.

I brushed my teeth, got dressed in my heartbreak-smelling clothes, and sat on the couch to fidget and stare at the wall. Everything hurt and my body felt like it was burning inside my flesh, like if I listened hard enough I could hear the crisps of skin falling off as the monkeys in my brain shrieked in chorus.

I tried to remember what was going on. Right . . . I was going to my mother's because I couldn't take care of myself. Ellen was taking me. That was the plan.

"What should I do?" I'd asked my mother on the phone the day before. "I can't face this weekend alone and without Tavi. I don't know how to be in the world."

"Well, you could come out here?" my mother had said. "We're hosting a grief retreat . . ."

Of course she was. For the past decade, my mother and her wife have opened their property for use as a communal retreat space they call Sacred Groves, a land of work-trade transients and millennial artists. My childhood home has been turned into a hippie retreat destination, and I've mostly adapted to the fact that on any given weekend, there might be a bunch of girls singing around a campfire at a coming-of-age ceremony or a group of boomers discussing conscious aging as part of an elders circle. Sometimes when I've visited, I've heard people through the woods participating in something called a "wailing lodge," part of the weekend-long grief retreats.

"But I'm not grieving, Mom," I'd said into the phone, trying to find the energy to argue with my mother like I always did. "No one died. My husband just walked out, and now I can't keep my shit together. That's not grief."

"That's loss," my mom had said. "Grief is just an acute experience of loss, and it seems like you're feeling this loss pretty deeply. Why don't you just come?"

I wasn't sure what else to do, so I'd agreed.

I heard Ellen let herself in my front door, and she led me like a child around my own home. She handed me my bag and a coat. She pointed me toward the door and walked me through it. She helped me get in the car and drove me down the west face of Seattle's Capitol Hill to the waterfront, where we waited to drive onto one of those picturesque Puget Sound ferries that's really just a floating bus.

I sat perfectly still for the half-hour ferry ride, silent stony panic in the passenger seat. Catatonic, dissociated, and disoriented, the only movement I could muster was a slow drip of snot down my face while Ellen patted my hand. She'd wrestled through a bipolar diagnosis and her own divorce, surviving her own high-grade shit-shows, so she got it.

"Thank you for being my crisis doula," I managed to say.

Once docked on Bainbridge Island, Ellen drove me the ten minutes through the forest, over the glacier-carved hills, and down the one-lane road that leads to the ten acres of second-growth forest where I grew up. The driveway was filled with Priuses and old Subarus, and I could hear people crying before I even walked through the door.

That's what happens when your mom runs a retreat facility: when your life abruptly falls apart and you try to go home for some consoling, you end up attending a grief retreat.

Shitshows take you all sorts of places you never imagined.

WHEN AVOIDING THE PAIN STOPS WORKING

Generally speaking, Western culture likes to deny pain. We try to avoid and ignore illness, death, poverty, and grief to bypass the difficult associated emotions. Author of *The Other Side of Complicated Grief: Hope in the Midst of Despair* Rhonda O'Neill says that this cultural predisposed alienation from our own misery only amplifies our suffering.

Instead of retreating into isolation or distraction (which is what our culture expects—The Man wants you to hide your pain!), it's mission critical that you find people who can be with you in your suffering.

I'm not gonna lie: this can be HARD. Your friends and family might want to help, but sometimes they can be too close to the situation to effectively provide the support you need. Sometimes your pain triggers their pain and then you're in a shitshow echo chamber, which, needless to say, isn't an especially comforting environment.

If your shitshow involves grief (either because someone died or because your loss is so intense that you're having physical symptoms), you may want to investigate grief support groups in your area. Groups dedicated specifically to assisting people through this kind of experience will have the tools and strategies you need and help you combat the isolation that so many of us experience when we're in pain.

It may feel awkward to seek out these groups, or they might seem like they're not meant for you, or the folks at support groups might not seem like "your people." Part of this process is understanding that loss is the great equalizer. It can be hard to let that information in (especially for those of us who have prided ourselves on our offbeat-ness), but it's true: when you're grieving, other grievers are your people.

I never *ever* thought I'd go to a grief retreat (again, no one had died—what was I even doing there?), but when you're ripped open and torn down, comfort shows up in different shapes than your previous self might have expected. The dominant cultural aesthetics of loss may not match your vibe (religious quotes and fuzzy pictures of candles, anyone?), but for your own survival, you *must* find and allow comfort.

Speaking of cultural aesthetics, I may love my moms and Sacred Groves, but it's not really my scene.

The hub of Sacred Groves is a yurt-like roundhouse that's almost forty feet across with a huge circular skylight in the center. Filled with a mix of discarded Goodwill furniture, the structure's decor includes a four-foot drum made from a tree stump, a bison skull, and multiple swaths of prayer flags painted with goddess vagina art. The main room is anchored by a woodstove to the east and a huge bank of windows to the west that look out on the permaculture garden and the two smaller yurts rented out on Airbnb.

It's lovely, but I lean more toward the tidy modern lewk, y'know? I thought of myself as an urbanite, a media maven, an internet obsessive . . . or at least that's who I had been. I had no idea who this sobbing, wobbling woman was now.

I said my goodbyes and thank-yous to Ellen and walked into the roundhouse. The thirty retreat attendees were milling around the large room, with folks ranging from shaven-headed twenty-somethings to suburban dudes in sandals with socks, and more than a few wild-haired middle-aged women. Several of us were already crying, myself included. There were cedar boughs and twinkly lights and an altar with candles.

Even in my catatonic state, my inner bitch was rolling her eyes. I know how these kinds of workshops go, with lots of talking circles and mending times for broken people. Growing up with hippie parents, this kind of new-age stuff was what I spent my youth rebelling against. It's lovely and valuable for some people—it's just never been my thing.

Then again, being in a state of emotional pain so intense that I could feel it eating away at my body's tissues and warping my sense of time had never really been my thing either, and yet there I was.

The workshop attendees gathered into a circle to talk over the weekend. I learned that, traditionally, the social aspects of loss have always revolved around ritual. In *Grief and Loss Across the Lifespan*, Carolyn Ambler Walter and Judith L. M. McCoyd discuss studies showing that grievers get a sense of control over their mourning when they engage in specific behavior and performance involving other people, symbols of the loss, and activities that are "out of the ordinary."

Out of the ordinary. Like a grief retreat in a yurt, I guess. I learned that we were going to do something called "keening," which is basically wailing for what's been lost. Keening also felt solidly out of character for me, but it would be the first of dozens of out-of-character things I would eventually try in my attempts to heal from the catastrophe of my life.

Sitting in a circle, we were asked to introduce ourselves. There were people who'd had parents die recently, and a young woman who was mourning the death of a friend who'd been tortured and killed while doing international aid work. There were sexual assault survivors, parents of stillborn babies, and folks dealing with losing a job while also caring for adult children with disabilities. A couple people were there to mourn climate change. My loss seemed so small, and yet it was hard for me to focus on anything other than the shouting inside my head—all the details! All the unfairness! All the things that had gone wrong!

When you're in the thick of a full-life face-plant, your mind desperately wants to focus on all the little details—who said what and why, how could you have stopped it, what did you do wrong, why is this so unfair, how can you fix it?

But those little details are traps. That's your brain trying to make itself useful, telling you that if you could just figure it out, you could change it. That's your mind bargaining: if you review the details of what happened just a few more times, the result might be different.

For now, see if you can set aside the little details of what went wrong.

For now, just see if you can allow the feelings to be felt, separate from the story.

For now, just see if you can allow yourself to understand the depth of the loss.

I know it sucks and it hurts worse than anything, but you can't skip over this part. You must feel all the feelings so you can heal all the healings.

FIND YOUR AFTERGLOW

At the end of each chapter, I'm going to hit you up with some questions. These are the true meat of this book. Reading is cool, but in order to transmute the pain of your shitshow into a new life, you have to make the effort to get real with yourself, face some pain, and hold yourself accountable for how you're going to find your afterglow. Then—and only then—can you find that light, the glowy feeling of knowing you're good in the world again. It exists! You can get there! But there's stuff you've got to do first.

Think of it this way: You've fallen into a hole. You can curse, haul yourself out of the hole, and run for the hills, but unless you take the time to figure out what's down in that hole, how it got there, and what you can learn from it, you're probably going to keep running in circles and falling into that same damn hole.

So, here come some questions. I know some of these are uncomfortable, but, hey, guess what? You're already uncomfortable, and avoiding it just prolongs the pain, so let's dive in together.

◆ What's the physical sensation of your loss? Separate from the story of what happened, just tell me this: What's the shape of the pain you're in? (Is it sharp and searing? Dull and aching?) Where do you feel it in your body? (Is it a panic in your chest or a sinking in your stomach?) I know you don't want to feel, but just for a moment, see if you can allow yourself to experience the sensation of pure loss, without resisting it or making a story about how it happened or where it might be going.

◆ How disoriented and confused are you? You're in a transitional state, which can be upsetting if you're a person who likes things feeling settled and secure. What if being in transition is exactly where you're supposed to be right now? How does it make you feel to know that you might be entering a transitional period that could start a whole new phase of your life?

◆ Who in your life do you trust to witness your shitshow? Often, a crisis leads to surprising social shifts—folks you expected to be there for you just don't quite know how to handle the situation. Meanwhile, people you barely know may randomly step up in ways you never expected. Who in your life now do you feel safe enough to be vulnerable with? Who might be able to be a crisis doula, witnessing without fixing?

◆ If you don't have anyone in your life whom you trust to support you, what small steps could you take today to start to establish the kinds of connections you want more of in your new life? In adulthood, friendships and community don't just happen. They take daily effort, which often can be as simple as looking up from your phone and saying hello to the people around you. Or you might want to google a grief or loss support group in your area.

I'm not going to offer you any easy Band-Aids or glib assurances here, sweet friend. The simple reality is this: you're entering a new life. There's no going back. The details of how you got here matter, but what matters more is how you're going to use the experience to move yourself forward, toward contentment and feeling the lightness of life again.

We're going to help you find your afterglow.

Chapter 2

UGLY CRYING

GOING FOR GOLD AT THE PAIN OLYMPICS

SO THERE I WAS, IN A COUPLE PLACES I DIDN'T WANT TO BE: GOING THROUGH A SHITSHOW, attending a grief retreat.

The second night of the retreat, one wall of the roundhouse was transformed by huge cedar boughs curled against it, creating an open tent of sorts. Kneeling cushions faced an altar that we had decorated with reminders of what had been lost. Photos of dead mothers and friends, letters from lost lovers, drawings of unborn babies . . . and one of my wedding pictures. I'd built a whole business on those dang wedding pictures! They are all over the internet for godsake! Now they were part of a grief altar? Fuck my life.

We were instructed to drum, sing a repetitive folk song, and dance in the empty half of the room. Then when we felt called, we could come forward, kneel on the pillows in front of the altar, and loudly do whatever wailing we needed to do while everyone else kept singing and drumming. I like karaoke just fine, but this sure as hell wasn't karaoke and I wasn't into wailing.

And yet somehow, when the drumming began, I felt com-pelled to be one of the first to the altar. This was unlike me (um, you guys, I don't really *do* ceremonies?), but I hadn't slept in days and had lost track of who I was, and I couldn't remember how to be the person I was supposed to be (i.e., the kind of person who's super NOT into this kind of thing).

So I stepped up and knelt at the altar and started swaying as I sobbed. The drums and singing got louder. I swayed harder, and cried harder. I lost myself.

My sleep-deprived mind filled with the image of being on my knees at a deathbed. My eyes slid closed and rolled back as I fell forward onto all fours, rocking, seeing myself at the bedside of the life I'd known.

I saw my life up until this point embodied as a separate entity, a person I'd nursed and nurtured, celebrated and shared, built a life with . . . and that life, that person, had died.

The beloved body was stretched out in a bed in my mind's eye, and I could see all the hopes and dreams and future-schemes, and as I held the gnarled hand of my former life, I could feel the body cooling. I felt myself holding on to the stiffening flesh as I sobbed, "Don't go. Stay with me. Stay here with me. Just stay. Just for a while."

But this body of my previous life was already dead, and all I could do was sit and watch it cool and gently collapse into itself.

I was only half-aware that I was on all fours at an altar, in a round room, in the woods where I grew up, and that I was keening and growling, pleading and ugly crying. The round room was filled with the sound of the drums and singing, so all my wailing barely registered. It was a relief to be drowned out.

Shit, maybe this was grief. Someone *had* died, and it was me. I gritted my teeth and bore down, screaming. I pushed hard. The visions crystallized, and I lost my grip on reality completely.

I was at a deathbed, *on* a deathbed, but I was also birthing something. Screaming on all fours, pushing something new and pink and tender into the world and it hurt worse than anything I'd ever known. The pain was blinding, and I started rasping out the breathing exercises I'd learned in preparation for my son's birth.

Time passed or didn't pass. I couldn't tell.

Eventually, I rocked back a bit on my heels and blinked, trying to clear the hallucinations. My body was in so much pain. Was I having a heart attack?

No, wait, I thought. *Maybe I'm dying, doubled over on a dirty* zabuton *at some hippie grief-ceremony thinger at my mom's. This is not the way I wanted to go.*

But nah, I wasn't dying. I was just ugly crying my face off, drowning in the loss of the life I'd known. I wobbled myself to standing and stepped back from the altar. I tried to take a breath into my new lungs.

WHY YOU SHOULD GET STOKED ABOUT CRYING HARD

Since you may be crying way more than you're used to, let's nerd out on this for a second. There are three types of tears: basal tears that lubricate the eye, reflex tears that flush out irritants, and emotional tears. These tears have different stimuli, but emotional tears also have a different chemical composition: they're way richer in hormones.

This is to say that hard cathartic crying feels drastically different from crying over chopping onions because it's not just emotionally different—it's *biologically* different.

Beyond releasing hormones, hard crying serves another purpose. Evolutionary psychologist Oren Hasson at Tel Aviv University believes that crying signals shared emotional attachments and solicits sympathy and aid from bystanders. Crying may be your body's way to physically express to others "I need help!" (And, oh, you do. I'm glad you're here with me.)

Again, we get a lot of cultural messaging telling us to keep ourselves together and stay strong—but screw it. Part of this process is fully embracing it and allowing yourself to be *completely* undone. You must be dissolved. You must let your tears flow. You must empty yourself over and over again so that you can make room for different emotions to come through.

Psychiatrist Colin Murray Parkes said that in times of intense loss, "the familiar world suddenly seems to have become unfamiliar . . . and we lose confidence in our own internal world." This knock-you-on-your-ass uncertainty marks the start of your path of rebirthing your new self.

In the moment, grieving doesn't feel profound or productive. You might obsess over strange things, get profoundly angry over seemingly unrelated events, have anxiety spikes that feel petty, or catch yourself looping over trivialities.

Personally, my favorite thing to do when I was miserable was hate myself. It would go like this: something would hurt, and then I would rip myself apart for being hurt by it. This self-abuse had the lovely side effect of making me hurt even more!

Buddhists call this phenomenon the "second arrow." The first arrow is the initial pain, the injury that just happens. Then the second arrow is you resisting the pain, hating yourself for somehow allowing it to happen, railing about the injustice of it all, berating yourself for bleeding, and making plans for how you can exact revenge, etc. Even if you're not a fan of beating yourself up like I am, you might still wrestle with believing you don't have a valid reason for feeling as awful as you do.

According to *Grief and Loss Across the Lifespan*, this type of disenfranchised pain is a result of a culture that acknowledges some forms of loss as more legitimate than others. There's nothing illegitimate about what you're experiencing. No matter what caused the feelings, *they exist*, and you're suffering and hurting as a result. Your emotions are valid. *Your loss is valid!* The idea of competitive Pain Olympics or loss hierarchy does nothing but make what you're going through even harder.

"Grief is visceral, not reasonable: the howling at the center of grief is raw and real. It is love in its most wild form," writes Megan Devine in her remarkable book *It's OK That You're Not OK*.

"The reality of grief is far different from what others see from the outside," Devine explains. "There is pain in this world that you can't be cheered out of. You don't need solutions. You don't need to move on from your grief. You need someone to see your grief, to acknowledge it. . . . Some things cannot be fixed. They can only be carried."

Getting to your afterglow means first wholeheartedly accepting the invitation to your shitshow. It means not running from the pain or numbing out. It means understanding that the only way to really get through it is to fully feel *all* the feels, even the ones you're ashamed of or want to deny. Actually, *especially* the ones you're ashamed of and want to deny.

As for me, one of my first waves of shame was that I was a midlife cliché, keening at a new-age grief retreat.

But despite my shame, I came to understand that my loss needed to be felt, seen, and given an outlet . . . and the retreat provided that. "True comfort in grief is in acknowledging the pain, not in trying to make it go away," Devine writes. "Companionship, not correction, is the way forward."

There's no right way to feel like crap, but there is such a thing as "good" emotional recovery. The best kinds help you learn more about yourself and how you fit into your new world, helping you grow from the pain and all the other overwhelming feelings.

Accepting your feelings doesn't mean you have to *like* them, or like what happened to you. It's not about silver linings or denying pain. It's about learning about yourself, and using the information to power your journey.

This is about healing *forward*. I can't take away your sorrow or fix your problems, but I can help you carry them. I'm here to support you in feeling it all, so that you can use the momentum of that loss to fuel you forward.

FIND YOUR AFTERGLOW

Before we can get into the glowy stuff, it's mission critical to take the time to feel the rough stuff. This is unpleasant but necessary to get where you want to go. Want to call it wallowing? Go ahead. Wallow your way forward.

One perspective on why certain losses feel so overwhelmingly huge is that they tap into a well of unresolved, unattended sorrow from old hurts. Think of all the times in the past when shit happened and you just stuffed your emotions, brushed yourself off, and told yourself you were fine, *just fine!* All those little unattended sorrows add up, and then your shitshow hits and—*BLAM*—you can no longer stuff it.

Now it's time to unpack it. Ready for some questions? Take your time with these, and let yourself actually feel the answers:

◈ As you wrestle through the specifics of your current situation, what *old* pains are resurfacing? These old hurts could show up as thoughts (for example, a miscarriage somehow reminds you of your grandmother's death), but these hurts may also be sensations in your body. Can you allow yourself to feel and acknowledge those old hurts?

◈ Consider the second-arrow concept: How are you making more pain for yourself by resisting it? Sure, something awful (or several awfuls) happened, but how are you hating on yourself for feeling bad, resisting the fact that you feel bad, or trying to push away the bad feeling? How are you stabbing yourself with a second arrow, and what would happen if you just let yourself feel how you feel? (One arrow is enough, friend!)

◈ Shitty feelings desperately want to get *out*. They need to be witnessed and acknowledged, and can be a strong creative force, even for people who don't identify as artistic. How does your loss want to be expressed? You may find that you start with one format like writing and then move into some other format like dancing or photography. Allow *all* creative impulses to move through you without judgment! The quality of the output isn't important—what's important is the act of expression. Get your shit OUT.

In these early chapters, this stuff is dark and rough. Stay with it. We have to dig down a bit before we can glow up.

Chapter 3

SLEEP

SILENCING THE FUCKING DEMONS SO YOU CAN REST

THOSE FIRST FEW WEEKS, I JUST STOPPED SLEEPING. IF I MANAGED TO DRIFT OFF, I'D WAKE up writhing a couple hours later with a physical pain that I could never quite identify . . . Was it my tendons aching? My skin hurting? A stroke?

Then there were the fucking demons, haunting me all night.

And I do mean "fucking demons." I would wake up with a start and could see them over my bed . . . fucking, taunting me, laughing at me while I cried. The demons that haunted me were always having epic, back-archingly amazing sex, while I just had to lie there in bed and watch them over me, like the worst threesome.

After weeks of hallucinating instead of sleeping, I realized that the situation was starting to interfere with my ability to effectively parent my son. I called my doctor's office and learned that my primary care provider was on vacation.

"Can I see someone today?" I begged, unable to keep my cool. "I'm in a state of personal crisis and not sleeping and I'm scared."

My voice shaking, I realized that I was somewhere between hyper-lucid and hyper-insane. The receptionist asked me if I was a danger to myself ("I don't think so . . . ?" I said, more a question than an answer) and got me an appointment with an on-call doctor that morning.

I drove to the clinic, crying. I sat in the waiting room, crying. A nurse came out and called me back into the clinic, and I shambled down the hall behind her, crying. I couldn't walk in a straight line. The nurse weighed me (I'd dropped ten pounds that week) and wrapped my arm to take my blood pressure.

"One forty-six over eighty-four," she noted, gently ripping the Velcro cuff off my arm and looking at me maybe a little too closely, and leaving me with a mental health form, which asked me to check boxes about my brain.

Did I feel hopeless? Yes. Problems with appetite? Yes. Was I sleeping? No. Experiencing anxiety? YES!!!! 11!!! OMG!! Was I having trouble concentrating? Yes. Heart palpitations? Yes. I checked the boxes, crying. I waited for the doctor, crying.

I'm normally the Best! Patient! Ever!, asking all the questions that need asking, taking notes, curious and engaged in my own medical care. This time, as a doctor I'd never met before walked in with her brown ponytail swinging, I could barely look up.

"I'm Dr. Adams," she said, sitting down and looking at the checkboxes on my form. She peppered me with questions, mostly around whether I was a self-harm risk.

"I thought about throwing myself off a cliff," I said, ashamed. "I'd never do it, but I've never thought about suicide ever in my life."

Dr. Adams listened with incredible patience considering she'd never met me before. Then she diagnosed me with something called "adjustment disorder."

Later, I read up on it: "Adjustment disorder is a short-term condition that occurs when a person has great difficulty coping with, or adjusting to, a particular source of stress, such as a major life change, loss, or event." Yep, IT ME.

The list of things that can lead to adjustment disorder is remarkably similar to the shitshow on-ramps I listed in the introduction:

◆ Ending of a relationship or marriage (ooh ooh, that's mine!)

◆ Losing or changing a job

◆ Death of a loved one

◆ Developing a serious illness (yep, I've done that one!)

◆ Being a victim of a crime

◆ Having an accident

◆ Undergoing a major life change, such as getting married, having a baby, or retiring from a job

◆ Living through a disaster, such as a fire, flood, or hurricane

This all makes sense, right? A person with adjustment disorder has emotional and behavioral symptoms as a reaction to a stressful event. It all sounds so simple (something stressful happened, and you're reacting!), but it feels like your world is truly ending.

Part of adjustment disorder is that the reaction to the stressor is greater than what might be expected. For some of us, adjustment stress tastes great with a dollop of shame. It's that second arrow again—you're hurting, and then there's the sense that you're hurting more than you really should be. And there you go again, making yourself hurt even more. It's a sneaky hate spiral.

Adjustment disorder symptoms generally begin within three months of a precipitating event and don't usually last for more than six months (there's an end in sight!). But those six months can be brutal, because the symptoms interfere with your ability to function—stuff like sleeping, working, or even just basics like reading.

You feel broken, ashamed, and unable to function: yikes!

The doctor told me I could have symptoms of physical shock for weeks or even months. We talked through sleep meds, and

I was lucid enough to explain that I was terrified of developing chemical dependencies.

"The last thing I need is to become a pillhead on top of this disaster," I said as I wiped snot on my sleeve and tried a half smile. Smiling felt foreign, like my teeth were about to crack and fall out. I've always tended toward anxiety, but suddenly I realized . . . oh shit, this bleak gray nothingness is what depression feels like. I saw no bottom, and no end. This loss felt like my new forever.

Dr. Adams prescribed me two different sleep medications so that I could toggle back and forth, to hopefully avoid getting dependent on one, and a low-dose prescription for Xanax, for use when the panic and anxiety got especially bad.

THE NO-BAD-VIBES BED AND GOOD VIBRATIONS

Obviously, if your sleep is borked, pretty much everything is going to suck even more than it already does. Lack of sleep, or poor-quality sleep (like, oh I don't know, the kind that has you hallucinating demons over your bed, for instance), affects stuff like your

◆ cognitive abilities, like learning and remembering;

◆ emotional well-being, by causing you to be more depressed or susceptible to mood swings;

◆ physical well-being, by compromising your immune system; and

◆ decision-making ability, which can feel especially dangerous when you're going through difficult and stressful periods.

Sleep problems can also affect your appetite, not to mention your ability to work, hang out with friends or family, or enjoy any of the things you used to enjoy.

The insidious thing about shitty sleep is that it permeates all aspects of your life and its effects are exponential. Even a small disruption in a healthy sleep schedule can leave you messed up for days. If you're already struggling in a vulnerable state? Well, everything's just going to feel worse. If you have the resources to do so, talking to a medical professional about sleep problems can be a smart idea, especially if those sleep problems start affecting your ability to function in everyday life.

But what else can you do?

Well, first, you can make a No Bad Vibes bed. When you're going through a shitshow, bad vibes can't be avoided (and SHOULDN'T be avoided—you must accept your situation and attend to your sorrows!), but you can try to give your bad vibes a home somewhere *other* than your bedroom, designating your bed as a No Bad Vibes zone.

Some folks say that your bed should only be for sleep and sex, but it's more like you should keep it to anything that helps you feel comforted and comfortable. If reading in bed helps relax you, that's great. If social media in bed pisses you off, it's banned. Try to establish your bed as an island where you intentionally focus on caring for yourself and being comfortable.

Every night before you get into bed, try to do the same things, carefully and with intent. This isn't just a routine—it's a ritual. You know how most children need regimented bedtime routines? You need something like that right now. Think of it like a ceremony that initiates the next part of your day: rest.

Tell yourself it's time to go to sleep and that you're going to start your ritual. Try to concentrate only on what you're doing, when you're doing it. This kind of regime trains your body to start winding down when it gets the signals. Even mundane everyday hygiene like brushing your teeth can be part of this ritual. You are tranquil, and you got this.

Consider enacting a "no phones in the bedroom" rule. No phone at all is a great goal, but many of us are attached to using certain apps in the bedroom (for example, your alarm or a music app). You can have the tools you need (without the distractions you don't) if you designate an old smartphone as a bedroom phone.

How to set up your No Bad Vibes bedroom phone:

◆ Find an old smartphone. Cracked screen? Outdated hardware? No problem.

◆ Do a clean install of the operating system—you want the phone wiped and fresh.

◆ Set the phone to Wi-Fi-only. You don't need to make calls with this device, so you don't need to pay for service. This is essentially using a smartphone as a bedroom remote.

◆ Install only the apps that support your rest and sleep. On my bedroom phone, the only apps are a meditation timer, audiobooks, music (and sometimes porn). There's no social media, messaging, email. The goal is minimalism!

◆ If your old operating system offers it, set your phone to dark mode for a mellower screen experience.

◆ Bonus: set your phone wallpaper to something soothing.

Remember that phones are tools, and you get to choose how you want to use them! You must watch your behavior closely, though: if you notice your bedroom phone becoming yet another distraction that keeps you awake, then *you've* become the tool and your phone is using you.

Next, can we talk about getting hands-on with some sleep help? Yep, I'm talking masturbation. Your hand or vibrator absolutely may become a crisis doula. When you have a lot of anxious energy to burn, jacking off can really, really help. Some folks just aren't interested in sex (even solo sex), and other folks might find sexual energy triggering (Fucking Demons, I'm looking at you), but for many of us, rubbing one out can be palliative care to help us calm down and rest.

Plus, masturbation is a mindfulness practice: you're concentrating on one thing—and it's pleasure. Whether you're using toys or porn or just your hand, your focus is on your pleasure and building toward an orgasm. Distraction becomes less likely in this head-space, because your body and mind are working together toward a clear, sexy goal. After all that focus (lookit you, sweet little trau-matized adjustment-disorder bb—you're focusing on something!), your mind might be a little clearer, helping you slip into sleep.

If you have an orgasm (which, hey, if it doesn't happen, that's okay, too!), that can lower your blood pressure and release en-dorphins, both of which can further help you drift off to sleep. Orgasm endorphins are natural stress-killers, and the emotional catharsis is powerful. Come! Cry! Tell the demons to fuck off!

There are other benefits that don't relate directly to sleep and relaxation:

◆ Pain killing: menstrual cramps and other aches can be alleviated by orgasms thanks to the muscle contractions and also the hormones involved.

◆ Reconnecting to what your body likes and needs during sex: it helps you become more aware of yourself and how you can get off during sex, too!

◆ Putting you in touch with your body: literally, of course, but how many times a day do you touch yourself in a way that really focuses your awareness on finding joy in your physicality? More about this in Chapter 24.

Finally, as part of your evening routine, take a few steps to feel ready for your morning. Los Angeles artist Gabi Abrão suggests being "physically prepared" to deal with difficult wake-ups during times of heartbreak and hardship. "Have lots of water by your bed for when you wake up. When your mood is lower than usual, ev-ery little bit counts. A slight dehydration can make a sad morning into a devastating one."

"You will wake up and recognize yourself again someday," she says. "And it will be grand. It will be bigger than anything."

She's right.

You don't have to believe it today, but she's right.

FIND YOUR AFTERGLOW

Sleep can be challenging for many of us—even when we're NOT living through an existential train wreck. Twenty-first-century technology, overpacked schedules, and a roller coaster of emotions all conspire to keep you up at night, but sleep is nonnegotiable. Here are some questions to help you find ways to get the rest you need, so that you have the strength to heal:

◆ How are you using (or abusing) technology at night? How might your evening change if you turned screens off an hour before going to bed?

◆ Many of us experience looping thoughts when we lie down to sleep. Writing your thoughts (on paper!) can be a great way to prevent them from keeping you up. Write a letter to someone with no intention of sending it, or journal to drain the words out of your head and onto the page. No one is going to read this writing—you could even burn it or tear it up once you're done.

◆ What elements of your bed area could you arrange to help yourself feel more safe, comforted, and cozy? Even if you only have ten minutes, what tiny changes could you make right now?

◆ Imagine your ideal bedtime. Now, pick just three elements that you could try committing to doing each night. Start tiny, but write them down and put the note up in your home, then see if you can stick to it for a week.

Thinking about something as basic as sleep might feel silly when there are so many other, more urgent problems to react to, but it's a core foundational ingredient that will make the rest of this exhausting endeavor feel more feasible. Think of your recovery as a marathon: you gotta pace yourself and get your rest.

Chapter 4

TALK THERAPY

WHEN SOLO STRATEGIZING STOPS WORKING

THANKS TO ACTUALLY SLEEPING, AFTER A FEW WEEKS, MY BRAIN STARTED REBOOTING AND was back to its old tricks: I suddenly decided I could strategize my way out. I could outsmart this situation! I could put a shape to this horror!

My friend Ashlee took me out to dinner at Smith, the hipster bar/restaurant around the corner from my home, with its taxidermized animal heads on the wall and cozy booths. Ashlee is a boss-ass bitch, a hardworking curvy redhead who directs a marketing team for an international construction company.

The waiter brought our first round of drinks, a Moscow mule for Ashlee and a ginger beer for me (I was already drunk on doom and felt too emotionally unstable to add booze to my disorientation). Ginger beer in hand, I leaned in because that's what boss-ass bitches do when confronted with a challenge: we lean in and we strategize.

"Okay, here's what I'm thinking," I said. "Not to get too midlife horrors on you, but the simple reality is this: if the first forty years are about building things up, the next forty years will be about slowly letting them go. This year has been a pretty intense crash course: my health, my youth, my marriage."

Ashlee nodded and took a sip of her cocktail. Her father had died abruptly the previous year, and then a few months later her husband had come down with meningitis, and then things had gotten really rough with her daughter, and yeah—she understands life implosions.

"The next few decades will include losses like losing friends, losing my son as he grows up and moves out, losing my parents as they get older and eventually die, losing my own physical abilities, and eventually the big loss I'm one hundred percent guaranteed: my own life!"

I waved my drink at Ashlee for emphasis. Even sober, I was on an unstoppable ramble, panting a little.

"So, here's my strategy: What if I can use the loss of *this* situation to practice dealing with all the inevitable *future* loss situations? What if I view this as loss training?" I had this figured out! I had a motherfucking plan!

"You want to practice so you can win at losing?" Ashlee asked, and I nodded.

"Exactly! There are other options, of course. Instead of dealing with the pain of this loss, I could just avoid it and steel myself against life so that future losses don't feel as painful. But that just trades the sharpness of full-blown loss for a low-grade chronic loss. If you disengage from life to protect yourself from pain, you're in a state of *daily* loss. I don't want to avoid the pain—I want to lean into it so I can get better at dealing with it! See?! Loss training!!"

Ashlee swallowed and looked at me. "I mean, sounds like a great idea, but it hasn't even been a month since your marriage ended. Maybe hold off on strategizing till you've had some time to just, like, *heal?*"

She was right, of course. I was sweating in my seat a bit, and realized that my strategizing sounded a bit unhinged . . . maybe a lot unhinged.

"You should get into therapy," Ashlee told me lovingly. "Let me give you my guy's number."

She did. The next day, I called.

Finding a good mental health professional can be tough (why isn't there Tinder for counselors?), and this is doubly true if you're still in the thick of unfolding chaos. Here are a few things to try:

- Ask all friends and family for referrals, and specifically what they like about their counselor. Bonus: you destigmatize seeing a mental health professional by being open about seeking treatment!

- Read online reviews. These can help you get a sense of a counselor's style before you call for a consultation. Keep in mind that therapy is subjective, so use reviews only to look for red flags, and take them with a grain of salt.

- Remember that many folks do counseling via Skype, so you don't have to be limited by who's in your area.

- Have a sense of what you're looking for. Are you interested in cognitive behavioral therapy, mindfulness, acceptance therapy, a mixture, something else? Not sure? Your consultation is the time to ask your potential therapist what techniques they use and how they would help you through your specific situation.

- Investigate free resources! Ask friends, medical professionals, or your wellness center at work or school for references to free resources. Doing a Google search can help you find online crisis support and even therapists who can talk with you for free—just be sure to do your due diligence and go for a trustworthy source, like the NAMI HelpLine in the US.

Know that it can take time to find a good fit. This is important. Try to not get discouraged if you meet a therapist, pour your heart out, and feel like you get nothing in return. Meeting with different therapists can be difficult when it involves reliving painful experiences, but the payoff will make it worthwhile when you find someone who gels with your needs.

As you're searching for a counselor, you may encounter some judgments or a sense of stigma. Even though some corners of North America are more progressive about mental health, many American communities are still working to normalize therapy—and the global outlook on mental health has an even longer way to go. The stigma around seeking treatment for mental health issues acts as a harmful barrier for folks getting the care they need.

There are two layers of stigma: the public stigma, and then self-stigma. Both types involve stereotypes, prejudice, and discrimination, whether focused outward or internalized. Because of this, those of us who are suffering from grief, mental illness, trauma, or significant life changes can suffer twice: first from the situation itself, and again at the stigmatization.

While the overall prevalence of mental illness is the same across races, different cultures and ethnic communities have different beliefs about mental illness and seeking help.

So consider this a reality check: not everyone dealing with emotional turmoil has the same path to help. If you have the access and resources to pursue mental health care with a professional, you've got an incredible privilege—*don't waste it!*

THE WONDERS OF A BLUE-HAIRED THERAPIST

I sat in my new therapist's waiting room, perched in a chair beneath a colorful quilt on the wall that was stitched with the words WE'RE ALL GONNA DIE. Atta opened the door to his office and shook my hand. He was a compact guy with black glasses, a handlebar mustache, gauged earlobes, and leather boots. His dark hair was dyed blue.

"C'mon in," Atta said in what I learned was a Kentucky accent. I sat down on the leather couch across from his armchair, and I told him my story.

"The days when I feel the most okay are the days when I'm fooling myself into thinking surely I can get my old life back somehow. Surely by releasing my marriage with compassion, I can

somehow save it? Surely if I take good care of my body, I can prevent other organs from exploding, and stay healthy forever? Surely
if I do everything just right, my life can go back to how it was?"

"I hear you," Atta said. "But I can't make your life go back to
what it was, and I don't think you can either. What I want for you
is to come out of this feeling like you have grown and benefited as
a person. How does that sound as a goal?"

"Ooh," I said. "I'm down with that. I mean, I *feel* like I want my
old life back . . . but maybe I just want to feel like my life is okay
again? I can't control the situation, but I guess I can make choices
about how I want to grow?"

Atta looked at me and smiled, and dude might as well have
been like *DING DING DING*.

"I believe in you, Ariel," he said.

At the end of our fifty-minute session, I walked out feeling on
top of the world, with an appointment for the next week. For that
moment, I felt like I had a little agency in my life. I got to choose
where to focus my attention, and *I chose growth*. What a revelation!

Of course within an hour of getting home, I was on my floor,
sobbing on all fours over how intolerable the emotional pain
was . . . but, hey, an hour was a start!

The next week, after patiently listening to a fast-talking bar-
rage of my loss-training strategies, my new motto of "expect the
worst, CRY FIRST," and my concept of "pre-grieving" where maybe
I could be really sad now to avoid being sad later, Atta interrupted
me.

"Slow down," he said. "Have you tried any sort of meditation
or mindfulness exercises?"

I rolled my eyes. "Have you been talking to my hippie parents?"

"I just think you'd do really well with it, seeing how your brain
works," Atta said. "But my big question this week is this: Can you
slow down a bit here?"

I immediately burst into tears. I call these kinds of tears "truth
tears," when someone hits you with a loving callout so accurate
that there's no point in defending yourself. All you can do is cry
and nod.

"I see you trying so hard to learn as much as possible, as quickly as possible. I see your poor brain spinning nonstop trying to bargain and strategize and make sense of all this . . . but I'm asking you to please, please slow yourself down. Basically, you were just in an emotional car accident. It was abrupt and traumatic. Picture yourself in a full body cast. Rest and heal. Think of animals after they get hurt: they just crawl into a hole and rest. That's all you can do to heal. You can't outthink this."

I nodded, crying. I heard what Atta was saying, but secretly I was sure that I could prove him wrong. My brain had gotten me this far in life, and I was still convinced I could outthink this nightmare.

If you're reading this book, you too might be a thinker and strategizer, a schemer and planner. You might use words to feel safe, carefully laying out intellectual plans to escape emotional discomforts. You may prefer to talk about pain than actually feel it.

That big beautiful brain of yours is a wonderful tool, but your toolbox has the potential to be so much deeper and more robust. What I want for you is to find a breadth of tools so you don't lean on your favorites so hard that you break them.

FIND YOUR AFTERGLOW

Since a shitshow burns down your identities and often shows how your old coping methods don't work anymore, it can be terrifying. Your old self and old ways are no longer relevant—YIKES. But there's vital intel in this mess. Let's poke around in there a bit.

◆ What's your default reaction to stress? Do you go strategic and anxious? Fuzzy and catatonic? Depressed and confused? Do you reach for a distraction, or numb out with drugs or alcohol or screens? What if you tried to make a different decision—if you normally ramp up, can you try slowing down? If you normally check out, can you try staying engaged with your situation just a little bit longer? The goal here isn't to radically shift your reactions, but to be aware of what your defaults are, consider other paths, and get a taste of taking one. It'll feel unbearable at first—that's okay! Try in small bites.

◆ What is this time in your life potentially teaching you about loss training? What are you being challenged to let go of? What identities are being stripped away? List them out and take the time to feel the loss of each one. (I know it's hard, but stay with the discomfort if you can—it needs to be felt!)

◆ How do you talk about your mental health? What language do you use to describe the state of your mind (i.e., words like *crazy, unhinged, manic,* or *fucked up*)? How could you be more compassionate toward yourself? How could you speak more kindly about the totally understandable, completely human experience of suffering?

◆ What are you looking to get out of therapy, no matter what form that therapy takes? What's your ultimate wish list? Allow yourself to be as over-the-top as you want— imagining the ideal therapy situation can help you navigate finding the help you need. Therapy is everywhere.

The behaviors and reactions that you default to during times of crisis are super revealing. If you can find some awareness about your old coping methods, you'll gain a little room to make new decisions to use new tools. It takes time, though. For now, just acknowledge that there might be other ways besides your defaults. That's a great first step.

Chapter 5

MINDFULNESS

WOO-FREE MEDITATION

WHEN I WAS ELEVEN, TWO BIG THINGS HAPPENED. I GOT MY FIRST PERM AND MY PARENTS took me to a family meditation retreat led by Thich Nhat Hanh, a Vietnamese Buddhist monk and activist. I didn't really understand who or what he was, but I understood that he was cool and famous for meditating. But I refused to meditate at the retreat.

In fact, I didn't just not meditate . . . I prided myself on rejecting the whole idea. Meditation was something for stupid old hippies. "You have such a monkey brain," my mom would say to me in my teens, and I would scoff, "I like the monkeys! They're my friends!" In my early twenties, I watched my friends discover meditation, and I still scoffed. In my thirties, aging ravers I knew did silent Vipassana meditation retreats as rehab, and I was like, "Yeah, yeah, that's cool. You go sit for a week. I'm going to be over here building my career, making shit happen."

Meditation struck me as a denial of my mind's power, a dismissal of my ambitions, a way to round off my more aggressive corners, a cult-y plot to make me more passive. Funny how a shitshow makes you reconsider everything. And by funny, I mean humbling and embarrassing and awful.

A month after the shit went down, I would tell myself that I was doing a bit better (I was sleeping! I could go a few hours without crying!), but there I was in bed, and it was four a.m. again, and I was freaking out . . . again.

Tavi was at his father's for his half of the week, and I had been in my bed panicked, terrified, and unable to sleep for hours. I'd tried all the brainy tools I had: thinking, journaling, reading, crying, sleeping pills. My next therapy appointment wasn't for days. I lay in bed, feeling the fucking demons circling. I cried so hard that I started panting. Then I started talking to myself.

"You're fine," I said out loud. "No one is hurting you right now! Calm down."

It didn't work.

For the first time, I started to recognize that the monkeys in my brain were not always my friends. Grinding my teeth and hyperventilating into the darkness, I realized that I was feeling myself go insane. Not figuratively insane, like "You're so crazy!" "This is a crazy sale!" "Wow, that's sooooo crazy!" This was not hyperbolic cray-cray. This was me losing my grasp on reality. I could feel it happening, the cords of my own mental coherence slipping through my fingers.

Like many of us, I have an extensive family history of mental illness. I could feel my anxiety pulling me under, and it felt like I was following in my maternal grandmother's footsteps, which ultimately led to her being institutionalized for a decade. My family also has paranoid schizophrenia, anxiety disorders, and some bipolar II tucked into the lineage; chances are decent that yours has similar.

Lying in my bed, I felt myself standing at a mental cliff, staring over the lip of my grasp on reality. The monkeys were going to shove me right off the edge.

I got out of bed. I woke myself up all the way. I went to the kitchen to put on water for tea and continued my out-loud conversation with myself: "I need to stop thinking like this because I am literally driving myself crazy." Desperate for a distraction, I checked my phone and found an email from a friend that included this Thich Nhat Hanh quote:

> You are hurt. And you want to punish him or her for having made you suffer. The mantra is to overcome that: "Darling, I suffer. I am trying my best to practice. Please help me.". . . And if you can bring yourself to say that mantra, you suffer less right away.

Suddenly, just like that, I was ready to try meditation. The suffering was too much for my usual coping strategies of overthinking, strategizing, and busy-making. I stood in my dark kitchen, gritted my teeth, and tried repeating it: *Darling, I suffer. I am trying my best to practice. Thank you for this practice.*

It didn't work.

I tried to clear my mind (SHUT UP, MONKEYS!) and counted my breaths, making it to three before I got lost.

It still didn't work. I sucked at this, but there was nothing else to do but keep practicing. It was either that, or go off the cliff.

Oh wait . . . is that why it's called a meditation *practice*?

If anyone gets that meditation can be an intimidating and irritating concept, it's me. Lots of us have that reaction, which is probably why the word *mindfulness* has gained popularity recently. Mindfulness is just a form of meditation, but the name has a less esoteric sound to Western ears, so it's less likely to scare away those wary of "woo-woo."

But even the term *mindfulness* can be a turnoff for those of us who aren't sure about quiet minds. And it's certainly become trendy recently, which can be a turnoff for those of us who are skeptics or think of ourselves as offbeat. If you've been curious about the benefits of mindfulness but reluctant to try it because phrases like "clearing your mind" don't resonate with you, you're not alone.

But mindfulness and meditation aren't necessarily about not thinking, or clearing your mind. Psychologist Dr. Ellen Hendriksen, author of *How to Be Yourself: Quiet Your Inner Critic and Rise Above Social Anxiety*, explains, "Mindfulness is not . . . a vacant mind. Your mind is designed to be anything but vacant. All day we think, notice, and concentrate. Mindfulness isn't asking your mind not to think, it's asking it to focus its attention."

So mindfulness is not trying to reach Inbox Zero in your head or chastising yourself for having a monkey brain . . . so WTF is it, then? Professor Jon Kabat-Zinn, an expert on mindfulness in Western medicine, defines mindfulness as "paying attention in a particular way: on purpose, in the present moment, and non-judgmentally."

Let's break this down:

◆ **Paying attention on purpose:** This just means making a conscious choice to focus your mind, rather than letting your thoughts wander around on their own.

◆ **Paying attention in the present moment:** Acknowledge the thoughts and feelings that are happening in you right now and recognize that they'll change; you haven't always thought or felt this way, nor will you always think or feel this way in the future. It's like you're at a bus stop and your thoughts and feelings are buses passing you on the road—*you don't have to get on the bus!*

◆ **Paying attention non-judgmentally:** There's no need to analyze, fix, or judge your thoughts and feelings. This part is freaking hard. Our brains spend all day problem-solving, theorizing, hypothesizing, and even conspiring against us. It's hard to just watch your thoughts go by, not get on the bus, and not get mad that it's THAT stupid bus again—*I hate that bus!*

Let's be clear: mindfulness doesn't stop you from feeling anxiety or other sucky emotions, but it can change the way you *relate* to them. This doesn't sound huge, but it is. You can step back and just recognize that there's a thought in your mind or a sensation in your body—completely appropriate and understandable, but also not something you have to make a story about. You don't have to get on the bus.

With even just two minutes a day of practice, you can start to get some space from your thoughts and feelings. Your discomfort can be a bus that you stand on the sidewalk and watch go right on by with curiosity and compassion—without getting on it.

Well, that's how it works in a perfect world, anyway.

THE "THIS FUCKING SUCKS" MEDITATION

☑ Set a timer for two minutes.

☑ Sit down, take a breath, close your eyes, and for just two minutes try to *feel* how you actually feel right now, whatever it may be. Worried, hopeless, resentful? Feel it. Impatient? Irritated? Woot, there it is. Full of rage, resentment, fear? Yep, that makes sense.

☑ Try touching the mood and then feeling your way around the edges of the sensations the mood brings up in your body. Try to resist making a story of why those feelings are there, or judgment about whether they should be, or questions about the anxiety that's making your butt tingle. Just feel the sensations.

☑ Now, recognize it: *this fucking sucks*. It's an agonizing experience, especially if you have trauma in your body, like many of us do. Give it just one moment more to focus on the discomfort that feels like a lump in your gut or a pang in your chest. *URG.*

☑ Now try this on: What if this experience of discomfort is not a problem? Can you relax and just feel it? Don't tell yourself a story about it ("I hate this! Why am I like this? This is going to kill me! I can't handle this!"), but just take a few breaths, allowing yourself to experience the discomfort.

☑ Okay, open your eyes. Take a breath, stand up, and shake your body a bit to clear that gunk out.

Now consider this: What if the chronic misery that so many of us live with isn't actually from those uncomfortable feelings you just sat with, but from how you *relate* to them? The sensations are just there, and the real pain comes when you judge the feelings as bad, reject them, tell yourself you can't manage them, shame yourself for feeling them, or push them away and wish you were feeling something else. If you don't mind feeling miserable, what happens to the misery?

By practicing just a minute or two of sitting with the discomfort of things sucking, you're building a practice of allowing sensations to pass through you . . . and when you let them pass through, then there's room for different feelings.

SUCKING IS PART OF WHAT YOU'RE PRACTICING

Here in the twenty-first century, of course there are tons of meditation apps to help you start meditating. For me, it was the Headspace app that finally got me to settle into a seated practice—and the thirty-day series on anxiety was life-changing for me. (Not being hyperbolic, here. It literally changed my life.)

If having a disembodied voice talk you through breathing exercises isn't your thing, you can start small and just practice awareness during your daily routines. While you're brushing your teeth, focus on how the toothpaste tastes, how the bristles feel, how your bones and muscles move your hand, the sounds that surround you.

Your mind is going to wander. That's what a mind does! You're going to feel like you suck at first—that's totally normal. Remember that every time you notice yourself thinking about how much you suck at meditation, you're winning because you actually noticed yourself thinking! Awareness of being distracted is a major, massive accomplishment.

Practicing mindfulness is going to be hard, and it's going to feel like it's not working. Remember, that's why it's called a practice: *because you suck at it at first*. It's going to feel silly. It's going to feel like you are the only person in the world for whom mindfulness cannot possibly work. Keep trying. Slowly, you'll start to notice a shift. It feels agonizing, and like you're getting worse, but it's because you're noticing, which means you're getting better.

A few weeks after I first tried meditating, the demons came again. I felt myself start to freak out, and tried to put on my observation hat and just notice what was happening. It went something like this:

"Oh no, here it comes again. Okay, let's just be curious. What is the sensation in this moment? I have a stab of fear in my chest. Hmm. That makes sense, given everything that's happened."

I took a breath.

"Where am I actually right now, though? I am in this bed: warm, comfortable, quiet, safe. Sure, there's fear in my body (that's appropriate given that scary things have happened recently!), but the fear bus can just go by."

Then I lost the plot and just freaked out for an hour. It sucked. A shitshow provides endless opportunities to practice sucking.

There will be days when you feel overwhelmed by the understanding that a time in your life that you loved dearly is gone forever. Take a breath and remember that *this* time, too, this existential turmoil, is also going to be gone at some point. It's all temporary!

Everything you hate, everything you love—it's all temporary!

Thank fucking god!

But also, fucking tragic?

If things feel tangled up, like the joy and the pain are indistinguishable? It's confusing, but you're doing it right.

FIND YOUR AFTERGLOW

I know firsthand most of the reasons that your brain will tell you that you "can't" meditate, because my brain gives me all those reasons, too—still! Your brain may tell you that meditation is too boring, too new age, too trendy, too hard, that you suck at it. All these excuses are your mind being like the Wizard of Oz, shouting, "Pay no attention to that man behind the curtain!" Your brain hates change and desperately doesn't want you to see what it's doing behind that curtain.

When you practice observing your mind during a shitshow, it can be upsetting to actually witness the horrific things your brain is doing—yelling at you, shaming you, distracting you. It's all normal, and you should still meditate. Let's talk about it.

◆ When you think about meditation, what doubts come up? Some of us like to berate ourselves for being distractible, some of us spin in doubt and worry that we're not doing it "right," some of us get snarky about how the whole idea is dumb. What are your mind's favorite stories about why you supposedly "can't meditate"? And what if you recognize that this is your mind defending itself—it's making up stories to put you off the track of observing it and recognizing that it's not always right.

◆ What are your brain's favorite buses? Everyone's mind has its favorite awful stories it likes to tell. List your mind's three favorite disaster stories, and see if you can do it without judgment: you might hate these buses, but for now, we're just acknowledging the express routes you're working with. (Some common favorite awful buses: I'm flawed, I'm unlovable, I'm worthless, I'm insignificant, I'm incompetent, I'm unsafe, I'm bored, I'm vulnerable, I'm fucked up, etc.)

◆ What hackneyed advice has started to feel irritatingly relevant? Are there any clichés ("The only way over is through!") that are starting to take on new meaning in your life? What things that you never thought you'd try are starting to appeal to you?

You're probably starting to see that a big part of this journey is learning to notice your mind's tricks—awareness of your habits, awareness of your old stories, awareness of your excuses. This is true mindfulness, and sometimes it's really hard to look at this stuff! Be gentle on yourself and know that just by noticing, you're making impressive progress. All you need to do is notice. It will feel like you're getting worse, but remember: sucking is how you practice. I believe in you. Keep going!

Chapter 6

SHAME

WHEN YOU FAIL IN PUBLIC

NAVIGATING AN EMOTIONAL RECOVERY CAN FEEL LIKE TRYING TO WALK THROUGH A MAZE blindfolded while randomly getting punched in the gut when you go around certain corners. Less than a month after my life imploded, I got the double gut-punch of Thanksgiving and my son's sixth birthday. Shitshow holidays and birthdays are the stuff of shitty legends, and . . . yep, those legends are accurate.

In that first month, I'd been trying to manage myself (sleeping! therapy! trying to be mindful!) and was only crying a few times a day. I was trying to stay in the moment and breathe. Once the holidays rolled around, however, I looped back to acute brokenness. The demons reappeared and I reverted to the mode of having no idea what to do at any time.

I worked from home most days (read as: crying and puking and bumping into walls), with my coworkers contacting me only with the most pressing of questions, asked in the simplest of sentences.

I used mapping apps when driving even just a mile across town, because deciding between freeway or surface streets felt utterly insurmountable. I doubted everything, especially my own choices—I thought I knew what my life was, I thought I had a trustworthy foundation, but I guess I was wrong? What else was I wrong about?! I thought I knew? I don't know anything! Thanksgiving? My son's sixth birthday? Can my mapping app tell me how to navigate these emotional land mines?

Unfortunately, there is not an app for navigating a family holiday after a shitshow. Before Thanksgiving dinner with my extended family, my mother gathered us into a family gratitude circle. We sat on her assortment of Goodwill cast-off couches and stained rugs. I sat between my parents and silently dripped tears as we went around the circle.

"I'm grateful to be out of jail," my cousin said. He'd had a rough year.

"I'm thankful I survived that cancer scare," my aunt's boyfriend said. He'd had a rough year.

"I'm grateful that my son is out of jail and I'm almost healed from that surgery," my aunt said. She'd had a rough year.

My hierarchy of needs was offended by my own pain. My hierarchy of needs understood that my family members were being grateful for surviving actual *real* problems. My hierarchy of needs wondered where the hell was my perspective?

I had no perspective, like a lost child sobbing three feet from home.

When my turn in the family gratitude circle came, I couldn't even talk (*me?* unable to talk!?) because I was so leveled by loss that no words would come out. I silently shook my head, snot bubbling down my chin like a preschooler. My brain collapsed in on itself, thinking, *I know I should be grateful to be alive, but sometimes that just doesn't even feel like a gift.*

This was not gratitude. This was darkest thoughts and deepest heartbreak.

After a Thanksgiving dinner that I chewed and swallowed but couldn't really digest, and some time sitting mutely by the woodstove while my family chatted with each other, my son and I drifted into the guest room of the roundhouse.

I sat down on the queen-size guest bed while Tavi hopped onto the twin bed against the other wall.

"Do you want to have a slumber party with me in the big bed?" I asked my son.

Tavi jumped from his little bed into the big bed, and we burrowed under the blankets together.

"Ready for whispers and kisses?" I said, desperate to stick to our bedtime routines even as I could feel myself sinking under the surface of my own depression.

Tavi nodded and curled up in front of me. I nuzzled my face into the back of his little neck and tried to stay in the moment, breathing in his hair and whispering stories I made up as I went. I kissed his head and felt his little boy body twitch as he drifted off to sleep.

Then, as he snored in my arms, I saturated his Rainbow Dash pajamas with tears as I tried to rock myself to sleep.

I tried breathing exercises and that Thich Nhat Hanh *Darling, I suffer* mantra I'd just learned. Nothing worked, and after two hours of watching the monkeys in my brain scream, of trying to let the anxiety bus just go on by, of failing and getting on the express route to Abandonment Story Town, and then hopping on a different bus headed to I Will Die Alone Station, and then observing the speeding bright-red RAGE BUS with its flaming exhaust pipes, I watched this thought bus go by: *This is like watching an open wound rotting.*

How could I be this tormented in my head when in this moment what's really happening is that I'm snuggling a child I love, in the home of a family who loves me?

Who am I to be this destroyed by a shithow? Real people had real problems—getting out of jail! Cancer scares! I was just some forty-year-old lady freaking out over common life shit.

Oh look . . . it's the express bus to Shameville.

Remember that by definition, a shitshow *feels* like your life is over—even when you know it's not. That's part of what makes the whole situation so awful: even as one part of your mind is like,

"It's over! My life hath ended! Everything is awful!" another part of your head is scoffing and impatiently judging itself for being upset.

You might say things to yourself like "Yo, I know it's hard when we lose our job, then our aunt dies, and then we get evicted [or whatever your particular on-ramp might've been], but it's not like we're in a refugee camp! It's not like we got a terminal diagnosis! People have it worse than us, so we need to stop wallowing and STFU!"

This is that second arrow of shame. It's understandable, but it doesn't help you get over the stress of your life changing, or help you focus on your recuperation. Remember: if you shame yourself into not experiencing these feelings now, they'll just bide their time and wait to take you down later.

You may find these words from Bay Area mystic L'Erin Alta comforting: "Trauma doesn't happen in isolation, and neither does healing. When done with intention, love, and wild devotion, our individual healing is collective healing."

So rather than yelling at yourself in your head for being broken, consider that your brokenness and healing is a road to help you gain compassion for others who are in pain, and to contribute to the healing of us all.

Your shame doesn't help anyone, but you know what does benefit others? Using your suffering to help you gain compassion for the suffering of those around you. You know what else helps? Knowing that by tending to yourself, you're contributing to the healing of others.

But that's a lot to take on when you're still in the emotional weeds. We'll get to concepts like healing it forward in Chapter 29. For now, just know that your feelings are valid and need to be felt in their full awful entirety.

CELEBRITIES: THEY SHITSHOW JUST LIKE US!

No one is exempt. Life crises are truly the great equalizer, and it doesn't matter how rich and famous you might be. Actor Mark Ruffalo underwent successful surgery to remove a brain tumor. He described it: "The whole experience of getting close to mortality changed my perspective. I thought I deserved more, and I wasn't grateful for all the great shit that had happened to me."

Writer Glennon Doyle, author of *Love Warrior*, describes herself as a "Recovering Everything." She dealt with addiction, bulimia, a divorce, and then coming out of the closet—all in the public eye thanks to her popular mommy blog.

In an extreme example, Keanu Reeves's partner Jennifer Syme gave birth to a stillborn baby, and soon after she was killed in a car accident. Talking about the tragedies, Reeves said, "Grief changes shape, but it never ends. People have a misconception that you can deal with it and say, 'It's gone, and I'm better.' They're wrong."

Clinical psychologist Melanie Greenberg, author of *The Stress-Proof Brain*, says that experiencing trauma can deepen how you relate to others and bring spiritual change and newfound personal strength. Screw silver linings, but understanding trauma as an awful opportunity feels more feasible when you see folks who have gone through it and come out of it forever changed, but with a sense of peace.

VACANCY AT THE NOT-PAIN MOTEL

The morning after Thanksgiving, I was the first one awake. I shuffled into my mother's kitchen, made space on the counter between the wheat germ and dried nettles, and steeped myself some black tea in a chipped cup.

I sat with my tea in an enormous pink chair covered with an old afghan and cracked open Stephen Levine's book *Unattended Sorrow*: "Grief calls us to open our heart in hell. When hope is wounded and life spins out of our control—when we're stunned from bewilderment and dismay—our nerve endings seemingly burst into flame." I underlined that part.

Underlining! I was almost functional! Until I wasn't. An hour later, I was lying in a heap on the guest bed, sobbing to myself like ya do when it's the day after Thanksgiving a month after your life slides off the rails. In that moment, I recognized that I'd moved into a place beyond vulnerability, to a place where I was so stripped down and raw and completely helpless that it actually frightened me.

I was scared for myself. I recognized how at-risk someone in this state was. ("Someone in this state . . ." Ha! Me! UGH!)

I suddenly had an insight into how folks in crisis can go really, really far off the rails. I was in such a state of concentrated emotional pain that any brief moments of relief felt ecstatic. Ah, sweet not-pain!

You may feel like pleasure has become a foreign country, you've lost your passport, and your vacation standards are suddenly very, very low. You may find yourself in a crappy metaphorical motel, luxuriating on a threadbare comforter, your toes digging into the stained carpet. Welcome to the Not-Pain Motel—it might not be much, but when you're going through personal hell, any small not-pain feels amazing.

You may notice that any experience that brings you a sense of "not pain" immediately becomes a rat lever to which you'll return. A friend who offers a kind word, you may call again and again and again. A book that feels comforting, you may reread and underline every other sentence. Your stack of self-dev books may eventually threaten to bury you.

This is where you have to stop and ask yourself: Is the Not-Pain Motel a stop on the road to the land beyond loss . . . or a roadside-attraction scam?

I knew to stay away from alcohol and hard drugs and TV evangelicals, but I gained enormous compassion for how damaged,

SHAME

disoriented, vulnerable people are at such high risk for addiction, exploitation, and self-harm. I was so addled that I frequently couldn't even make basic decisions, and that meant that I was basically a cult leader's wet dream.

Now I understand how easy it is for the emotionally vulnerable to be sucked into an exploitative church, or a toxic relationship, or a bad time-share. (Spoiler alert: I fell prey to one of these three.)

As you move through your shitshow, you must be aware of and responsible for your emotional vulnerability. While the rawness can make for remarkable leaps in personal development, desperate moments can lead you to make questionable decisions.

Recovery after an emotional undoing isn't the same as recovering from a chemical dependency, but there are some similarities when it comes to managing the vulnerability of a new life. Alcoholics Anonymous advises recovering addicts to avoid new romantic relationships for at least a year, because latching on to a new person can mess up a recovery process. You may be wise to follow suit (although, full disclosure: I didn't).

Some days, I felt courageous. I had my toolbox (crying when I needed to cry, recognizing there was no fixing things or controlling them, trying to be patient with myself and the passage of time, trying to have faith in the fact that everything is temporary, asking to be held when I couldn't sit up anymore), and I was starting to feel the glimmers of an afterglow, like just maaaaaybe I could do this.

Other days, I paced the edge of my mental pit in tighter and tighter circles. I digested myself in my own self-loathing acids. I keened on my kitchen floor. I tried to count my breaths and ended up panting and nauseated.

You must remind yourself of this as often as you can: feeling this discomfort is a vital part of the process.

I hate that truth! But if it hurts, you're probably doing it right. If it's confusing, you're doing it right. If you feel embarrassed that you're this devastated—ugh, that's shame, and it ain't right, but it's *normal*. And if it feels intolerable and like you don't know who you are anymore? Yep, exactly. You're nailing this thing!

If it doesn't hurt, you might be probably in denial. If it's not confusing, you're tricking yourself into thinking you have control over it. If it feels tolerable, you might be numbing out. If you don't know who you are anymore? That's identity death, and unfortunately that's exactly what needs to happen.

There's a new you waiting. The longer you're in denial or avoiding it or pretending you can control your fumbles toward that new life, your eyes blinded with tears, tender new skin raw and pink, arms outstretched . . . the longer you put off being embraced by that new self.

Your potential is waiting patiently for you.

FIND YOUR AFTERGLOW

Oh, gratitude and shame, gratitude and shame. You have to hold both the realities that there is so much to be grateful for (even in the middle of a shitshow) while also recognizing that there's nothing to be ashamed of about feeling pain. There's a friction there, and it gets even more complex when issues of privilege are involved. If you're learning anything in this book, it's that discomfort is the name of the game with growth, and if you can be brave and stay with it, discomfort can be such amazing fuel. Here are some questions to consider:

◆ What shameful feelings are coming up for you? What if you just let yourself recognize that you're an imperfect human, doing human things, making human choices and human mistakes?

◆ Are there any times in the past when you've judged others for being in "too much" pain? How is your experience now helping you gain compassion? How might you use that compassion positively in your life?

◆ How can you keep yourself emotionally and logistically safe during your shitshow? Who can you trust to help you navigate your options in your new life? Who could you ask for gut checks when you feel unsafe or unsure?

◆ How is this shitshow giving you the awful gift of getting exactly what you've always wanted, but in the worst way? (For example, I realized that the fifty/fifty custody that initially felt excruciating ultimately gave me the time I needed to focus on personal development. For other folks, a serious illness forces them to take time off—time that they desperately needed but didn't want in *that* way.) This question isn't about finding a silver lining to a shitty situation (screw that), it's about recognizing the ways that you sometimes get gifts you've always wanted wrapped in super-ugly wrapping paper.

As you start to peel back the shame to see what's underneath, you might find that there are things you want from this new life that you've been denying, or didn't want to admit to yourself. The sensation of shame can feel intolerable, but sometimes it's telling you there's something you've been avoiding that wants your attention. Don't be afraid to stare!

Chapter 7

GRATITUDE

PULLING INTO APPRECIATION STATION

OKAY, SO MAYBE I WAS TONGUE-TIED DURING THE THANKSGIVING FAMILY GRATITUDE CIRCLE, but the idea planted a seed and I decided that even if I was still stumbling, at least I could stumble from one desperately grateful moment to the next.

Thank you until the end of time I owe you a rainbow unicorn and free pony rides forever, I texted one of my coworkers when she covered my ass for the hundredth time because my brain still didn't know how to make a decision.

(I watch this bus go by: "I thought I knew how to make decisions. I thought I knew how to watch for things, but I must have had my eyes closed or willfully unfocused. Clearly I did something wrong. What did I do wrong? How can I never ever do that again?")

"Thank you for caffeinating me," I said to the floppy-haired bespectacled barista at Ada's Technical Books when he remembered the kind of milk I like in my spiced chai latte that I call the Midlife White-Lady Special.

(And I watch this bus go by: "I thought I was a generally appreciative person before. Maybe I didn't say thank you enough in my life? Maybe I didn't sing the Appreciation Song enough times? Clearly I did something wrong. What did I do wrong? How can I never ever do that again?")

"Thank you for listening when I can barely put sentences together," I sobbed to Ashlee over the phone after she'd listened to me go on for another hour and a half about how lonely I was when Tavi was gone and I was by myself rattling around my home, leaving heavy piles of wet Kleenex behind me in each room.

(And there goes this bus: "I thought I was a good person, but maybe I didn't listen enough? Maybe I should have asked questions more often? Maybe my friends are all about to leave me, too. Clearly I did something wrong. What did I do wrong? How can I never ever do that again?")

"Thank you, sweet potato," I said to my son when he brought me a cup of tea one morning during one of his weekends at my house.

(The parenting bus goes by: "We're doing a good job of holding each other up, and the play therapist I hired to work with Tavi said he was transitioning really well, and we have a lot of support from extended family and he seems fine and he's such a good boy and so agreeable, but then again sometimes agreeable people are actually quite unhappy for a long time before they start to show signs. So I'm still worrying. Did I do something wrong? What did I do wrong? How can I never ever do that again?")

Most days that winter, I walked to and from my Capitol Hill coworking office (progress: I could get dressed and leave the house!), umbrella over my head, my feet counting out the mistakes I'd made. Right regret, left remorse. Right failure, left disaster. Right catastrophe, left existential disintegration. There was nothing to do but keep walking and keep breathing and try to stay in the moment of feeling my tears of regret mix with the Seattle rain.

I found it difficult to be merciful with myself. I was starting to find tiny windows of okay-ness for a few minutes at a time, but I spent most days loathing myself for every mistake, every misstep

I'd ever made. Clearly I had done so many things wrong or this wouldn't have happened. If I wasn't The Worst Person Ever Born, surely my life wouldn't have gone off the rails. My mind was sure I deserved this misery.

If you're staring down a regret black hole, try bending your perspective a little. Does regret benefit you or others in any way? Probably not. Say it out loud to yourself: "Those situations are in the past, I can't do anything about them." Shout it if you need to.

You can, however, resolve to be self-reflective, recognize where you made mistakes, and use that awareness as a learning experience. This means hell YES for holding yourself accountable for your choices and the consequences, but hell NO to regret and shame. Let your regret be a bus. Watch it pull up, note it (ooh, there's regret in the system right now), and let it pass you on by. Remind yourself that you'll have opportunities in the future, and that because of the effort you're making today, you'll be better able to kick ass when the time comes.

I tried to be merciful with myself in my regret. I tried to be merciful with myself in my distrust of the entire world. In my *la-la-la rainbows* life of middle-class first-world privilege, I'd always been a relatively trusting person . . . but now I was guarded and skittish, suspicious and scared of everything.

Even when good things happened, I didn't quiiiite trust the good feelings.

"I can't ever let my emotions be dependent on outside inputs," I fretted to Atta. "I need to do more work on getting myself completely independently rock-solid so that this will never happen to me ever again."

I'm human, though. Mammalian. Despite my fears, I was a soldier willing to fight to the death for human connection, and all I could do was keep reaching out and saying thank you, thank you, thank you. I lobbed loving grenades of communications at everyone I cared about, exploding my heartfelt shrapnel across the country.

Mornings were my most difficult time of day. I'd wake up and generally start crying first thing as I remembered my new reality.

But then I'd crisscross my emotional machine-gun belts across my chest and fire off the rounds, sending texts to friends and family and people who matter to me:

> I miss you!
>
> I love you!
>
> I appreciate who you are and the time we spend together!
>
> I'm thinking of you!
>
> I hope that hard thing is feeling softer for you today!
>
> I know you have that fertility treatment today I'm sending your uterus good thoughts!
>
> I am lucky to know you!

Pulling into Appreciation Station felt good (it feels nice to put some love out into the world when you're hurting), but it also brought up even more shame—when did I get so pathetic and desperate?

I tried to remind myself that I've always been a communicator, and I've always tried to be an appreciator. I hoped I'd been a kind, loving, grateful, valuable member of my community, but I realized that perhaps, before my life fell down, I didn't fully understand how much I needed people.

Reaching out and being vulnerable can be one of the most emotionally awkward parts of going through a crisis. Isolating yourself can seem attractive when you're soldiering through pain and sadness. You may think no one wants to put up with your emotions, that it's unfair to be a burden. You might not want to put your already-vulnerable ass on the line again.

But you need a network for support, and these people need to be compassionate, trustworthy, ride-or-die friends. Here's how to assemble a support crew:

◆ Make a list of your ride-or-die folks, the people in your life that you can rely on no matter what. The people who would give you a ride to the airport at five a.m.

◆ Tell them explicitly how important they are to you, and that you may need them. You may not know exactly how they can help yet, but vocalizing that you see them as part of your support network will help you and them.

◆ Remember that you chose your folks for a reason. You're going to feel like a burden, or like you should be able to handle things on your own. Imagine if one of your crew came to you for help—now try to give yourself the same compassion you'd give them when you need to ask for help.

In her book *How to Stop Feeling Like Sh*t*, Andrea Owen calls these people "compassionate witnesses." These are people who can respond to your needs with empathy instead of trying to fix, distract, one-up, or gaslight you. "Empathy," Owen explains, "is about feeling *with* someone."

Assembling a shitshow support crew is about being okay sharing your experience so you can sort out your feelings. It's about someone bearing witness to your struggle. About being seen and heard in your pain. You might not even know yet what you might need, but you definitely need your shitshow support crew of compassionate witnesses.

Once you understand that it's okay to need people, things get easier. It's okay to, for instance, beg a beloved geighbor (that's a gay neighbor) to come over and hold your hand while you cry. (Not that I or my beloved geighbor would know anything about that . . .)

YOUR GOAL: MAKE NEW MISTAKES

I was back in my therapist Atta's office on the dark brown couch.

"I wish I was more evolved," I sobbed. "I'm just so sad and angry but I wish I was more compassionate, in less pain, less raw, less angry, less grabby, less shove-y, less conniving, less attention whore-y, less needy, less immature . . . just less *me*."

Atta's hair was colored teal that week.

"Try to have compassion for the distance between where you're at right now and the place where you want to end up. You're doing all the right things to get there, you just have to be patient with the process."

I wiped my mascara across my cheek and choked out, "Ugh, it's hard to level up a soul. A friend sent me a quote that was like, 'When you fall, it's the arms of your future self that are waiting to catch you,' which, I mean, cool story, bro. But I don't trust myself to catch anything! Clearly, I did something wrong. How can I trust myself to not keep failing?"

"Life's a series of failures," Atta replied. "Maturation is just being able to handle them in new ways. Make new mistakes."

"Make new mistakes," I repeated. I would repeat this line over and over and over as the months went on.

I went home and swayed in my living room, coat still on. I hated myself for struggling so hard, for being in so much pain, for being so angry.

Sobbing, I took off my coat, walked myself into the bedroom, and flopped on the bed.

I tried desperately to be more compassionate with myself. I was still convinced that if I thought REALLY HARD about this, I could fix it. *Think more compassionately right now, Ariel!*

"More mercy, you stupid bitch!" I said out loud to myself.

Wait, I was doing it wrong.

"More patience with the process, you asshole!"

Aargh, no, that wasn't right at all.

"Stallings!" I barked at myself. "Be less broken!"

Crap. I was failing at self-compassion. I took a breath. I tried to focus on how the breath felt in my belly. I tried to talk to myself like I'd talk to my son.

"I am where I am and it's all understandable and appropriate and makes sense. I'm getting there."

There. Whew. Finally nailed it.

When you're going through a shitshow, being mid-process can be excruciating. Your brain will tell you that, sure, maybe lots of people have been through this kind of thing, but surely it didn't suck like this for them? But you know what? IT DID. Despite having all the information, knowing the destination, and understanding that you can't rush it . . . you still just have to be where you're at. It's agonizing.

I was the scorned divorcée who couldn't help but spit out her story of woe to a cab driver who was like, "Uh, yeah, so have a nice flight today!" (Scorned woman doesn't want to small talk! Scorned woman has fucking *feelings*, cabbie!)

I was the raw exposed nerve on the business trip who started crying on an airplane when I saw over my seatmate's shoulder that he was sending an email about a serious medical issue with his kidneys, asking people to pray for him. All our bodies are failing, every day! I could have another organ explode at any moment! This plane could crash! We're all so flimsy! I bathed in the human fragility of coach class.

I was the scowling woman in headphones fuming on the bus about intuition, grinding over the fact that I knew, I knew, I knew and I felt like I was gaslighted and intentionally distracted from my own knowing.

I was the stupid entitled bitch who dropped her son off at his lovely school and walked to her coworking office while muttering angrily, strolling past the gorgeous homes of her friendly neighbors under the moist gray sky of her favorite city in the world, crying and hating everything.

The monkeys screamed inside my head: "I didn't want this to be my life! I didn't want to be dealing with midlife bullshit! Why has this been forced on me!? Why can't I stop thinking about how much this sucks?"

And here's where that distance between where I was at and where I wanted to be came up: I would *like* to just stop thinking about it! I *could* just stop thinking about it! I *should* just stop thinking about it! I saw that. I felt that. I wanted that. But that awareness didn't mean I could magically make it happen. I couldn't magically transport myself ahead in the maturation process.

I could see where I wanted to get (Magical Mature Unicorn Who Does Not Get Bogged Down by Petty Interpersonal Bullshit or Fear of Health Problems), and it was unfathomably difficult to be where I was actually at (Magical Immature Unicorn Who Gets Completely Derailed by Petty Interpersonal Bullshit Because I Was Betrayed and Left Godammit and It's Not Fair and Wasn't Life Supposed to Be Fair Where Can I File a Unicorn Lifetime Fairness Appeal?).

Even more difficult? Holding compassion for myself being right where I was. No sense in yelling at myself. Mercy, mercy, mercy.

You're going to want to speed ahead, past the ugly stops on the map to the green pastures you can just make out on the horizon. Bad news, though: it just doesn't work like that. That said, when you're struggling with impatience, you don't have to beat yourself up. Just watch the buses go by, even when your feelings are ones you don't want to own, ones that make you feel shameful, ones that make you question who you even are anymore.

Even when the gap between where you are and where you want to be feels huge—even *those* feelings are valid, and even *those* feelings are temporary. Acknowledge them (ooh, there's the impatience-and-self-loathing bus going by!) and try to look at yourself mercifully and acknowledge that you're not there yet, but you're on your way.

What you focus on grows. If you focus on the gap, you'll only get more gap.

FIND YOUR AFTERGLOW

Gratitude is one of those concepts that's gotten a little too much Vaseline on the lens. It can feel inauthentic, like you're #blessed (or #bragging). But seriously: it may be the most valuable daily practice. When you're falling apart, it can be a major challenge to find the time to notice things to be grateful for . . . but it's an incredibly valuable way to retrain your brain to recognize when there's an absence of suck, and find a tiny moment of being grateful. Just a tiny one.

◆ What are you grateful for in this moment? Writing down five positive thoughts before bed can help you hold the gratitude in your mind in a conscious way that just thinking it to yourself never could. Remember, this is for your eyes only, so go wild. Nothing is too silly or too small to be grateful for. "I AM GRATEFUL I SHOW-ERED TODAY." "I AM GRATEFUL I REMEMBERED TO TURN OFF THE STOVE." "I AM GRATEFUL TO HAVE WARM SOCKS." This practice will make it easier for your brain to be appreciative by rewiring synapses that don't get enough traffic during a shitshow. Your thought-pattern ruts will slowly shift, and eventually speaking your gratitude aloud will feel easier.

◆ How do you talk to yourself when you're feeling down? Would you speak to anyone else this way? In your life, who spoke to you this way in the past? When you're feeling down, how do you WISH someone spoke to you? What would your perfect beloved say to you in your lowest moments? Write down three comforting things you wish someone else would say to you, and then read them aloud to yourself.

◆ Try Atta's suggestion: What if your goal isn't to *avoid* mistakes, but to make NEW mistakes? Committing to new kinds of mistakes keeps you moving forward, and gets you unstuck from both perfectionism and your old default behaviors and mental loops.

If you're starting to feel exhausted by all of this, you're doing it right. I promise you, this grind pays off. You're building the foundation for your future self. Pace yourself and stay with it. You deserve this.

Chapter 8

PANIC ATTACKS

WHEN YOUR IDENTITY IMPLODES

I WAS WORKING OVERTIME ON MY SELF-DEVELOPMENT, DESPERATELY TRYING TO MEDITATE every day ("There are screaming monkeys in the system. The anxiety bus is going by. There are hallucinations! In this moment, I am drowning in cortisol and feel like I need to run away as fast as I can! I am breathing. I AM BREATHING!!"), desperately trying to sleep every night, desperately talking to my therapist, desperately trying to keep track of how to stay alive, desperately trying to stay safe, desperately trying to stay grateful (life isn't that bad! I'm down an ovary and a husband, but I still have my child and my home and my job!) . . .

And then I had my first panic attack.

I'd known all about panic attacks, of course. I'd counseled a friend through one fifteen years earlier when she was coming down off a bender at an outdoor music festival.

"I think I'm dying!" she'd gasped, and I held her hand and told her to put her feet in a river.

"You're not dying," I'd said. "You just really shouldn't do coke again."

"Just feel your feet in the river and breathe with me," I'd said. "And seriously, stop doing coke."

So I thought I knew about panic attacks.

I just didn't *know*.

It was early evening and I was the last one working at the co-working office when I first noticed that the ever-present crushing anxiety in my chest was turning into something else.

I was exhausted from my workday, but in my efforts to get to Inbox Zero, I was finishing by answering an email from a friend. She wanted to talk through her social anxiety about her birthday party: Should she invite both me and my newly estranged spouse?

I was trying desperately to be nice to everyone. I had immediately agreed to amicable co-parenting plans and then spent hours pacing with my heart racing, fighting the urge to run as fast as possible to get away from the crushing terror. I would push down the terror and focus really hard on *being nice*! Everyone wants this situation to *be nice*. This is the West Coast! We believe in conscious uncoupling and namaste niceness, right?

At my desk, in the empty coworking office, I felt my breathing speed up as I tried to be as nice as possible answering this email.

Thank you for putting so much thought into this, I started to type, but my fingers were shaking and my chest hurt. I closed my eyes and tried to focus on my breathing. *I probably don't need to answer this email right now.*

I'm not sure if I have a good answer about who you should invite to your birthday party, I typed, but it was getting harder to ignore the constriction in my chest. The breaths were coming quicker.

I closed my email. I got a glass of water and tried to focus myself by watching the surface of the water ripple from my shaking hands. I tried to slow things down.

At my standing desk, my legs started to feel weak. Despite all my efforts, my breathing sped up. I packed my bag; my hands wouldn't stop shaking and my breathing deteriorated into gasps. The monkeys in my head started screaming, and I felt my nervous system lean forward, *hard*.

This was bad.

THE PANIC ATTACK THAT ATE MY EGO

As I walked out the door, I started sending up flares in the form of text messages. Between the gasps, I started sobbing.

I texted Ellen: Are you home? I think something bad is happening and I'm scared to be alone right now.

It was only a few blocks to walk home. You can do this, I told myself as the monkeys shrieked *RUN!!!*

I texted Ashlee: Freaking out in a way that feels different and awful. Don't know what to do.

Walking down the sidewalk felt like a catastrophe waiting to happen. My urban neighbors had seen me silently crying on those sidewalks for a couple months, but this time I was wheezing and bawling . . . I felt naked and about to cause a scene.

I turned down an alley to hide. It was rush hour, so all my friends were in cars and buses and busy. Life doesn't stop for a shitshow.

Next, I texted Ben, my friend who identifies as a bipolar genderqueer unicorn. Starting to have trouble breathing. Maybe panic attack? Scared.

I'm getting in the car right now, Ben texted back immediately. I'll be there in less than 10 minutes.

I put my phone away, looked up, and try to focus on the alley I was walking down.

In this moment, I tried to practice, but it was pointless. In that moment I felt like I was dying. The monkey-scream chorus was in full swing. The edges of my vision went dark and my knees buckled and I grabbed a dumpster to keep from face-planting. My sobbing and gasping upped the pace to panting. FUCK.

Did I need to throw up? I couldn't even tell. I tried to focus on one foot in front of the other. Just get down this alley. Just get home.

By the time I walked in the back door, I was in a hellish hyper-ventilation loop. I was locked in tunnel vision. My arms ached and my chest constricted to the point that I thought I couldn't keep breathing. I sat on the couch and shook.

Ben arrived a few minutes later and sat next to me on the couch, holding my hand as I wheezed and frothed. They've had panic attacks. They know.

I touched my face—why was it tingling?

Why were my extremities numb? I wanted to ask Ben, but I couldn't really talk because all that I could get out of my mouth was a subhuman wheeze. I felt like a corpse, expelling gases caught in its cavities.

I was reduced to strings of saliva and burning lungs, muscles shaking with fatigue and chest feeling crushed. I understood now that my loss-training strategies were pointless. I was the woman burned down. This was the fall of the empire. I was snot bubbles and panting and tingling hands.

I could barely walk to the bathroom. Even mid–panic attack, I was angry at myself for how broken I was. Ben had already seen me sobbing for weeks and had told me, "I've known you for a decade, and other than happy tears the night Obama was elected, I've never seen you cry, *ever*." The person I used to be never even got misty-eyed. It just wasn't a thing that happened. But now? I was the person who couldn't stop crying, who couldn't stop wheezing, who couldn't talk, who could barely walk. I was the person who needed someone to hold her hand to keep her from feeling like she was dying from panic.

Who the hell is this particular person? I thought, hands shaking as I held on to the hallway walls to try to get back to the couch. *I've never been this person before.*

My mind spun, looked desperately for an answer, reeled, tripped, and tipped over. Things got weirdly quiet.

When I could finally talk half an hour later, I managed to say to Ben, "What's going on with my hands? It feels like my life is burning out of my palms," and I could feel it. My hands had stopped shaking, replaced by a strong throbbing in my palms. Was that just another panic attack symptom?

After another half hour, the attack slowly ran out of fuel. The panic attack ate my ego. I felt completely emptied. The monkeys in my head had stopped shrieking, had fallen out of their tree, and lay limp on the ground.

"My brain broke," I told Atta a few days later, trying to explain the panic attack. "It felt like I died. Honestly, I think a part of me DID die. I can't be nice or pretend I'm okay anymore!"

Atta nodded from his chair, his hair pink that week. "Conserve your energy if you can. Going through something like this is a major endurance test. You need to rest, Ariel. We talked about this. Treat yourself like you've been hit by a truck. Just *rest* and let yourself heal."

"The panic attack made some things clear to me," I said. "I think it's beyond my mental capacity to hold both 'healing' and 'hope' that I can get my old life back . . ."

I started crying. My palms were still throbbing, and I flexed my fingers a bit. My mouth tasted like the darkest loss, but also a sense of relief.

Atta teared up with me. "I know it hurts to let go of that hope, but I think you have to focus on healing."

My mind couldn't fix this. My thoughts couldn't make this better. I couldn't outthink this situation. I had to use other tools.

YOU'RE NOT DYING, IT JUST FEELS THAT WAY

That panic attack was a turning point for me, a bottoming out and an awakening all at once. It became clear that I had exited the zone of rational thought and being nice and was walking into the realm of trauma.

That word feels big, but trauma is just your body's natural reaction to being overwhelmed by more stress than your nervous

system can take in, and panic attacks are a super-common traumatic response.

Panic attacks have lots of different symptoms, from palpitations to nausea to chest pains. The Anxiety and Depression Association of America offers some solid advice on how to deal:

- ◆ **Find a quiet place with little stimulation.** Close your eyes.
  Hold your hands together.

- ◆ **Regulate your breathing:** breathe slowly and way down
  into your belly, concentrating only on your breath. You
  can try to breathe in through your nose and out through
  your mouth, or breathe in for the same number of seconds that you breathe out. In for four seconds—out for
  four seconds. Repeat.

- ◆ **Relax muscle groups:** focus on your neck, your jaw, your
  hands, your shoulders, your back—anything that seems
  tense. Notice and acknowledge each of these parts of your
  body.

- ◆ **Recognize it as a panic attack that will pass.** Say it out
  loud to yourself: "This is a panic attack. I'm not dying.
  This will pass." (Having a unicorn friend be there for you
  helps, too.)

Now, let's talk a bit more about the science of trauma: it's
individual and *totally subjective.* A situation that overwhelms your
nervous system could be totally par for the course for someone
else. This can feel embarrassing if you find yourself traumatized by
events you don't deem "traumatic enough."

Picture me standing up at the trauma party, saying, "So, I was
trying to answer an email about a birthday party? But I couldn't
be nice enough and so my brain, like, broke?" So yeah, I get the
shame, but you know what? *Give it up!* You don't control your
trauma response. It's a nervous system reaction.

For those of us prone to mental spirals, one of the awful gifts
that trauma provides is that it forces you to recognize that you

can't think your way out of every problem. Once your nervous system flips into trauma mode, you're past the realm of conscious thought.

From a physiological point of view, trying to outthink trauma *simply won't work*. Atta had been trying to tell me this for months, but I was still convinced that my big ol' brain could outsmart the nightmare I was living through. Having a panic attack finally made me realize that my brain had lost the battle.

Trauma lives in your body, beyond the control of your desperate braining. This is why so many of us who try to heal with only talk therapy can feel like we've hit a wall.

Trauma demands that you get creative with nonmental, nonverbal treatments. For many of us, that happens in and through the body, either through somatic therapies or movement practices.

As trauma researcher Bessel A. van der Kolk observed, "Trauma victims cannot recover until they become familiar with and befriend the sensations in their bodies. . . . Physical self-awareness is the first step in releasing the tyranny of the past."

Many of us deal with trauma as part of our shitshow—that's why this particular kind of crisis pushes you over the edge: your brain tools stop working. This doesn't mean that mental coping strategies like talk therapy, journaling, mindfulness, or gratitude practices are useless. It just means that talking about it, writing about it, breathing through it, and feeling #blessed aren't enough to get you where you need to go.

Brains are great, but once trauma gets into your body, no amount of mental tools are going to move you forward.

You can't think your way out of this.

You have to shift the focus *to* your body so you can move the trauma out *through* your body.

FIND YOUR AFTERGLOW

A shitshow pushes you past capacity, and your life may have you scrambling to learn new skills. Old identities crack off (sometimes abruptly!), and the skin underneath is real pink and soft. It can be excruciating. When breakdowns show up, it's a time to be extra gentle with yourself. Hitting rock bottom hurts like hell, but that pain holds valuable lessons.

- In what ways are you still trying to "keep it together," be nice, save face, or otherwise maintain an image of competence, even when dealing with crushing stress? What would happen if you let that go and allowed yourself to truly FEEL where you're at right now, even if it's hopeless, depressed, raging, or panicked?

- What are you being challenged to let go of? What are you being asked to surrender? Which old identities are cracking off?

- If you're having physical symptoms of stress and trauma, what do you think your body is trying to tell you? Try this question: "If my body could ask me for something, what would it want?"

After a breakdown, do your best to treat yourself softly. Remember what Atta said: Think of yourself as having been hit by a truck. Find ways to rest, sleep, and soothe your body. We'll be talking much more about this in coming chapters.

part two

BODY

GETTING BACK TO BEING HUMAN

Chapter 9

ATTACHMENT THEORY

UNDERSTANDING NIPPLE PANIC

AND SO MY SHITSHOW WENT ON. ON ONE OF MY MANY "ALONE DAYS" WHEN MY SON WAS with his father, I found myself sitting on the couch in my living room that faced the gray, wet Seattle alley that is my backyard.

I took stock: My immediate family and extended family felt like a rock, and it was amazing how my circle of longtime friends swooped in to catch me and Tavi. Ben delivered jars of peanut butter at six a.m. when I was too scattered to stay on top of groceries and I couldn't make Tavi's lunch. Ellen sat on the floor next to my bed and read me Pema Chödrön's *Taking the Leap* and Stephen Levine's *Unattended Sorrow*. My parents helped with childcare. I kept going to therapy with Atta. I kept doing my best to feel my feelings. I kept crying every day, and I tried to notice myself breathing every day.

I sat on the couch and read over things friends had sent me, like this line from *Infinite Jest*:

He could do [this] pain the same way: Abiding. No one single instant of it was unendurable. Here was a second right here:

he endured it. . . . He could just hunker down in the space between each heartbeat and make each heartbeat a wall and live there.

Yes, I kept hunkering down between the spaces of each heartbeat. Yes, I resolved not to drink or get baked in the hopes of not numbing the pain. Yes, I kept doing my mindfulness exercises. *In this moment . . . I am not crying!*

Another friend sent this quote from Rumi: "Do not worry that your life is turning upside down. How do you know the side you are used to is better than the one to come?" I hated this quote because I was sure the old side had definitely been better.

Spoiler alert: I was wrong. But in that moment, I missed absolutely everything about my old life. The missing ate into me, consumed me, left my heart pounding with the effort of just trying to stay alive. I bled love, and the stains were all over the house, pooling in brown clots behind me on the sidewalk and getting crusted in my son's hair during whispers and kisses at bedtime.

Somehow, recovering from the emotional injury of my marriage ending felt more difficult than the time I'd spent rehabilitating from the exploding ovary and emergency surgery. The week in the hospital of tubes hanging out of me, the time of being unable to walk, the month regaining my strength to make it across the room? That felt easier than the emotional pain. The knife of heartbreak cut deeper than the surgeon's blade, and the roping scars left behind were much longer than the eight-inch line the surgery had left up the middle of my belly.

Sitting on the old couch, I read another message I'd received from a friend:

> If it helps to make sense of it at all, the adult attachment circuits in your brain run on the same neural fibers as the attachment circuits that formed when you were an infant. So when your primary attachment figure leaves, even as an adult, it activates the same kind of life-and-death panic that a baby who has been abandoned by its mother would feel.

Our human, mammalian brains are wired to treat attachment and belonging as extremely important—probably even more important than a physical injury.

This reminded me of some neurobiological attachment theory stuff that I'd read. Even after the panic attack broke my brain, my mind was still chewing over why my marriage ending felt so *physical*, why my nervous system was so shot, why my whole body was wobbling. The insights didn't ease the pain, but at least they gave me something to do while I convalesced.

I thought back to the day my son was born, remembered holding him in my arms and watching him root around for my breast.

I remembered his desperate newborn grunts, his little bobble-head wobbling with surprising strength as he tried to latch on to the nipple. The instinct was so remarkably animalistic and fierce. I held him in my arms and thought, *What the hell, this isn't a baby . . . this is a desperate little beast that's trying to stay alive.* This is nipple panic.

This is biology. This is instinct and survival. This is the essence of life, trying to stay alive.

Here's the thing with attachment: We don't just attach to people like caregivers and partners. Our minds form psychological attachments to concepts and identities, too! These psychological attachments are usually around stuff like achievements, status, or beliefs, and we lean on them for a sense of comfort, building our identities around them.

You might have thought of yourself as a breadwinner, and now you're unemployed. You might have seen yourself as strong, and now you've been sick with a chronic condition for six months. You were a homebody, and then your house burned down.

As psychologist Steve Taylor explains in his book *The Leap*, "These attachments are the building blocks of a person's identity, and as the attachments dissolve, the person's identity also begins to dissolve."

Do you feel like you're dissolving? Cuz I totally did.

Understanding these psychological attachments helps explain why, even if your shitshow doesn't involve a breakup or death, you may feel a sense of heartbreak and mourning. You're not grieving the loss of another person, you're grieving the loss of your psychological attachment. You're grieving the loss of your identity. You're mourning your own death.

But if you are dealing with the nipple panic of a relationship ending, it can be helpful (and comforting!) to learn more about the science of how attachment theory plays out in your adult relationships. This is dense stuff, but worth the effort. It's a potent tool for understanding the mechanisms of your heart and brain.

Attachment theory was first developed by Mary Ainsworth and John Bowlby to describe infants' tendencies to frantically cry, cling, and search for their caregiver if separated. In the '80s, researchers started applying attachment theory to their studies of adult relationships. Turns out that infant-caregiver relationships and adult romantic relationships are remarkably similar, which means that many of us adults are acting out relationship patterns we learned as babies. Aww, it's both cute and sad.

Adults act out one of these attachment styles:

◆ **Secure:** You feel confident that your partner has your back and you're comfortable letting your partner depend on you.

◆ **Anxious-preoccupied:** You easily become upset when you feel your needs aren't being met and worry that others may not entirely love you. (This is me! I'm clingy and chase-y, and prone to panic.)

◆ **Fearful-avoidant:** You want closeness, but are so afraid you'll get hurt that you often push people away.

◆ **Dismissive-avoidant:** You look aloof because you have a lot of pain associated with depending on others or being depended on.

Again, this is a bit intense to dig into if you're mid-chaos, but as you start to put your life back together, I highly recommend learning about your attachment type. Reading the book *Attached* by Amir Levine and Rachel S. F. Heller felt like finding a magical key—suddenly I had so much more understanding and compassion for the confusing things so many of us do in our partnerships. Knowledge is power, and this particular knowledge is extremely powerful.

HEARTBREAK: THE CORE MAMMALIAN EXPERIENCE

"The feeling of heartbreak might be the core mammalian experience," I theorized that week with Atta. "I mean, our mammalian bodies are born knowing that if you can't find another creature to feed you, you will die. *Literally!* If you can't find that nipple, you're dead. Find the nipple or die."

"Now you're working on attachment theory?" Atta laughed, baffled. "Didn't I tell you to rest?"

"I know, I know," I said, waving my hands at him dismissively. "But stay with me here. If you can't find the nipple? Panic, rooting, head wobbling. Every cell wall pounds with the nipple panic. Find the nipple OR DIE. When I feel the heartache coming on again, it's not even in my brain—it's in my body! I try to remember that it's nipple panic. Those sensations of pain aren't just the shared *human* experience of heartbreak—they might be the most core mammalian experience that there is!"

Atta let me go on. He was getting used to the way I knit myself dense blankets of words, wrapping myself in information to feel safe.

"That nipple panic connects me to every mouse and every whale and every horse and cow and elephant and bear and rabbit. All the mammals! Now I know how a heartbroken bat feels. I empathize with the lonely boar. Me and that dying baby rat? We're the same."

"I wonder if parasites share this feeling?" Atta said.

"HA!" I said. "Me and that tick? We're the same!"

When the panic came late at night, I tried to remind myself that I wasn't alone. That I was sharing an experience with bats and boars and dying baby rats. I tried to breathe mindfully with all my frightened mammal friends.

Sometimes it helped, sometimes I just felt weird. But at least it was a new kind of weird! I was making new mistakes.

Another part of my slowly evolving mindfulness practice included tracking moments when I wasn't feeling the panic. If I happened to notice that I wasn't on all fours on my living room floor, writhing and sobbing over Peter Gabriel's *Us* or whimpering my empathy for the lonely rabbit, I tried to actively *notice* it and be grateful for it.

"In this moment," I tried to say to myself when I could remember to be aware, "I don't feel like I'm dying of nipple panic."

Then again, other times all I could do was note the awful pain and do the best I could to ride through it.

It happened in my kitchen once . . . and I woke up enough to notice. My brain had started to loop on a particular cycle of suffering, and my heart was pounding again, *ugh ugh ugh*. My mental chatter was looping on this: *Sometimes? When I lay on my side at night? Waiting for the sleep meds to drag me away from the demons? I can physically feel my heart gently bouncing my body with fear.* It felt like my body was in a chronic state of running some sort of strange emotional marathon. Fight or flight was my daily bread, and hypervigilance was the soup I slurped between bites.

Wait, did I come in the kitchen to eat something? I couldn't remember. My body just hurt, and I paced. I bumped into the counter, steadied myself, and noticed how out of it I was. I tried to focus and started talking out loud:

"In this moment, I am standing in my kitchen."

I looked around. Yep, there it was. My mid-'00s yuppie kitchen. I felt the countertops against my hand and the cold tile floor under my feet. Noted the window facing north. The bare tree branches outside.

"In this moment, it's warm in here."

Yep, even though it was late winter, my house was not cold. That was a thing that I could still do: I couldn't always remember to have peanut butter in the house, but I could keep the house warm!

I scanned my body. "In this moment, I am hungry." Cortisol bread and shock soup were not enough to nourish me.

I grabbed a baggie of frozen stew from the freezer and stuck it in a bowl to microwave. My best friend from high school had come over a few weeks earlier and made me single servings of stew to keep on hand. Amazing! My friends are amazing! How am I so loved and yet feel so fundamentally unlovable?

Wait, I thought, trying to stay focused. "In this moment, I can't hear any gunshots."

It was true! I lived in a safe-ish structure in a safe-ish neighborhood in a safe-ish city in a first-world country. There were no gunshots outside, no one banging on the door, no one yelling at me or threatening my life. The house was quiet and calm, except for the beep of the microwave finishing my stew, and my waves of panic totally unrelated to anything in the present moment.

FOOD FAVORS

When things fall apart, many of us have friends and family who offer to help "in any way they can." It can be difficult to figure out what to ask these well-meaning volunteers to do, but if any wannabe helpers enjoy cooking, ask them to make a meal you can keep frozen for when you need it because you've forgotten to feed yourself. Many folks will jump at the chance to make you their fave emergency meal.

The next time someone says "Let me know if you need anything," try this: "There is something: if you could make an extra serving when you make your killer butter chicken, I'd love to not have to think about cooking one night." People who love to cook freaking *love* to cook, and will be stoked you asked.

Bonus: cooking an extra portion isn't even that much more work or expense for your friend, so banish any "I'm a burden" talk from your brain.

I pulled the bowl out of the microwave, got a spoon out of a drawer (I have spoons! In this moment, *I have spoons*!!), leaned a hip against the counter, and kept talking to myself, getting louder:

"In this moment, I'm eating food a friend made for me!" I hollered out.

AND IT WAS TRUE! I was totally standing there with a spoonful of stew! In my kitchen! Which was a comfortable temperature! In a safe place! I swallowed and tried to feel the food sliding down my throat, into my belly, nourishing me.

"In this moment, I do not have nipple panic!" I hooted.

I didn't feel like I was dying, and with the warmth of the food in my belly, I wasn't as desperate feeling. I scanned again. My head might have been a mess, but my body felt . . . not currently in pain!

"In this moment, I am wearing shoes that fit," I shouted to my empty house, "and my underwear are not up my butt!"

It was true: my shoes did fit, and my underwear were not currently up my butt.

This was transcendent mediocrity. I stood at the counter, spooning stew and contentment into myself. I felt at peace. Nothing was up my butt! Damn, this Not-Pain Motel felt great.

That was becoming my new normal: the moments when I didn't feel like I was dying were full of the blissfully desperate mania of self-discovery and introspection.

This is what it feels like when your afterglow starts to dawn. Your brain may feel like it has two settings: devastating, hallucinatory misery OR hyperactive honor student trying to get your A+ in a course called Finding the Silver Lining of Your Personal Apocalypse.

In that particular kitchen moment, I was in the A+ zone! My belly filled with stew and peace. The A+ feeling lasted maybe two minutes, and then I was back to crying and bumping into walls and freaking out. But those two minutes were golden!

My hope for you as you start to feel the heaviest clouds lifting is that you find these tiny A+ moments for yourself. It might just be two minutes, when you happen to notice the way the rain is shining off the sidewalk. It might be just thirty seconds, when your crying slows down long enough that you notice one of your eyelashes on a pillow and get lost in the wonder of it all. (Think of all the microscopic mites living there! It's amazing!) It might be just awareness of a bird singing. Just one bird, this one time. A+ for you!

These peaceful moments are like small, shy children: if you look for them too hard, they'll hide. All you can do is notice, keep your gaze soft, and breathe a little gratitude for a two-minute stretch of not-pain.

You can build a new life out of those two-minute stretches. Just keep noticing them.

FIND YOUR AFTERGLOW

Okay, this might feel weird because you're reading this book and probably up in your brain right now, but let's take a body break. Take a moment to be aware of your own "In this moment . . ." observations. Take a breath. What are your five senses experiencing *right now*?

Now, let's dig in a bit more . . .

◆ Where does your suffering live in your body? Take some time to close your eyes, take a breath, and get into your quiet space. Where do you feel tenseness and discomfort? Is it a tight chest? A knotted stomach? An electric shock through your veins? See if you can just sit with the sensation for a moment, without resistance. Just for five breaths. Just to acknowledge it. It's torturous, but stay with it if you can, and breathe into it. Sensations just need to be fully felt before they can move through. Your body is talking to you! (In future chapters, we'll explore working with those sensations and moving them out of your body, but in *this* moment . . . just see if you can establish a relationship with where in your body the discomfort is hanging out.)

◆ One of the great lies of human suffering is how it tells you that you alone feel this level of pain. Think about this: suffering is in fact one of the most basic experiences of being human—or rather, of being a mammal! Or maybe just of being alive. How does it change the shape of your misery to understand that it's the sensation that binds you to the rest of life on this planet? What if, in your most isolated miseries and pain, you are actually more connected to everyone and everything on earth?

◆ Did you recognize yourself in any of the attachment styles? How do your adult relationships repeat the patterns you experienced with your childhood caregivers? Know this: you CAN change your attachment style. It demands a lot of awareness and patience and compassion with yourself, but it's fully possible.

◆ Have you had any A+ moments? Not the distracted moments when you managed to forget what happened to you, but the moments where even in full shitshow-awareness mode, you still found a sense of peace in the middle of it all. Take the time to notice and appreciate each two-minute moment! What's the shape of the moment? What's the feeling in your body? What do your moments have in common?

By understanding that everyone hurts and noticing tiny moments of awakened peace despite the pain, you're building a new life where your pain doesn't isolate you, where you find contentment anyway, and where you start to see the shape of what brings you joy. Even if it's just a minute of noticing that your underwear is not up your butt right now—GET THAT JOY.

Chapter 10

MAKEOVER

WHY INSIDE-OUT THERAPY SOMETIMES WORKS

AT WORK ONE WINTER DAY, I TRIED TO NOTICE AND SET ASIDE MY NIPPLE PANIC (*hmm, the anxiety feels like a jolt down my arms today. Interesting . . .*) and focus on my to-do list. I'd put off this task for weeks, but it was time to buy the plane tickets for my two months of business travel coming up: I was going to spend my first winter as a newly separated woman traveling across the country to coproduce eight alternative wedding expos.

My job at these expos was mostly marketing and promotion beforehand, but then also attending the events, chatting with vendors, greeting newly engaged couples, keeping the vibe high, trying to not cry on anyone, and looking fancy . . . Ugh, what the hell was I going to wear?! Nothing fit anymore. My crisis had consumed me from the inside out, and my clothes hung off me like tents, stretched-out fabric draping awkwardly where my boobs used to be.

I booked my flights that morning and then took the afternoon to walk down the western slope of Capitol Hill to a local boutique called Pretty Parlor. It's on a corner near one of Seattle's 133 Starbucks, with a striped awning and midcentury furniture in the window. They sell a mix of vintage gowns, retro reproduction dresses, and clothing meant for burlesque dancers, drag queens, and those of us who aspire to look like them.

I walked through the gold doors into the pink-walled boutique and tried to smile.

The owner of the shop was behind the counter and looked up to greet me. Her name is Anna Banana (that's her legal name, yes), and her hair was pink that month. Between my therapist and my shop owners, I lived in a gray city filled with rainbows.

"Ariel!" Anna smiled. "How are you?"

In my hollowed-out state, I lacked the energy to be anything other than grossly honest.

"I'm a disaster," I rambled. "My husband left and none of my clothes fit and next month I have to fly all over the country doing these wedding expos and I don't have anything to wear and how am I going to handle all those engaged people wanting to talk about their weddings when I'm broken and I just need to find a couple dresses that fit me so that I can put on a brave face and I don't even know what's going to look good on me anymore because I also had this crazy surgery earlier this year and I don't have the same body I've always had and do you have any Kleenex because oh look I'm crying fuck I'm a shitshow."

I was a walking catastrophe of TMI. I was a fountain of verbal diarrhea and pain. Even in a pink-walled boutique, I was cracked open and crying and unable to maintain any sense of decorum.

This person, too: I have never ever been this woman who cries in boutiques.

Anna Banana was unfazed and immediately swung into action.

"Oh god, I've been there. Later I'll tell you about the time I was half-homeless, peeing on a pregnancy test in an alley. I understand shitshows. But let's focus and find you something fabulous," she said. "Something sparkly that fits like a glove."

Anna started pulling dresses off the racks. I was sent into the pink-curtained dressing room with arms full of color and texture.

I wiped away my tears and tried to avoid getting wet mascara on the insides of any of the dresses.

I walked out in the first one, which had a pencil skirt made from a stiff, stretchy fabric that held me like a jealous wet suit.

"MARVELOUS!" Anna shouted from behind the counter.

I looked in the mirror and was both aghast and amazed. A scrawny woman with frail little bird arms stared back at me in a dress that was meant for crawling across a detective's desk, husky-voiced and persuasive.

"You look amazing!" Anna shouted, almost louder than the monkeys in my head that told me all day every day that I was a worthless monster who deserved everything that happened.

I looked up at Anna, running my hands along my flanks, touching my oddly bony hips through the fabric.

"I do?" I asked.

I looked back in the mirror.

I did.

Back in the dressing room, I put on the next dress, a floor-length sequined gown with a huge mermaid flare at the bottom. I felt it slide over my skin (not-pain, I see you!) and looked in the mirror.

I couldn't get over the contrast between how I felt and how the dress looked on me. I felt like the bag of sagging mom-breasts, left on the curb. I felt like the crone, tossed when the lines started showing. I was the old wife, put out in the alley for something better. I was worthless and unlovable . . . but fuck if those sequins didn't make my worthlessness sparkle!

"Maybe it's too much for a wedding expo," I called through the curtain, and what I meant was *Maybe it's too much for the garbage that I am.*

I looked in the mirror, saw the person I still didn't recognize looking back at me. I was trying on self-worth to see if it fit.

"Maybe it's easier this way," I told Atta in therapy that week. "I don't recognize myself anymore because I've never been this person before. I keep trying to find the old self that I recognize, because I keep thinking I want my old life back. But maybe it's easier to just be a new person."

Atta nodded. I noticed that he'd gotten a new tattoo on his wrist—two small arrows. *I see you, second arrow.*

"I can't really reconcile what happened with my life," I said. "I can't even fully look at it without my eyes hurting. Last year I had a healthy body and what I thought was a happy marriage and now I have scars and loneliness and panic. I feel like I've been burned down completely, like I'm just a foundation and a few sooty black two-by-fours leaning into the sky at awkward angles . . . and I keep trying to find my old self, but maybe it's easier to rebuild myself completely new from scratch. The sequined gown was a completely different person that I've never been before."

"So are you going to buy it?" Atta asked.

"Of course not," I said. "I can't afford it."

Three weeks later, a couple friends pooled their money and bought me the gown as a Christmas gift.

"You might feel like shit," their card said. "But you look like a million bucks."

UNDERSTANDING YOUR NEW SELF THROUGH SHITSHOW SELFIES

If you catch yourself taking more selfies than you used to, let me block that second arrow before you stab it into yourself: shitshow selfies are totally normal and even valuable! One aspect of recovering from loss is figuring out who this different you is in your new world.

There's an odd joy in not knowing who you are anymore (growing into new identities is part of healthy maturation! You didn't need that ol' persona anyway!), but not knowing yourself is confusing. One way to learn more about who you are now is to understand what others are seeing.

Thus, shitshow selfies.

Sometimes these selfies are the faces of grief. As Seattle author Tricia Romano wrote after her boyfriend died in a motorcycle accident, "Each time I went to the bathroom and looked in the mirror, I was shocked anew by what I saw. I did not recognize this person.

My face seemed to be carved into a permanent state of sadness. The light was out of my eyes, my smile erased, a new crease forming in my forehead from my eyebrows being knitted together from being in anguish 24 hours a day, seven days a week. I looked like this even when I was not crying and that's what scared me the most, . . . that I would never look like myself again, or be myself again.

Sometimes these shitshow selfies look like what *Emergent Strategy* author adrienne maree brown calls "self-pornography." Taking nudes of yourself for yourself can be liberating, and help you understand this new self as a sensual being that may someday be capable of pleasure. adrienne describes her process with self-pornography this way: "i had to learn to desire myself, my body, my skin, my rhythms, my pleasure . . . i started with my face—how did i look smiling? happy? turned on? shut down? laughing? i took photos of every part of myself until i felt i knew more about my body, could tolerate myself, even like what i saw . . . they were not for anyone else's eyes, opinions or desires. that was radically important. the energy of them was purely self-adoration."

Your shitshow selfies may just look like you playing with silly filters, trying to see yourself in a new light. They might be erotic photos to help you imagine how your new self will love in your new world. They might be victorious survivor photos (not dead today!) or studies in depression. As with all therapeutic creative expression, the result isn't the point: the value is in the act of expression and learning how your new self wants to be seen.

I will say this, however: be extremely judicious about sharing on social media. The skin of your new self is still pink and uncalloused. The world isn't ready for you yet.

On the last day of the year that burned down my life, I started parting my hair on the side. I snapped a selfie. It was an insignificant superficial shift that likely no one noticed, but it felt huge.

When I looked at the photo I'd taken, I saw a different person. In that photo, maybe I saw someone who wasn't *done to*, but someone who made choices and had a sense of agency. I saw someone who wasn't a victim of a medical emergency and a marital collapse and an identity implosion.

WHY A CHANGE ON THE OUTSIDE HELPS THE INSIDE (AND HOW TO KNOW WHEN IT WON'T)

Here are two truths: going through a shitshow feels completely out of your control, and physical makeovers and drastic shifts in personal style are stereotypical expressions of folks going through major life changes. Why are makeovers so common? Because, duh: you get to control *something* and see immediate results!

When you're climbing out of the depths of grief, loss, or trauma, having a bit of control over something tiny in your day, and making a change (instead of having change thrust upon you!) can be empowering and exhilarating.

You can't spackle over stress with sartorial splendor, though. A quick makeover might take the edge off, but it will never replace internal changes. So, sure, go for that drastic haircut or those sexy-ass leather pants—but stay diligent with your self-development! A makeover looks and feels best when it reflects internal progress.

I started to feel a shift. The fear that had crept through my bloodstream started to gel into something else: *agency*.

Since a shitshow feels like it happens *to* you, it can shatter any illusions of control you may have had. This is extra rough on those of us who pride ourselves on being in control and having our lives together. HA HA, joke's on us! Accept it: you do not have control over where your life goes (body parts and relationships and entire lives explode without warning!), but you still have the capacity to *make choices*. You don't have to just sit there, hypervigilant and frozen in terror.

When you're dealing with a lack of control, making even minuscule decisions can help build your confidence and feeling of ownership of your life. This is known as a sense of agency—the ability to want something, make a choice, and then take action to make that choice happen. Instead of just observing and reacting to life as a passive bystander or victim, agency helps you regain a sense of owning your life path. (Spoiler alert: you still don't have any control, but at least you can make choices!)

Finding a sense of agency can be terrifying, especially coming off an existential burn-down, so start by making tiny plans, small choices, and keeping little promises to yourself. Try just one easy promise a day—it should be something that only takes five minutes of effort. When you can keep one small promise to yourself, you're teaching yourself that you're worthy of effort. It's a great feeling, and you can get it in itty-bitty daily doses.

The confusing upside of having your life fall apart is that it opens things up to potential, to new lives you could be living. This isn't to say you should be okay with losing your old life—loss is loss, and it must be grieved fully. But as you start to look forward, think about ways that you can find agency in shaping your new life.

Try these steps:

◈ **Desire:** What do you want from your future life? What would a perfect day *feel* like for you—not what would it look like (vacation in Hawaii), but what would it FEEL like (relaxed, unrushed). Focus on the *sensations* of your perfect future day, not specifics. For me, I imagined a new life for myself where I felt comfortable with my emotions, strong in my body, and securely connected to beloved people in my life.

◈ **Plan:** Consider what small daily actions now could contribute to the sensations you desire in the future. If your ideal day involves feeling connected to people in meaningful ways, devote time to reaching out and making plans. If you want to feel more strength in your life, find moments in your day where you can push your abilities, wherever they may be. Remember, keep your plans very small and manageable. What could you do in five minutes today, and again tomorrow?

◆ **Act:** Execute on those plans! Again, if you're focusing on sensations ("I want to feel relaxed") instead of specifics ("I want to go on vacation"), many desires are instantly attainable: you might not be able to afford a vacation, but hopefully you can schedule fifteen minutes for an extra-long hot shower. Pro tip: If you feel like you just don't have enough minutes in the day, try reducing your screen time! You'll likely find many, *many* hours you didn't have in your life.

For me, having a sense of agency meant making time every day to *feel* my emotions instead of running from them (even when they were painful and sucked!) and making time every day to move my body (even if it was just five minutes wiggling around my living room and crying to an emo pop song). It also meant spending less time on social media and more time contacting friends directly to make plans with them.

By focusing on small ways to create the sensations *today* that you want from your future life, you're actively constructing your future self. You become an active agent in your life, one small choice at a time. Those small choices will eventually help you build a big new life.

Even if the first little choice is a new outfit or parting your hair differently.

FIND YOUR AFTERGLOW

Releasing control while finding a sense of agency is a rough balance. Ultimately, control is an illusion, while agency is just the sensation of being able to take action in your life—even if you don't know how those actions will play out.

Makeovers are silly and only superficial, but if shifting your appearance helps you feel like you've got the ability to take action in your life, then that's forward momentum and it's freaking awesome! Plus, makeovers can be fun, and you know what every afterglow needs? SOME FUN.

◆ If your shitshow was a movie, what would your makeover scene look like? What would the montage soundtrack be? What new you would emerge from the dressing room? Give yourself a moment to indulge the fantasy.

◆ What you focus your attention on grows. Spend some time to consider what in your life brings you the most joy. Then find ways to focus more of your life on those things, even if it's just in very small increments.

◆ What tiny changes could you make in your life to free up more time for the things you value? Even if it's just in five-minute increments, what can you do today to introduce more of what you want in your future life? Again, think small.

◆ What familiar old stories are you telling yourself right now about why you can't make any small changes? We all do this, and the key is recognizing the patterns in the self-limiting stories you tell, recognizing that it's an old script, and recognizing that it might not be relevant anymore. Some common favorites: "I can't because I'm too busy" (are you really, or are you "busy" watching Netflix and scrolling on your phone?), "I can't because I'd just get rejected" (so you're rejecting yourself first? Stop being such a jerk to yourself!), "I can't because I'm broke" (remember, focus not on things but *sensations*. You don't have to go to Hawaii to relax—it's free to open the window and take five slow breaths!). All you have to do is recognize your favorite old stories. Awareness is enough.

Are you starting to feel some glimmers of what's possible? Yes, you still want to be feeling all the feelings, but hopefully you're starting to get some healings in there, too.

Chapter 11

BURLESQUE

CONVERTING HUMILIATION INTO CONFIDENCE

AS I STARTED TO SEE THE FIRST GLIMMERS OF AN AFTERGLOW, I TRIED TO FIND MOMENTS when I could sit very quietly and open some space for my new life unfolding.

What if instead of catastrophe, this awful transition was an opportunity?

As I tried to get through the mess that my life had become (and was still becoming, because then one of my incisors started wobbling and eventually came out. I was a woman crisscrossed with scars, going through a divorce, *and now missing a tooth!* YAHTZEE!!), I tried to be as patient as I could with being where I was at, which was . . . tentative. Tentative healing. Tentative hope. Tentative fun. I was still fragile and there was so much work to do . . . but I tried not to mind the gap, in my smile or my life.

I tried not to look too far ahead, and I tried to stay mindful. While working the floor at one of the wedding expos, I tried to notice how it felt to be in the Not-Pain Motel for a few minutes, meeting *Offbeat Bride* readers and advertisers and seeing if I could tolerate a break in my months of sobriety with a sip of whiskey.

I toddled past the booth for a Seattle dance studio called the Academy of Burlesque. They were there both to perform at the expo and promote the bachelorette burlesque parties they throw, and I was tickled beyond belief to see that the studio owner and I were wearing the same sparkly dress!

"Sequin twinsies!" I shouted, maybe a little too loud, maybe a little drunk on not-pain and my sip of whiskey.

Word had gotten out about my divorce, and I felt like everyone was staring at me. The weight of public perception can feel crushing when your life is falling apart. I have one friend who got a job promotion two days after learning her husband had sexually assaulted someone. Months later, the day her then-estranged husband's criminal case went public, my friend received another promotion—this one very prominent and highly visible. Talk about everyone staring . . .

As for me, the slightly tipsy recent divorcée wearing sequins and laughing too loud while working the wedding expo, I had to wonder: Was I embarrassing myself? All indications pointed to yes, but compared to how I'd been feeling, all indications also pointed to my not really caring.

Private shame felt hot and claustrophobic, especially coming off the mind-bending initial shock and the dense gray death-fog of depression. Compared to that, public humiliation felt like a vacation.

One burlesque dancer, a petite classically trained ballet dancer named Inga, did a performance at the expo where she took off her vintage dress and finished by spinning tassels on her butt. (I later learned that these are known as "assels," because of course they are.) I watched in awe. At home on the nights when my son was gone, sometimes I would find myself in my underwear, dancing around the house, trying to feel something . . . *anything*. Despite her petite size, Inga's dancing was huge and confident. I wanted to feel like that.

Suddenly inspired, I approached Inga after her performance.

"You're my favorite," I gushed. "Teach me your ways! I want lessons!"

WHEN YOUR THERAPY BUDGET INCLUDES STRIPTEASES

Appointments with Atta were expensive and out of pocket, and that winter I'd already reallocated all my travel, entertainment, and shopping budgets into a new bucket called "therapy." As I tried to figure out who this traumatized, lonely woman was, I decided that maybe some movement therapy might help.

What is your overall/long-term goal for studying at the Academy? Inga emailed me.

Confidence! I typed back. I have this scrawny new body that I don't really know how to move, and I feel really devastated after my past year. My goal is to relearn how to be in this new body in these new times!

I felt a jolt of conviction. This needed to happen. (Lookit me! Making a decision for myself! First parting my hair on the side, now this?! Baby steps, baby steps.)

I wanted to relearn how to inhabit myself.

Dr. Bessel van der Kolk explains in his book *The Body Keeps the Score* that "many traumatized individuals are too hypervigilant to enjoy the ordinary pleasures that life has to offer, while others are too numb to absorb new experiences. . . . In an effort to shut off terrifying sensations, they also [deaden] their capacity to be alive."

Those of us recovering from trauma often disconnect from our bodies in an attempt to control the negative feelings. It makes sense for a while, but ultimately you gotta get that trauma OUT.

Paired with talk therapy and mindfulness, the physical aspect of healing is integral to the emotional and mental aspects, Dr. van der Kolk stresses. Integrating multiple systems of healing is the most effective way to overcome trauma.

Reconnecting with your physicality is one of the most useful tools you can work with as you recover from a shitshow. This reconnection could involve practicing physical movement, physical changes like getting a haircut or tattoo (more about that in Chapter 22), or physical connections with other people.

Your goals are to reestablish your sense of agency, regain a sense of ownership through physical movement, and mostly just feel the sensations in your body. These are all small steps toward reclaiming your body as something that can bring you joyful sensation.

THE MINDFULNESS OF VERY SLOWLY TOUCHING YOUR OWN ARM

The day of my first lesson with Inga, I drove to the Academy of Burlesque and found the studio tucked off an alley around the corner from a restaurant called SAN FERNANDO ROASTED CHICKEN in Seattle's Rainier Valley.

Inga opened the door to let me in. Of course I know that burlesque dancers are normal people when they're out of costume, but onstage, Inga has an enormous presence, a sparkling, jiggling explosion of rhinestones and swinging assels. The petite woman standing in front of me was barely five feet tall, clean-faced and unassuming.

"Come on in," she said, adjusting the turban she wore over her short hair. The Academy of Burlesque was a one-room dance studio with two mirrored walls and curtains hiding tubs with labels like "Bump 'n' Grind Costumes."

Inga sat me down in a blue chair shaped like a high heel, next to a bookshelf filled with titles like *The Lusty Lady* and *Carnival Strippers*, and I started babbling.

"I've danced for my whole life," I rambled. "But it's always UNSEXY. Musical theater in high school? Not sexy. Raving in the '90s? I wore phat pants and huge hoodies and kept my eyes down. Not sexy. The hippie Jazzercise classes I take? Not sexy. I'm just sort of always in my own little bubble."

"I totally get it," Inga said. "Let's see if we can break you out of that bubble a bit."

Inga placed me in front of the longest mirrored wall and put on Prince's "Cream."

I stood side by side in the mirror with the ballet dancer/burlesque queen and we rolled our shoulders out together.

"It's all about the eye contact," Inga explained as we warmed up. "Yeah, your person is looking at your body, and if you turn away of course they want to see your butt—but really, they're watching your eyes."

"Ugh, eye contact," I whined.

Inga gave me a stern look. "Practice."

"Okay," I said. "Practice eye contact: check."

In *The Body Keeps the Score*, van der Kolk writes that trauma victims must "befriend" the sensations in their bodies if they are to recover from trauma. Feeling safe with yourself and other people is, according to him, "the single most important aspect of mental health." He recommends approaching your body and sensations with curiosity by asking yourself to take notice of feelings, rather than hiding from them.

So, okay: I took note of how difficult eye contact felt.

Inga pulled out a chair and told me to pretend "my person" was sitting in it. (I noted her gender-neutral language.)

"Start by walking up to your person and introducing yourself," she instructed. "Then set an expectation about physical contact."

I tried to saunter seductively up to the chair, but in the mirror, all I saw was a depressed middle-aged woman in stretch pants and a missing tooth. I felt awkward, like my old skin didn't fit my new self. I took a breath and resolved to embrace the awkwardness instead of shying away from it.

I leaned forward to the empty chair and said, "I'm Ariel. No touching." I glanced over my shoulder at Inga, crossed my eyes, and grimaced at her.

"Good," she said. "But don't make that face."

Then she taught me something she called "the stripper sway," which involved standing with my legs hip-width apart and just swaying my weight from side to side, sort of tracing an infinity symbol with my hips. It was incredibly simple, and I was incredibly unable to do it.

"Go slower," Inga said, and I tried to think about a sleepy stripper.

"Slow it down way, way more," Inga said. "Go so slow it feels silly, and then slow it down even more."

"Ugh," I whined again. "I'm so impatient!"

"Practice," Inga said again, sternly.

"Okay," I said. "Practice slowness: check."

"Now try this," Inga said. "Touch yourself—your arms or your stomach. Stop for a second and REALLY feel your hand against your skin."

So then I was *this* new person: a lonely woman standing in front of an empty chair in a dance studio in Rainier Valley, touching myself and feeling stupid.

I glanced at Inga. "Like this?" I said, running the fingers of my right hand along the inside surface of my extended left arm.

"Sort of," Inga said. "Think to yourself, 'This arm is the most amazing arm I've ever touched.' Then do the other one, and think to yourself, 'Now THIS arm is the most amazing arm I've ever touched.'"

"Oh my god," I said, forgetting about my arm. "Is this burlesque mindfulness!?"

Inga laughed. "I guess so? I never thought about it that way."

"Sexy dancing is like the triple threat of things I am really uncomfortable with: eye contact, going slow, and being present. What's next?"

"Okay, so once you've done the touching," Inga continued, "just stop and take a breath."

TAKE A BREATH?! This really was mindfulness practice. Therapy is everywhere!

In this moment, I'd done the touching, and I was stopping and taking a breath. I imagined myself walking across my bedroom, slowly. Breathing, slowly. I imagined myself looking at my person. I tried to imagine that I might *have* a person someday, that I might be able to trust someone again someday . . . it felt impossibly far away, sort of like my ability to make eye contact and breathe and move slowly without bolting.

I stood in front of the Academy of Burlesque mirror and kept touching my own arm, blinking back tears.

That night, I had a dream. I was in my sequined dress, running into the flames of my burning-down life.

"Slower," I told myself in the dream. "Maybe just saunter in! Touch your arm like it's the most amazing arm you've ever touched, even as the skin burns to a crisp and peels off the bone! Take a breath! SAUNTER SLOWER, STALLINGS!"

As Inga instructed, practicing body-mindful awareness can be as simple as concentrating on your breath and touching your own skin. This can be a helpful practice, especially when negative or distracting thoughts bubble up. You can let them pass and refocus on what you can feel with your fingers, noticing the rise and fall of your chest.

Try it for yourself: stand in front of a mirror, put on a song you love, and just see how it feels to breathe and touch your own skin to the music. This doesn't need to be seductive or erotic at all—the goal here is just to combine a little touch, a hint of movement, and focused breathing.

For me, dance was an excellent first way to calm my nervous system, move some trauma through, and feel my way into my new life. If dance is something that speaks to you, then by all means, start dancing!

But maybe the idea of moving your body to music horrifies you. I totally get that, too! The key here is to find ways that YOU find pleasure being in your body—for some of us, it might be taking our dog for a long, slow walk, where you focus on the sensation of each step beneath your feet and how the leash feels in your hand. Other folks might love going for a hard run. Even just taking the time to indulgently smell your food before you eat it can be an exercise in moving back into your human body.

Here are a few different kinds of embodiment methods to consider:

◆ Sensory awareness, which means just noticing sensations. This could just be a soak in the bathtub, where you really take the time to pay close attention to how your body feels in the water.

◆ Mind-body movement, which for some folks could mean yoga or tai chi, and for others could mean weight lifting or boxing.

◆ Human touch, which could be massage or other body work, or something as simple as *really* taking the time to notice how good it feels to hug someone you care about.

The goal here is just to find small, sustainable ways to give your body some loving, positive attention. It's worth the effort, I promise. As van der Kolk notes, "Self-regulation depends on having a friendly relationship with your body. Without it you have to rely on external regulation—from medication, drugs like alcohol, constant reassurance, or compulsive compliance with the wishes of others."

So many of us are dissociated, our big brain balloons floating around in screens and media all day, with our sadly ignored bodies dangling limp and ignored underneath. Those of us who've got trauma trapped in our bodies can be even more disconnected . . . it's crucial for each of us to find ways to make friends with our bodies.

Your body loves you. It's waiting to be your BFF.

FIND YOUR AFTERGLOW

Hopefully you're understanding now how trauma is stored in your body, and how traumatized bodies can struggle to feel pleasure or sensuality. This means that even if your shitshow didn't involve a self-esteem-crushing heartbreak, many shitshows come with trauma that messes with your ability to experience pleasure in connecting with your body. So let's talk about moving back into your body.

◆ Reflect on moments when you most feel in touch with your physicality or sensuality. (These moments might be very small, like enjoying the feeling of the wind on your face when you drive with the window open.) How could you increase the frequency of these in-touch sessions?

◆ What are your boundaries when it comes to physical sensuality and exploration? What do you want to try?

◆ Think of three things you love about your body today. Consider using this question as a daily gratitude practice. Every day, can you find something new to love about your body?

◆ What stories are you telling yourself about why you can't find pleasure in your body? What excuses do you have for why your body can't feel joy? Are you noticing any patterns in your self-limiting scripts? Are they starting to get boring? Are you ready to let them go? Letting go of old stories can be hard—they're like shitty friends who are irritating but predictable.

Remember that even those of us managing significant disabilities, illness, and chronic conditions have infinite capacity to find physical pleasure in our bodies. Find the edge of your pleasure, and commit to exploring it.

Chapter 12

SELF-CARE

CARE AND FEEDING OF A YOU

IN MY MARRIAGE, MY HUSBAND WAS THE COOK, AND ONE OF THE MOST IMMEDIATE SHIFTS IN my shitshow was that I was solely responsible for feeding myself and my son.

At first I wasn't hungry at all, and I focused on feeding Tavi. After four months or so, my appetite came back (it was like my body decided, "Oh, hey . . . maybe I *don't* want to die?") and I slowly began to assemble a new way of eating.

It was simple and straightforward, with a focus on protein and produce, nourishment and color. There was almost no flourish, no recipes, no single-use kitchen tools or elaborate appliances. No dish had more than five ingredients. My and my son's most common meals were a tour of healthy college cooking, stuff like scrambled eggs with salad, sweet-potato hash browns with cheese, and Insta-pot stews made from frozen chicken and precut veggies.

When Tavi was with his father, I'd sit and eat alone. Eating alone changes a lot of things.

In these quiet moments in my empty house, chewing my simple food, I realized that what I was doing was learning about care and feeding of my own inner . . . ugh, I can't believe I'm typing the words *inner child*, but there ya go.

It's totally normal that aspects of your personality get stuck in younger forms. Those of us coming out of long partnerships might have a few more stuck inner children, thanks to our tendency to "lock in" certain dynamics and behaviors from the age we were when we first shacked up.

I started recognizing my stuck inner children in almost every aspect of my life, and I was a mean mommy because I did NOT like these inner children.

Chewing my food alone in my quiet house, I ran through my family of inner children that I hated: The young adult desperate to prove she was in control and superior. The bratty teen always tryna push back. The awkward kid sure she was being rejected by everyone, all the time. The demanding toddler and her pathological need for attention. The baby who wasn't sure of her worth.

I chewed my simple food more. Swallowed. Took a sip of water.

Remember, you don't have to fix this mess today. You *can't* fix this mess today.

I took another bite.

DRINKING AWAY YOUR BAD FEELINGS

I'm talking about drinking *water*. When you're in a shit-show, dark thoughts can wallop you any time of day. You may find yourself obsessing about shit in the past (rumination, regret, and shame) or freaking out about shit in the future (anxiety, fear, hopelessness).

While mindfulness is one way to deal with these dark thoughts of the past and future (. . . so, what's happening in THIS moment?), you can also experiment with something simple: drinking more water.

Try this: the next time a dark thought comes up, take it not as a cue to *think* more but as a cue to *drink more water.*

It's a small miracle that most of us have potable water available at any time! Go get yourself a glass and take the time to notice the water coming out of the faucet. Take the time to feel the glass against your lips. Take the time to feel the water in your mouth. Drink the whole glassful! Take a breath when you're done. Has anything changed?

Even if your emotions are still dark, something HAS changed: you're better hydrated.

One of the inner children I was struggling with was my childish tendency to make someone else responsible for my moods. It's not intentional or malicious, but when my mood takes a downturn, it's a *lot* to deal with. I'm not a yeller or screamer, but I do have this way of blossoming black petals of misery and unhappiness that seem to make a room change temperature.

For the first half of my life, my response to a troubling mood would be blaming someone else, or begging someone to help me fix it. What a miserable, thankless task! Usually there's not even anything really wrong that needs to be *fixed*. The mood just needs to be held tightly until it passes—like a ThunderShirt, one of those weighted vests to keep dogs calm during storms.

These dark moods are sort of like a gentle emotional seizure. I'm okay, and it'll pass on its own, and it'll pass extra quickly if you hold me even tighter when I try to shove you away . . . because I always try to shove you away, because I'm predictable like that. (I'm a walking textbook example of that anxious-preoccupied attachment behavior that we talked about earlier. The shove away is so common that it's got a name: "protest behavior.")

As I sat there alone chewing my simple food, my self-loathing took a sharp downward turn. I felt the tears come up and I could feel the black petals blossoming. One of the many inner children looked up at me from the darkness of my own mind, in the corner where I'd banished her for years, her eyes huge and pupils dilated with fear.

Sitting at the table, I kept chewing my food. I took a sip of water. This inner child? She's my responsibility. I imagined turning on a light and smiling at her, holding out my hand.

I imagined holding her close and telling her I love her unconditionally, even when she makes a mess. I imagined myself stroking her hair the way I did with my son. I suddenly understood that my wish to have someone fix my emotions ("Outside Person should DO THIS THING so I'd feel better!") was actually an invitation to my own adult self to handle the broken baby parts of me that felt overwhelmed.

You can't control other people's actions, but when you find yourself wishing someone *else* would do something (or being disappointed they haven't yet), you can use it as an opportunity to do that dang thing for yourself!

When you feel a dark mood coming on, hold yourself accountable and step up to the task of self-soothing and self-regulating. Before you inflict your mood on someone else, consider these simple self-care lists:

◆ **HALT: Hungry, Angry, Lonely, Tired:** This one is borrowed from twelve-step programs. The theory is that an addict is at highest risk of relapse when they're hungry, angry, lonely, and/or tired. When you feel yourself on the verge of a meltdown, ask yourself: Is there a chance I'm just hungry, angry, lonely, or tired? And if so, how can you take care of *those* needs, rather than go down a dark spiral of anxiety and self-loathing or lashing out at someone? I'm prone to hangriness, and have learned that I need to always have snacks in my bag, just like I did when I was the mother of a toddler. What I'm saying is that sometimes the solution is as simple as goldfish crackers.

◆ **DREAMS: Drink, Rest, Eat, Air, Move, Socialize:** This one is from Atta—drink some water, take a rest, eat something nourishing, breathe in some air, move your body, be social. These are simple ways to soothe yourself through painful feelings that can't immediately be solved. You may learn that sometimes when you're sad, a few songs' worth of stretching will let the mood pass.

Of course, like everything else, you have to practice before these solutions feel natural. Most of the time you'll default to your favorite unconscious and ineffective coping strategies. God knows I did.

Most times when I got sad, I'd still default to making plans and strategies and policies that would help me avoid future sadness. (I will outsmart sadness! I shall never feel sadness ever again!) Most times when I got anxious, I would frantically pace while my brain went down the rabbit hole of contingency plans.

Every once in a while, though, I could manage to just sit quietly at the table eating with my inner children, smiling at them compassionately while they screamed and dropped food on the floor.

FIND YOUR AFTERGLOW

Let's talk about your blossoming black petals of misery and unhappiness. Uncomfortable moods happen, and when they do, blaming others or hating yourself doesn't help anyone. We must each hold ourselves accountable for our difficult moods, and allow ourselves to feel them, attend to them, and soothe ourselves, allowing the moods to move through.

◆ Think back to the last few times you felt like you needed a ThunderShirt. What were your HALT factors at each of those times? Can you recognize any patterns so you can attend to those things before they get rough? If your emotions take over when you're hungry, try to plan ahead so you don't face stressful shit on an empty stomach. If getting even a little bit less sleep makes everything in your day more miserable, make sure to account for your tiredness when evaluating your mood.

◆ What DREAMS self-soothing tools do you have in your toolbox? What healthy, productive, nondestructive methods do you have for calming yourself? Sometimes it can be helpful to think about what you'd do for a child or dear friend who was melting down—would you wrap them in a blanket and play music? Make them tea? Draw them a bath?

◆ How do you treat the parts of yourself you don't like? How are you rejecting your inner children? Do you yell at them or shame them into silence? Do you punish them or ignore them? How do the ways you treat yourself reflect the ways you were spoken to by people in your life?

◆ When you feel disappointed in other people, what are the most common stories (i.e., they ignore me, they don't respect me, they reject me)? How can you start providing for yourself in the ways you've felt are lacking (i.e., never ignoring your needs, respecting your feelings, actively accepting yourself)?

◆ Sometimes working with the concept of an inner child is referred to as "reparenting," where you focus attention on being the parent you wish you'd always had. What kind of parenting do you feel like you wanted and didn't get? How can you treat yourself like the parent you wish you'd had?

The loving, caring person you've been waiting your whole life for? It's you, and you're right here!

Chapter 13

CONNECTING

FALLING IN TRUST

SHITSHOWS SMELL LIKE BETRAYAL. EVEN IF YOURS DOESN'T INCLUDE A STEREOTYPICAL BE-trayal like infidelity, there's still just this sense of feeling like you've been deceived . . . you followed the rules, and this *still* happened? Or, for those of us on the offbeat side of the coin, you made a point to *break* every stupid old-fashioned rule, and this same old-fashioned bullshit *still* happened to you?

You ate all-organic, and yet you *still* got gravely ill? You committed to the perfect social justice job in the nonprofit sector, and yet you *still* got totally canned as part of some office politics? You had an open relationship and flipped gender roles, but *still* your marriage ended? Yep. Shit happens, and when it does, your sense of trust can get destroyed.

For me, I spent months feeling distrustful and terrified of everything, and convinced I would be stuck that way. We've all heard the stories about people broken by a personal loss, folks who just never bounce back.

"I don't know how I'll ever trust anyone ever again," I told Atta. "I thought I could trust my body, and then it exploded. I thought I could trust my marriage, and then it collapsed."

"What if you think of trust as a muscle?" Atta asked me. "What if it's sprained but just needs some gentle exercise to regain its strength?"

"More practice," I said, feeling both exhausted by the idea but also a little excited because at least it was something to DO. I'm not great at just sitting around resting and letting myself heal, but exercises I could do.

I started my trust practices with myself. Could I make a small daily promise to myself and keep it? Today I will text three friends to tell them I appreciate them: check. Today I will meditate for five minutes: check. Today I will feed myself a nourishing meal: check.

Then I tried trust practices with my friends.

I have a business trip again next week, I texted my geighbor. It's so sad coming home to a cold dark house. Would you mind using my spare key to turn on my heat the morning I get home?

Of course, he texted back, and I came home to a warm house with a couple lights on. I noticed a sensation in my chest that felt cozy and pleasantly squished, like the trust was invisible arms around me.

Then I tested out making some new friends. Out with Ashlee one night, I invited a friend of hers over for drinks after the bar closed. She was a queer former cheerleader I would run into sometimes at my hippie Jazzercise dance class.

"Nice place," she said, walking up the stairs. "You live here alone?"

"Yeah, half the week," I said, still feeling sad about it.

"Niiiiiice!" my new friend said, and I blinked with confusion and looked around at my life with fresh eyes and thought, *Oh wait, maybe it is?!*

We smoked a joint (after months of sobriety, I was finally feeling okay with a couple drinks and a bit of Seattle's legal weed), and by the time we finally said good night at four a.m., I was woozy with the intoxication of connection. I'd invited a new friend over, and we'd had a great time! I felt giddy . . . there was an expansion in my chest, a quickening in my stomach.

It felt like I was falling in love . . . but no, wait, that's not quite it because it was completely platonic.

It felt like I was falling in trust with the world again.

IT'S HARD OUT THERE FOR A MILF

"You should get out there," Anna Banana told me when I was at Pretty Parlor doing my sparkle therapy. "Meet people. Get on Tinder or something."

"You need a boost," the new-age aesthetician told me as she slathered organic single-source oils on my face and extracted blindsided blackheads from my skin. "Get back out there!"

I was still struggling to make decisions for myself (a solid sense of agency takes a while, apparently), but when two people made the same suggestion, I figured I should probably do it. Is that how this trust-muscle idea works?

The last time I'd been truly single, it was 1997. I had a beeper, drove a Honda CRX, and wore JNCO jeans with thirty-two-inch cuffs. But there in early 2016, I was forty and technology had marched forward. One night after Tavi was asleep, I set up a Tinder profile. It was so easy! I uploaded a picture of me in sequins from a wedding expo photo booth and wrote a quick profile: Capitol Hill MILF, small business owner, dancer. Be interesting.

Profile active, I started swiping through photos of nearby folks. Left, left, left . . . right? Fish picture, "school of hard knocks," sports jersey, ooh helloooo jawline! I was quickly overwhelmed by all the people, whom I started thinking of collectively (and gender-neutrally) as Tinderellas. It felt sort of like auditioning a diverse array of beautiful people from interesting places in a vast rainbow of delights. Men? Women? Trans folks? Couples? QUILTBAG? Check all boxes that apply.

Tinder reminded me of Burning Man, back at the turn of the millennium when I used to go. Part of what made Burning Man remarkable was that anyone could ask anyone for *anything*—the agreement being that you had to be okay with the answer. It was an exercise in radical consent: ask for anything you want, without shame! The person you're asking can just be like, "Nope, that's not my thing!" but whatever, there's nothing wrong with asking. That's what Tinder felt like—like a digital temporary autonomous zone combined with a gaming console. Left, left, right, left, left.

As I started matching with people, the questions started coming.

What are you looking for? Tinderellas asked, and I said everything from someone to go dancing with to drinks and talk of mindfulness to personal trainer with benefits? Can we talk about whether you dance or perform and to what kind of music? Are you an Afro-Cuban singer down with new jack swing? Is your personality bigger than mine? That's a feat, so let's see what you've got. Are you leaving town soon, so you're not going to mess with this GO DEEP OR GO HOME self-dev adventure I'm on? Do you have a high tolerance for being amused by other high-intensity people going through high-intensity life transitions? PS: Not looking for new long-term partner.

I was self-aware enough to know that I was too reactionary, too raw, still in too much recovery to get into anything serious. Traveling musicians? Road trippers? Power lesbians on business trips? Touring stand-up comedians? DM me! Capitol Hill is dense and tourist-filled, so any given week, Tinder was packed with people passing through my three-mile discoverability radius.

I didn't end up sleeping with anyone, but there was a lot of making out.

THE SCIENCE OF TALKING TO STRANGERS

A life implosion can make you feel depressed and profoundly isolated (or hell, maybe that's just the twenty-first century in general?), and of course then the more isolated you get, the more depressed you can feel. It's a downward spiral.

In his book *The Upward Spiral*, neuroscientist Alex Korb talks about the research behind why talking to strangers can make you feel good. One study in Chicago paid commuters to either speak to a stranger or just sit quietly by themselves, and the results clearly showed that a quick conversation with a stranger led to better moods. Despite many of the subjects voicing that they were concerned that conversations with a stranger would be uncomfortable, they instead reported having a more pleasant commute.

The gentle lift from even a brief conversation with a stranger "is likely due to the fact that the oxytocin system supports the serotonin system," Korb explains. These two chemicals interact to help you get into an upward spiral. Being social (even with strangers!) can help you feel better, and feeling better helps you be more social.

And what is dating if not talking to strangers?! As my afterglow started to shine, I remembered that I liked being social, and so I mostly liked dating.

One night, I went on two dates with three people. First, I toddled to a wine bar in black kitten heels (literally: the toes have whiskers stitched into them) for a chat with a lovely early-thirties swinger couple from Bellevue, the upscale suburban city across Lake Washington from Seattle.

"It's so refreshing that you already know about how these things work," the female half of the couple said, under those impeccably drawn eyebrows that the millennial girls love so much.

I winked at her over my wineglass. This was definitely still a shitshow, but the show was transitioning from a tragedy to a dirty rom-com.

The couple gave me a ride home in their Mercedes, and I ran upstairs, swapped out my heels for Adidas high tops, and ran out the back door and down the hill to meet a Tinderella I'd been texting with that afternoon. He was the lead singer of a touring Afro-Caribbean band, and he had a flight home to LA early the next morning.

We met at a dive bar, smoked a joint, and enjoyed some dirty blues dancing to Motown music. He came back to my place for a drink and gave me a lap dance to a Jodeci song. At the end of the night, I paid for his car back to his hotel because I'm a gentleman like that.

Being a forty-year-old divorced wedding blogger on a dating app was an embarrassing stage, but it was also an appropriate one. With Tinder, I learned to roll the dice, stay safe, and rediscover amusement. I also had some crushing emotional defeats that set me back significantly—getting stood up, getting ghosted, and getting in over my head with people even more messed up than I was.

"I feel like such a cliché," I told Atta that week. "I mean, am I really *that lady?* The one going through a divorce, going on Tinder dates in short dresses? UGH, who is this woman? It's embarrassing."

The embarrassed feeling was starting to feel familiar. I was like a baby deer, wobbling around on little midlife lady legs, bounding through flowering fields of shame.

But in that moment, for a short moment, Tinder was exactly where I needed to be.

Now, you already know this: whether it's jumping into a new friendship, romance, hobby, or job, trying to replace something you've lost when it's too soon can set you back significantly. Sex and relationship therapist Chamin Ajjan explains that "dating with the goal of finding a new partner when you have unresolved feelings is selfish." For me, all I could do was be very, very direct about what I was looking for, but even then I was messy—and on Tinder, I was in good company.

A big reason people start dating soon after a big breakup is to help rebuild their self-esteem. Recovering from rejection, it's only natural to want to feel desirable again. But dating coach Laurel House says that without putting in the work on ourselves, that jolt of good feeling will reveal that the self-esteem we thought we were rebuilding was just temporary. She suggests being brutally honest with yourself, and looking "at the reasons for your breakup as opportunities to learn and grow."

If you're dating, be patient with yourself and clear with your intentions—both with yourself and with others. Remember that trying something new will *never* replace internal self-development.

Now, remember when we talked about that attachment system stuff a few chapters back? Know this: if you're not actively working on your attachment issues, your attachment issues will *work you over*. A triggered attachment system will make relationship choices for you, without you even noticing.

Dating without understanding how your attachment system works puts you at high risk for your system getting hacked. I don't mean to get all fearmongery on you here, but attachment issues play out in adult relationships in extremely predictable ways . . . ways that can easily be exploited. If you don't want to fall prey to manipulative people (and for women dating men, this can include Red Pill bros who use calculated systems of coercion to get women into bed), you need to learn how your attachment system works and stay awake enough to notice when your system is getting played.

For me, recognizing and working through my messed-up attachment dynamics was the most important lesson I learned from dating. Los Angeles artist and mindfulness author Yumi Sakugawa sums up my experience with this long, lovely sentence: "Imagine that you have already mastered the courage to fully step into confronting a relationship dynamic that makes you intensely uncomfortable, because it makes you really look at aspects of yourself that you really would rather not look at . . . but then you were able to be brave and speak up, and now this relationship dynamic is totally healed and transformed, because you were willing to fully experience those moments of extreme discomfort in your body, and feel those old outdated narratives fully leaving your body on an energetic and cellular level."

This is work that all of us can benefit from, whether you're celibate, dating, partnered, or otherwise. Understanding interpersonal patterns that show up in your relationships, holding yourself accountable for your quirks, and then attentively addressing them?

That's growth we *all* need, regardless of whether you're dating, partnered, or completely disinterested in romance. Understanding human connection is for all of us.

FIND YOUR AFTERGLOW

Connection with other people is a challenging issue for many of us, especially these days, thanks to the current state of social isolation and the loneliness epidemic that seems to be plaguing Western culture. And when you're going through a rocky life transition, connection gets even more sticky, regardless of your current partnership situation. Let's dig in.

◆ What connections in your life do you value the most? Can you think of any connections you want to rekindle, or new kinds of connections you're interested in exploring? There are so many different kinds of love, and our culture tends to overprioritize romantic love. Who are you in "friend-love" with? Where do you find subtle senses of connection in your day—the barber you wave at through the window, the neighbor who always nods when you pass them? Where do you find those small connections, and what could you do to cultivate even more of them?

◆ When you go seeking connection, where does shame come up? ("I can't ask my new coworker to coffee, they'll think I'm weird . . .") How can you hold those tender feelings with compassion and understanding instead of pushing them away? Watch the shame bus go by, and ask that coworker to coffee anyway!

◆ What stories do you tell yourself about being in relationship to others? (For example, do you feel like you're "always" rejected, or "always" disappointed?) What patterns can you see in the stories you tell yourself, and what might those familiar stories suggest about the work YOU need to do with yourself? For example, if you frequently feel rejected by others, can you find ways to accept aspects of yourself you dislike? What if you were the perfect lover you were looking for?

As you move out of the worst of your shitshow, you may find that you have more time and interest for cultivating connections. Even if you're an introvert, it's important to establish a new mesh of friends and acquaintances for this new life. These relationships can be small (a quiet smile with the person checking out your groceries may be enough for some of us!), but as you feel your new self emerging it's important to learn what that new self feels like in relationship to other selves.

Chapter 14

EXERCISE

WHEN SWEAT IS YOUR FLUID OFFERING

THE SPRING AFTER MY SHITSHOW, MOST MORNINGS STARTED LIKE THIS: DESPITE MY SLEEP meds, I'd wake up with a startle at five a.m., pick up my phone, triage work emails until seven a.m., and then get Tavi up and off to school.

On my way home from dropping him off, I checked my schedule to see what group fitness class I'd scheduled between my hours of emailing and other Offbeat Empire work. On this particular day, it was dance class.

When my life fell apart, my self-employment went from being the greatest blessing to being a confusing burden, with my life unscheduled and wide open. It helped my days feel less unmoored if I kept to a clear routine, and group classes helped give me structure.

I'd already redirected all my disposable income toward therapy, and these classes were categorized as "physical therapy." Plus, once I figured out that I was holding trauma in my body, I decided that when in doubt, I should just keep moving. The gods demand fluid offerings, and while the tears still came daily, it felt useful to add sweat (and come!) to the mix, too.

My favorite dance fitness class is taught in a basement on Capitol Hill's 15th Ave, with twinkly lights around the studio mirrors. We do basic choreography to wonderfully terrible pop music while my teacher Dina shouts at us to "focus on the sensation!" and "ground through your feet!" She's a counselor and hypnotherapist when she's not teaching this class that she calls "Bodyfulness," which I lovingly call "hippie Jazzercise."

That day, in that class, I kept moving, but I cried through the entire class and couldn't get up off the floor after the cooldown song.

Dina walked over after the room cleared and knelt down next to me on the floor.

"What's happening?"

"My life is falling apart," I sniffed through my tears, helpless on the floor.

Dina invited me to swing by her office later for a free hypnotherapy consultation. I would normally decline because hypnosis isn't really my jam, but that was the old me. New me didn't know what my jam was anymore, and if someone offered me something that might make me feel less like dying, I accepted. It was lovely.

The clusterfuck of my life had cracked off all my defenses. I was open to anything, which felt terrifying and confusing but also liberating and expansive. I just had to keep moving.

This is a big ol' "NO DUH" but here we go: exercise helps with stress, anxiety, depression, pick your discomfort of choice. But I want you to hear that and truly feel it. Dr. Emily Nagoski, author of *Come as You Are* and *Burnout: The Secret to Unlocking the Stress Cycle*, needs you to know this is straight-up truth: "Physical activity is the single most efficient strategy for completing the stress response cycle and recalibrating your central nervous system into a calm state. When people say, 'Exercise is good for stress,' that is for realsie real."

If you need more encouragement, the Anxiety and Depression Association of America reports that regular exercise can work as well as medication for some patients in reducing symptoms of anxiety and depression, and that the effects are not only long-lasting, but also immediate. (Can you imagine a pill that has that kind of efficacy?!) High-intensity exercise can alleviate symptoms of anxiety and depression for hours, and keeping a regular schedule may reduce those symptoms significantly over time.

High-intensity physical activity also releases those feel-good hormones and endorphins. Most of us have heard of the "runner's high," but even if you're not into high-intensity exercise (or it's not accessible to you due to disability or chronic conditions), your brain will benefit from incorporating mellow, loving physical activity into your life.

According to Harvard Health Publishing, low-intensity exercise sustained over time "spurs the release of proteins called neurotrophic or growth factors, which cause nerve cells to grow and make new connections. The improvement in brain function makes you feel better." By restimulating and making new connections in your brain, movement and physical activity *directly* and positively affect your emotional and mental recovery.

Most of us already know all this stuff already, but we find reasons to dismiss it. Here's the thing: if your defenses have been cracked off, now is the time to truly *feel* the truth. Seriously! Try standing up right now and doing five jumping jacks. Here, I'll do it too.

If you don't have the ability to stand or jump (I see you, friends working with different abilities!), just go for vigorous arm waving and hard, fast breathing. The point here isn't the specific activity—the goal is getting your blood and breath circulating in a different way.

It feels silly, but you'll feel different, and sometimes feeling different is better than feeling awful.

COMPENSATING FOR LACK OF SKILL WITH ENTHUSIASM

And as for me: I really, *really* wanted to stop feeling awful.

When my life fell apart, I was a soft, weak workaholic nerd who sat at a desk fourteen hours a day and danced for an hour or so a few times a month at Dina's classes. My spouse was the fit one; I was the one who looked at screens, my brain floating in a jar, my body forgotten, trying to support my family.

In my new post-shitshow life, where I only had to support myself and half of my kindergartener, where emergency surgery and then heartbreak sucked 20 percent of my body weight out of my breasts like a greedy grief baby, where anxiety and sleeplessness kept me in a state of half panic and mania, I was still a nerd—but I became a nerd who decided to sign up for a hip-hop dance class because I needed a break from crying on the couch.

The Monday night Intro to Hip-Hop class was at Velocity Dance Center, housed in a brick building on Capitol Hill's 12th Ave. The class is taught by a guy named Jaret Hughes, a former dancer for the LA Clippers and Seattle SuperSonics. I walked into the studio and felt a little less nervous when I saw that I wasn't the oldest student. Jaret put on Beyoncé and led us through a warm-up. Pop and R&B are my jam, so once the music was on, I felt myself settling into a comfort zone.

The comfort zone was abruptly yanked out from underneath me as Jaret moved into the choreography section of the ninety-minute class. He tried to teach us a move called "the snake" and my shoulders refused to move correctly. Some of the other students were classically trained dancers—I could tell by their postures and the way they held their hands. Interestingly, I watched them stumble through the unfamiliar movements, too, and reminded myself that we were all struggling in our own ways.

As for me, I compensated for lack of skill with enthusiasm and sweat. I was terrible at remembering choreography, but at least I had rhythm. I felt like a disaster, a forty-year-old white lady in a Monday night hip-hop class, but the music was loud and at least I felt different because I was moving and I was out of my house and not thinking about mortality and abandonment.

I was making my fluid offering.

CELEBRATION INSTEAD OF OBLIGATION

Many of us consider exercise to be a chore, or think it's about "no pain, no gain." In reality, all movement is good movement (say it again louder for the folks in back: *ALL MOVEMENT IS GOOD MOVEMENT!*), and you're more likely to get moving if you're enjoying yourself. Impromptu dance parties in the kitchen? Getting off the bus a couple stops early when the weather is nice just to enjoy the breeze? Catching up with friends while going for a walk (instead of getting drinks)? These are all forms of celebratory movement.

Moving for joy can help with that whole "reinhabiting your body after trauma" thing, and help you regain your sense of agency with your body and health in a positive, productive way. When you reframe exercise as nurturing and loving your body in ways that feel good, you shift fitness from an item on your to-do list to a treat.

Movement isn't an obligation, it's a *celebration*: YOU'RE NOT DEAD TODAY!

That said, moving back into your body can also be disorienting if you're not used to it. I was not an active child, and I hated gym class and avoided all sports. Until I was forty, my only consistent physical activities had been walking and dancing for fun a few times a month.

Then my ovary exploded, and after the emergency abdominal surgery, I did three months of physical therapy to help knit my sliced abdomen back together. The physical therapist I'd worked with taught me how to do an exercise called "Dead Bug" (google it!), and it completely changed my posture and how I walked.

After my marriage collapsed, my relationship to my body shifted again. The cortisol pumped through my veins twenty-four hours a day, and then there was that panic attack with the snotting and heaving, and come to think of it, that's when my hands first started throbbing. My hands went completely numb and started buzzing during that panic attack. My face tingled and I couldn't feel my nose, and it's all just hyperventilation, right? It's not my heart ripping out through my spine, the moment when I truly really crack all the way open and am split in two? Cuz that's what it felt like.

This combination of mortality check and emotional devastation pulled me into my body for the first time in my life—and it was a mysterious land in there. I wanted to get all the nervous trauma energy out somehow, so I went to as many group fitness classes as I could. As a bonus, it was nice to have people tell me what to do.

"YES YOU CAN!" my barre instructor SarahRose barked as I held my legs as still as possible in ballet postures, shaking until my bingo wings jiggled.

"DON'T GIVE UP ON THOSE JACKKNIVES!" the boxing instructor bellowed, and my brain clicked into "Expectation! Instruction! Execution! Sir yes sir!" mode and it was a relief that someone else was counting, and someone else had to keep track, and I didn't have to think for a change, all I had to do was move.

I moved into my middle-aged body with a desperate hunger. How had I never appreciated these muscles and tendons and the weathered veins on the backs of my hands? My motivation was less competitive or quantifiable or results-focused and more a race against time to get all the enjoyment I could out of having a human body.

It started to add up: all the dancing, all the classes, all the sobbing, all the walking, all the talking, all the breathing, and all the pacing around the house endlessly, and the burlesque practice, and the random jumping jacks I did just because I was like, *AHHH GET IT OUT GET IT OUT TOO MUCH LIFE HAPPENING, I HAVE TO GET IT OUT BEFORE I EXPLODE!*

I rattled myself like a jar full of pennies, trying to guess the value of what's inside. The stress stripped off my protective layers, and suddenly I could *see* how strong the muscles were underneath.

. . . Buh? I had muscles?! I'd never felt so strong.

Did you hear that? I was recovering from a shitshow, and I'd *never felt so strong.*

On a neighborhood walk with a Tinderella, we cut through a Capitol Hill playground.

"Can you do a pull-up?" my date asked me, squeezing my bicep. This one was a gun-slinging nerd on some cross-country survival-skills road trip, in town for a week for a class about pistol skills or chicken-skinning or something.

"I don't know!" I said. "Let's see!"

Then I jumped up, gripped my palms around the bar of a jungle gym, and pulled myself up! I started laughing so hard that I lost my grip and dropped to the ground, my feet landing with surprising stability on the wood chips.

"I guess I can?!" I said. I could not stop laughing. I'd never been this person before!

I'd grown muscles in places I didn't know existed. I didn't know what any of them were, but I knew how to stretch them in ways that felt good. (I was learning I could do things that made me feel good! Is that you, afterglow? It's me, Ariel!) I started learning how to isolate the muscles one by one, because it gave me something to do when I couldn't cry anymore and I was tired of my brain's endless looping.

After my burlesque training and the hip-hop classes, my dancing got cheesier, sluttier, more shameless. I had run out of time for shame. I was a divorced wedding blogger—now *that's* a shame. My ass-first dancing was nothing by comparison.

Movement for celebration instead of obligation is such a different experience. You may find yourself baffled most of the time: Look at what your leg can do! Can you make your leg do that thing again just for the joy of feeling it?

"Oh my god, your rhomboids!" the gunslinger cooed at me during a make-out, hands on my back.

"My what?" I said, still laughing.

FIND YOUR AFTERGLOW

Afterglow fitness absolutely is NOT about how much you can do. It's not about ability or goals. It's about finding the edges of what *your* particularly unique body can do, depending on *your* particularly unique abilities, and exploring and appreciating those edges. This isn't about body image, it's about body *sensation*. This isn't about weight or reps or calories, it's about celebrating what you can do today, listening to what your body has to say, and noticing as things change.

◆ Take a moment to just feel your body right now. No seriously, stop for a second and tune in. Shrug your shoulders, touch your arms, run a hand down your legs. YOU HAVE A HUMAN BODY! Seriously, can we just appreciate how amazing that is?!

◆ Write a love letter to your body. What has it survived? What has it taught you? What aspects of it do you adore? How can you show it you love it, just as it is, right in this moment?

◆ How do you talk about your body when it's hurting or not functioning how you'd like? How can you show your body that you appreciate it, even in its challenges? Your body is always listening.

◆ How are your abilities different now than they used to be? How can you celebrate the abilities you have today, knowing that inevitably they will change as you age? Imagine you're on your deathbed looking back—what might you wish you'd done when you had today's body and abilities? DO IT!

◆ What kinds of movement interest you? What steps can you take this week to get more of those movements into your life? Think small here; now is not the time to tell yourself you're going to go to the gym every day. The goal is movement that's a sustainable and joyful part of your life, not a crushing obligation.

◆ Again, take the time to notice the defenses your brain may be offering up about why you can't do this. Watch for the patterns in the ways you talk to yourself about why you can't make changes in your life.

My hope for you is that you're able to use the pain of your shit-show as momentum to get moving. How you move almost doesn't matter—the only result we're looking for is consistency and sustainability. The only goal we're aiming for is finding a way to celebrate that you have a body, and enjoying what it can do today.

Chapter 15

DAILY DEVOTIONAL DANCE

CELEBRATING NOT BEING DEAD TODAY!

WHEN I COULDN'T SLEEP (WHICH WAS STILL A LOT OF THE TIME), I WOULD DANCE AROUND MY bedroom in my underwear, emoting all over the place through full-body freak-outs. I would cry and crawl across the floor in agonized defeat, and then go around a bend and start hysterically laughing and jump up and down doing my dance moves I'd learned from Jaret, and then wind my hips doing the stripper sway I'd learned from Inga. I was messy, but I was feeling things and moving them through.

I needed my music LOUD to drown out the demons, but I'm also thoughtful about my neighbors so I always danced with headphones. If you'd been a fly on the wall, you would have heard only the sound of my breathing and crying.

I was unsure if the scene was hot or horribly embarrassing. Woman dancing in bedroom in underwear: hot! Completely silent dancing combining crawling, crying, late '90s rave moves, culturally appropriative hip-hop, and amateurish stripper sways: probably not hot?

My bedroom had big windows to use as a mirror, but the room is carpeted and much of my cry/crawling choreography had to be done in the small space around my bed. There was more space in the living room, but the mirrored windows weren't out there. I started fantasizing about having a dance studio and then hit another moment of disorientation: *This* is my life now? I was a nerd who liked to hang with the monkeys in my brain. Who was this person fantasizing about an in-home dance studio?

But now that I viscerally understood that organs explode and bodies die, that you could get hit by a bus or run over by an emotional freight train . . . suddenly it felt urgent. What other hobbies mattered?!

The dance studio was a new fantasy for a different kind of life.

One spring morning, I found myself where I usually was in the mornings: standing in my kitchen with a cup of milky black tea sitting on the countertop. My right leg was propped up on the counter next to the tea, stretching while I scrolled on my phone.

I shifted my weight, put my right foot back on the floor, and took another sip of tea. I put my left leg up on the countertop and stretched into the back of my thigh. The window was open and a sweet little breeze blew in, moving my hair against my cheek.

I took a belly breath, and in this moment I got a whiff of the festering alley dumpsters behind my building. Whatever. It was still a lovely breeze, and this was still a lovely moment. I rolled out my left ankle, felt it pop loudly, and took another sip of tea.

My kitchen counter was about the same height as the ballet barres we used in the barre classes I'd been going to, so I set my teacup down next to my phone, propped my palms against the edge of the granite, held my body in a flat plank, and did a few leaning push-ups against the edge of the counter.

It worked fine, but I wished I had a mirror to help me check my form—and now I had an idea.

I stopped my kitchen pushing-upping and thumbed a text to my friend Joel, a contractor who does shamanic work in his off-hours: What do you think about installing a mirror and a ballet barre on the wall of my living room?

Joel wrote back saying it'd be a relatively inexpensive project, and that's how a wall of my living room became a dance studio.

Like so many choices I'd made in my new life, I felt both a mix of clarity (I must do this!) and shame (*seriously?!*). I felt chronically both embarrassed and compelled by so many things. Left by husband? Embarrassing, but it happened! Trying to start meditating? Pathetic cliché, but five minutes a day was actually helping! Adding a mirror and a ballet barre to a wall of my living room? Indulgent, but I must!

The project itself was relatively straightforward. Joel came over and took measurements for the mirror, and we swapped emails about which barre style to order and what height it should be mounted at.

"It's a sound financial investment," Joel said. "Adding a mirror to that wall adds so much light to the room and really opens the space up . . . plus, sometimes you can peer into the eyes of your ancestors, or catch glimpses of your parallel lives, or even access other dimensions through a mirror!" Perfect. Every contractor should dabble in shamanism.

The five-by-six-foot mirror was mounted on the wall between the doors of my and my son's bedrooms, and it became clear that the idea wasn't just a self-indulgent middle-aged divorcée's whimsy (although it was that, too): the living room immediately felt twice as big. The contractor/shaman was right.

Inspired by the art in Atta's waiting room, I tracked down the artist who'd made it (Joey Veltkamp!) and got my own WE'RE ALL GONNA DIE quilt and mounted it on the wall facing the mirror. This reminder refused to let me ever forget my mortality. It was hot pink and teal, the colors so bright that they made your eyes skip a bit.

My queer cheerleader friend suggested calling the space Studio Haaay, as in "Hey, girl, haaayyyy!" and the name stuck.

Studio Haaay created a home for the mornings of my new life.

I would wake up, stumble to make tea, and go pee. Then I'd get myself to the living room, face myself and all my alternate metaverses in Studio Haaay, and my reflections and I would start our day together.

The movements shifted each morning. This wasn't yoga with its predetermined series of postures to be emulated. This wasn't dance class with its choreography to follow. It was just me, on this day, in this moment. It was just me, in this body, listening to it and being grateful that it was alive.

WE'RE ALL GONNA DIE the quilt on the wall reminds me, and my body shouts back, ". . . so we better move today!"

Most mornings, something would hurt, and I'd lean into the tight places and listen. Some mornings, I'd cry. Some mornings, there'd be lots of energy and I'd bounce around and flap my hands. Some mornings, I'd just sit on a mat and twist while I sipped my tea. Some mornings, I was sick with a cold or a stomach thing and all I could manage was lying on the floor and sticking my feet up and rolling my ankles until they popped.

The goal wasn't to do something impressive or interesting. The goal was just to show up every day and see what my body had to say. The goal was just to offer up the movement as a devotional to being alive and awake.

Quickly, Studio Haaay stopped being an embarrassment and became my morning devotional practice. In this home, we dance. In this home, we stretch and grow. In this home, we find what hurts and give it room to be, so that it can relax into something less painful. In this home, we make fluid offerings. In this home, we try to move the trauma out of our body, so that something else can come in.

CONSCIOUS DANCE FOR ABSOLUTE BEGINNERS

This kind of morning practice is a form of "conscious dance," which isn't a style like jazz or hip-hop, but more of a mindset. It just means that you're using movement as a mindfulness practice. It's available to anyone, regardless of age, physical ability, income, or access to a class or dance space. You don't need to be a "good dancer"—you just need to pay attention to the sensations of the movement in whatever body parts are available to move. If even the idea of dance is intimidating, rebrand it as mindful movement, free-form wiggling, sacred stretches, or any other name that feels safe to you.

Mackenzie Amara, a 5Rhythms dance teacher and embodiment coach in Zurich, describes it this way: "Conscious movement is not about doing anything in particular, more about letting yourself be *done* to. When you drop the need to act, think, control, change, shift, and simply allow your awareness to settle on the sensation of energy in your body, you find that the energy has textures, colors, and shapes all its own. From there, you can start to let your body be the tool for shaping the energy that's naturally there already. Embodiment is really a process of coming into greater alignment: head, heart, guts."

Here's how to get started:

◆ Find five minutes and a little space where you won't be interrupted. Your kitchen or bedroom work fine!

◆ Put on some headphones (that way you don't have to worry about anyone hearing you) and a song that makes you want to move. When in doubt, the Spotify robots have great playlists for every mood.

◆ I suggest closing your eyes. Conscious dance is less about how it looks (even just to yourself) and more about how it *feels*. With your eyes closed, you can focus on the sensations.

◆ Start small, maybe just swaying or moving your fingers.

◆ Do not push or force yourself—this is not the place for overexertion! Move in a way that feels safe, comforting, and natural. It might just be you gently waving your arms for an entire song—that's awesome!

◆ Keep your attention focused on your movement, and watch to see how your movements unfold (. . . or not!

That's interesting, too! Where do you get stuck? What thought buses go by? What familiar stories do you tell yourself about why you can't?). When your mind wanders away from your movement, just notice and gently refocus on a new body part—ooh, what's that left foot doing?

- ◆ If you become overwhelmed, take a break and keep breathing.
- ◆ Consider ending your practice with a seated meditation or journaling. What came up for you?

Doing this for even just one song a day can make a distinct difference in how that day feels. As Mackenzie told me, "In my experience, movement allows you to have profound therapeutic breakthroughs for complicated, persistent mental health problems like depression, anxiety, and trauma; breakthroughs that are off-limits without full utilization of the body."

If you find yourself enjoying conscious dance at home, you may want to see if there are gatherings in your area. Ecstatic Dance, 5Rhythms, Open Floor, and somatic movement are just some of the names associated with these kinds of gatherings—get googling!

As for me, having a daily movement practice transformed my mornings from my saddest parts of the day to something I woke up and welcomed.

My morning practice became a structure, an invisible internal framework that would hold me in its arms at the start of each day: my tea, my space, my movement. On the days when I had my son, I'd set my alarm half an hour early so I could have my time. The movement felt interesting even when I was a little underslept. When his alarm went off, Tavi would come stumbling out of his bedroom, lean his entire body over my outstretched leg, and yawn.

My morning dance practice was also part of relearning to trust my own intuition. What did my body need each morning? It would tell me if I listened closely.

For a while, I'd needed to go to classes and be told what to do with my body. I was unsure and terrified. But through my devotional dance practice, I slowly relearned what it felt like to trust my ability to know things. My shoulder felt tight, so I knew that it needed a little stretching . . . OMG, I *KNOW* THINGS!

Some mornings, I'd use my morning dance as a prayer, standing on one foot and tracing words in the air with the other. *TRUST*, I'd trace out with my toes and I felt myself relearning to trust my own body and my own wisdom. I couldn't control anything, and there were pains that would show up like hungry children, but I could find a sense of agency through choosing to listen to, understand, and move with the discomforts.

The joy of a practice like this is that there's no way to fail. There's no equipment necessary. There's no goal setting or results. You don't need any grippy socks or special mats or multisyllabic asanas. You just move in the way that your body asks, whatever your abilities may be.

You practice listening. You practice trusting. You practice breathing.

You practice not being dead.

FIND YOUR AFTERGLOW

Here's the challenge of the medium of a book: you're all up in your brain right now, reading these words. Can we take a break for a second to breathe and check in below the neck?

◆ What is your body telling you *right now*? Does it need to move? Rest? Stretch? Do a sixty-second body scan by concentrating on each part of you, from your toes to the top of your head. What is your body asking for? When was the last time you checked in on your body like this?

◆ What natural cues could you bake into your life to check in with your body? For instance, what if when you are stuck at a stoplight, you took a moment to take a breath and see how you were *actually* feeling in that *actual* moment?

◆ What kinds of movement make you happiest? Not everyone is a dancer, of course, so what activities make *your* body feel good? How can you find room for more of that in your life, even if it's just hints of it for five minutes in your home in the morning?

◆ What are your favorite ways of ignoring your body? Common faves are TV, scrolling on your phone, working, talking, drinking or drugs, focusing on caretaking others, or sleeping too much. What would happen if, instead of investing in these numbing activities, you practiced being in your body and paying attention to it—even if just for five minutes?

When you get a little bit of movement and body listening into every single day, things will change after about a month. You don't do this for how it looks, but if you move and listen to your body daily, you will notice small changes. When you start moving trauma and tension out of your body, it can change your posture or how you hold your face. You might notice differences in how you walk or how your muscles relate to your bones.

Stick with a daily movement practice for a couple months and other people will start to notice. People may comment that you look younger, even though you're aging just like we all are. They may ask if you've lost weight, even when you totally haven't. While these clumsy compliments can feel misguided (or even offensive), the reality is that when you're moving back into your body, people notice!

Again, this kind of daily movement is about how it *feels*, not how it looks. But when you're feeling good in your body, it changes how you carry and present yourself. Don't be surprised if people start asking why you're glowing.

Chapter 16

SURRENDER

RELINQUISHING CONTROL IN UNEXPECTED WAYS

I'D JUST DROPPED TAVI OFF FOR A SLUMBER PARTY WHEN THE TINDER MESSAGE POPPED UP on my phone.

Just finished the first week of rehearsals, it said. Wanna get a drink?

I clicked to view the profile of the guy who'd messaged. Giovanni. Thirty-eight. Opera singer. Oh right, *this* guy. When I'd swiped right, I'd thought, *Never met an opera singer. If nothing else, that's an interesting conversation.*

Sorry, I messaged back. I'm already in my fleece onesie for the night, so I don't think a drink is going to happen.

Are you joking about the fleece onesie? he wrote back immediately.

One does NOT joke about these things, I responded, and then sent the least sexy shitshow selfie ever: me in a hooded fleece onesie. There was no skin showing other than my smirking face, hands, and bare feet.

The opera singer responded with a photo of himself: he was a super-tall white guy . . . in a hooded fleece onesie. I barked out a laugh. *Really?!* This is a thing that happens in my life now? Swapping fleece onesie selfies with twinning Tinderellas?

Yep, that was a thing that happened in my life now. Afterglow in full effect.

We texted back and forth for an hour, riffing on how we should just have a date in our onesies, starting the relationship at the "just hanging out in our pajamas" phase with pizza and beer. Our second date could be a nice dinner, and then our final date would be meeting awkwardly for coffee and forgetting each other's names at the end.

We'll be like the Benjamin Button of Tinder, the opera singer texted, and I couldn't stop laughing. This one's funny!

We should absolutely do this, I replied. I don't know if I'm going to want to make out with you, but at the very least you're funny and have great taste in fleece eveningwear so that's reason enough to get together.

We made plans for him to come over in a fleece onesie for pizza and beer that weekend.

"Wait," I asked Ashlee on the phone later. "Is this safe? I'm inviting some rando to my house. Is this a bad idea?"

"Girl, it's 2016," she laughed. "Everyone hooks up with strangers on the internet. It's not a big deal. Just be safe about it."

I did some basic googling, determined the dude was indeed an opera singer in town for a local show. I texted his full name to Ashlee, letting her know I'd check in before and after the date.

At seven p.m., the call came from the front gate of my building, and I tiptoed barefoot through the rainy courtyard in my fleece onesie to let an opera singer into my home.

I opened the gate and immediately felt very, very small. He was a full foot taller than me, wearing his enormous fleece onesie and a pair of motorcycle boots. He was green-eyed, brown-haired, and had a chest so wide I could barely get my arms around him during my default Seattle welcome hug.

"Nice to meet you," I said, craning my neck up at him.

"You too," he boomed. This one was *loud*. I needed to get him inside before my geighbors started wondering. (Also, wait: Was I hanging out with someone *louder than me?*)

We walked up the stairs into my living room, and I gave the opera singer the waving tour of my place as I grabbed us beers. We sat on the couch in our onesies, and I curled around my bottle.

"So what's your deal," the opera singer said. "Divorce?"

"Yeah," I said. "Plus some other stuff; 2015 can suck a bag of dicks. I had the worst year ever."

"Fuck you," the opera singer teased, theatrically taking a swig from his bottle. "My 2015 was worse."

"Oh, you want to play one-lowmanship?" I said. "Okay, let's do this. Did *you* have a medical catastrophe that landed you in the hospital for a week with emergency surgery?!" I puffed my flat chest like a small, bitter goldfinch.

"Nope," he said, taking another drink. "Did your mother commit suicide?"

My face fell. Shit just got real with this Tinder hookup.

"Holy shit," I said. "I'm so, so sorry. You win this round. Uh, okay. So, moving on with our shitty years: Did *your* yoga-teacher spouse suddenly leave you?"

The opera singer looked up at me sharply, differently. "What did you say?" His voice sounded more human, performative veneer cracked.

"I said, did *your* yoga-teacher spouse suddenly leave you?"

"Uh . . . yes," the opera singer said. "Actually, that's exactly what happened to me last year."

We stared at each other.

"That's . . . really weird," I said, forehead creased. The opera singer nodded slowly, setting down his beer.

"Totally weird," he said and leaned in to kiss me. He smelled like cigarettes, beer, and abandonment.

My mind spun. In this moment, I'm on my couch making out with an enormous, heartbroken, grief-stricken opera singer in a fleece onesie. WTF?!

SURRENDER

The make-out intensified, and onesies were peeled down to
our waists. When I got up to pour us whiskeys (laughing about
how our exes had taught at the same yoga studios! The hilarity!),
the opera singer chased me across the living room, grabbed me
with one hand, and hoisted me onto his shoulder.

He kissed me harder, and I laughed around his tongue as he
pulled my onesie the rest of the way off with his free hand. I was
now in my underwear, on the shoulders of an opera singer.

"I'm taking you to bed," he growled into my neck. This
seemed . . . fast? Up until this point, I'd only really been making out
with Tinderellas. I hadn't slept with anyone since my ex-husband.

But years of boss fatigue caught up with me. I was so tired of
being in charge, of running a business, of supporting a family, of
trying to get my A+ in self-development. What if someone else
drove for a minute?

That's how I ended up in my divorced-lady bed, under the
bookshelves heavy with self-dev books, with an opera singer's face
between my legs, singing country ballads into my thighs.

I could not stop laughing. I wasn't sure if I was turned on or
just thoroughly entertained.

I needed a breather after a while, so I sat up and grabbed a
joint from the shelves by my bed, where it was resting on a Pema
Chödrön book. I lit it and passed it to the opera singer. He reached
across the bed to take it and tightly wrapped an arm around my
waist.

It was all very exciting and overwhelming and I was charmed
and a little starstruck but I also needed to catch my breath, so after
he passed me the joint back, I gently pushed him away and said,
"Okay, I just need a minute to chill . . ."

I leaned away to stub the joint out in a houseplant.

The opera singer growled theatrically and pulled me closer.

"Hey, now." I threw him a cautioning side-eye and leaned away
a bit. "Pause, please."

The opera singer cocked an eyebrow and grabbed my wrist.

"Easy, tiger!" I said, shifting my tone as I tried to pull my arm
away. He held on tighter and pulled me toward him.

I took a sharp breath in. My mouth went dry and my eyes went huge.

Suddenly, I was terrified. This could end very, very badly. My entire nervous system spiked; I stopped breathing and felt my limbs go cold. What was I thinking inviting this stranger into my house?! Women die this way!

Noticing my expression, the opera singer immediately released my arm, leaned back, and put both his hands in the air.

"Whoa, whoa," he said. "Holy shit. I'm so sorry. I didn't mean to scare you. I am not that guy. I'm a little drunk and a *lot* into this scene, but I am NOT that guy. I'm so, *so sorry*."

My breath came back.

"You scared me," I said, blinking back tears. He apologized again but I wasn't listening because my brain was talking over him, finishing my sentence in my mind: . . . *and I liked it*.

Getting honest with myself in my head . . . I liked it *a lot*.

I was completely out of my sexual wheelhouse. I was a naive divorcée, still cracked open and confused, and I could feel my synapses reconnecting in tangled ways. I could feel the pain and the fear and the excitement getting braided together into an unfamiliar rope.

"Here," the opera singer said quietly, completely shifting gears. "Just lie down and let me hold you. Let's just look at each other for a minute."

I settled into the crook of the arm of this enormous stranger and looked into his eyes as instructed.

We both reflexively sighed, and I burst into tears again.

"Shit," I said. "I'm sorry. I'm so raw." This was not how you were supposed to act on first dates.

"It's okay," he said, embracing me with a disarming tenderness. "Me too. I'm more fucked up than you are, actually."

For a few minutes, we just lay there, eyes wet, strangers who were stumbling through our respective catastrophes (mortality, divorce, yoga teachers), both trying to do the best we could to put our lives back together.

It was late and everyone was exhausted.

"I should go home," he said, and with that, the opera singer got up, gently tucked the blankets around my shoulders, and let himself out.

WHEN YOUR THERAPIST TELLS YOU TO GET SPANKED

A couple days later, the opera singer sent dirty texts suggesting he come over and spank me. I was intrigued, and immediately ashamed.

In therapy that afternoon, I twisted my hands in my lap.

"What's *wrong* with me?" I asked Atta. "My husband walks out, and now I want some huge guy who scared me to come over and, like, *be mean to me?!*"

"Ariel," Atta said patiently. "Sometimes after people have had an overwhelming emotional experience, they choose to process some of those emotions through consensual sexual scenes. This is called *role-playing* and it's really common."

"Oh!" I said, blushing and feeling naive. "Wait, *that's* what this is? I'm like some suburban housewife masturbating over *Fifty Shades of Grey* in the laundry room!?"

"I don't know that I'd be that dismissive," Atta said. "But yeah, this is a pretty common desire. You don't need to be ashamed about it. As long as you feel physically safe with this person, and take precautions to protect yourself against STIs, I think you're calling the shots with this one."

"*I'm* calling the shots?"

"You did your due diligence before meeting him, and he was willing to respect your boundaries when you made them clear. He's a classically trained performer who wants to role-play! If you like the scene he's proposing, seems like it's a chance to direct your own experience."

"Huh," I replied. "Sometimes I feel like such a powerless victim. Are you saying that I'm the one in charge?"

"I'm not worried about you," Atta said. "You're doing the work."

On the light rail home, I texted Ashlee: WTF, I think our therapist just told me to get spanked?!

Because I'm a nerd, I needed to know a little more. I did some quick googling and found a study led by Brad Sagarin, professor of psychology at Northern Illinois University, where researchers observed people engaging in BDSM who had been randomly assigned to "top" and "bottom" roles. The participants reported better moods and lowered stress after their sessions. Sagarin said this is partially attributable to how bottoms in BDSM scenes are able to safely relinquish control.

"This may be an effective thing for people who otherwise have a hard time getting out of their intellectual head," Sagarin wrote. "BDSM, because of the intense sensations and potentially because of the restriction of movement, may have the ability to put someone in the here and now in a way that they may find more difficult to achieve through other means."

I did need to get out of my head, so okay. I was working on how to be more in the here and now, so okay! Let's do this.

At eight that night, the opera singer showed up at my house again. I let him in the door, safe words having been determined via text beforehand ("fucking stop" is my safe word, I told him. Is that clear?).

At the top of the stairs, he made me kneel and take off his shoes, before roughly pulling me to my feet and pushing me up against my dining room table. I tried to kiss him, and he stopped me.

"No kissing," he instructed, and I tilted my chin back down, relieved to have a clear sense of what to do next.

"This could get really messed up," he said under his breath, almost to himself. I just gulped and tried to keep breathing, not thinking anything at all. (*Me!* Not thinking anything at all! It was working!)

"Get on the floor," the opera singer told me, pointing to the living room rug. I knelt down in the same place where, the year before, my husband had told me he didn't see a future for us.

"On all fours," the opera singer said, so I did.

Then he spanked me. *Hard.*

In this moment, I saw stars and smiled. Things felt . . . calm. I could feel my brain rewiring itself.

He spanked me again, harder, and I squeaked.

"Quiet," he instructed, and I kept my noises to myself.

There was nothing really for me to do but breathe and wait. I surrendered completely to that particular moment, and the monkeys in my brain went blessedly silent. I lived in the spaces between my own heartbeats and breaths.

I felt my hands start tingling. *What the hell—again!?* I flexed my palms against the carpet in between the spanks.

After a while, the opera singer pulled me to my feet, told me to pour us drinks.

I nodded and looked down at my hands, which were shaking and throbbing and felt like they were shooting lightning bolts. I looked up at him, mouth open.

"Why are my hands throbbing?" I asked him, completely baffled.

"Probably just energy moving through," he said, shrugging and completely blasé. "I did Reiki training a few years ago."

Did I just get Reiki spanked? Is that a thing?

After a drink and more spanking in the kitchen, the opera singer and I both broke from our respective roles and ended up just smoking a joint in my bedroom, telling each other dirty stories, cracking each other up, and deep-diving on death and loss. He recounted contemplating suicide after his mother's death, and I explained how I'd considered throwing myself off a cliff and how the only thing that made me reconsider was my son.

"Your son . . ." the opera singer repeated, eyes misty.

"My son!" I said again as the stoned opera singer grabbed my shoulders and put his face close to mine.

"You must think of your son!" he boomed at me, shaking my shoulders a little. "You must live for him! Sing to him every day!"

"Yes!" I said, crying again. "Every day!"

This was, without a doubt, the weirdest date I had ever been on.

Hours later, we eventually had sex. The opera singer was laid out beneath me, and he looked up and stretched his long arms over his head.

"I give you back all the power," he rumbled, my thighs vibrating from the timbre.

AN ODE TO WEIRD DATES AND BROKEN SOCIAL FILTERS

So, about weird dates. Part of why my encounter with the opera singer was so remarkable was that we were both so emotionally raw that neither of us had our "socially acceptable conversation" filters functioning. We immediately dove into shit you're *never* supposed to talk about on the first (or even tenth) date, and that raw authenticity facilitated the situation unfolding in unexpectedly delightful ways.

Getting into shit you're not supposed to talk about with new people is the best. For a while, my Tinder profile included "Tell me all about the self-development books you're reading." I felt like when you're leaning way, WAY in with your own journey of healing—unpeeling, unpacking, and rebuilding—the last thing you need is more small talk and false facades.

The world would be a better place if first dates (and first coffee hangs with new friends) included chitchat like "So, tell me all about your past failures and how you're applying what you learned?" or "So, how are you reparenting yourself?" Most folks will balk at this kind of emotional vulnerability, and you know what? *Those aren't your folks.*

For those of you dating, I encourage you to bring your most authentic, honest, messy self to every date you go on . . . and for those of you who aren't dating, I encourage you to bring your most authentic, honest, messy self to every casual social encounter. When you stop playing "nice" and start being vulnerable and honest, you can connect with people in unexpectedly delightful ways. It might not always involve Reiki spanking (and honestly, exploring BDSM with strangers ain't super safe—I wouldn't recommend it), but it will always be more interesting than talking about the weather. Weird dates are way, *way* more interesting.

The day after that particularly weird date, the opera singer and I traded texts.

What the hell WAS that? I asked him.

An exercise in trust, he said. Five hours of foreplay that was hotter than most sex I've had.

You wielded your power well, I said, feeling silly but also, I mean, he had!

That was all you, he said. I had no idea what I was doing. The power was all yours.

Wait, it was? Even when I was on all fours, the power was *mine*?

This felt big. I put my phone down, my hands feeling throbby again. This felt like it was about more than sex, more even than my body. If the panic attack made it clear that my mind wasn't the only way forward, this weirdest date of all time (the first new person I'd had sex with since 1997!) made it clear that something was going on that was more than just my body. Why had the surrender felt so good, way beyond sex or kink or even a physical experience?

Was that a sexual awakening, or a spiritual one?

I was itching to talk to the opera singer more about it, but he ghosted. I never saw him again.

FIND YOUR AFTERGLOW

If you get one thing from this chapter, let it be this: vulnerability has its rewards. You may not be interested in BDSM or role-playing (or even sex!), but the real value of these kinds of encounters is the vulnerability of relinquishing control in a safe context.

Vulnerability can take the form of being more raw with a new friend than you would normally be. Your surrender might just look like not reacting to a crappy text message that would normally set you off. That relinquishing of control could be dancing blindfolded around your living room.

That said, if you're thinking of exploring surrender and vulnerability in the context of consensual sexual play, here are some questions for you:

- ◆ What role does sexuality play in your shitshow? For many, trauma can either ramp up or shut off their sexuality. What's your experience? How is your sexuality shifting?

- ◆ Consider your physical connections, whether with yourself, a partner, or multiple partners. Where does your mind go during these experiences? What about directly after? What old, familiar stories show up?

- ◆ If you think of your sexual experiences as therapeutic, how does that change how you view them? What intention can you bring to your masturbation, your time with a partner, or even the smiles you share with people on the street?

If you're curious but inexperienced with BDSM, do your homework carefully. Read books and do your research. If you don't have a partner you trust, consider working with a professional BDSM practitioner instead of some Tinder bro. Your psyche is delicate stuff, and good BDSM pros really are like therapists—they know what they're doing and are focused on your goals.

Pros before bros!

part three

SPIRIT

WE'RE ALL ONE, BUT IN A SECULAR WAY

Chapter 17

SOUND HEALING

TRYING THINGS YOU USED TO SCOFF AT

IN THE FALL AND WINTER OF MY SHITSHOW, TALK THERAPY WAS GOOD, BUT IT WAS ONLY once a week and it wasn't enough. Atta dished out tough love and support at every session, but I needed to try other things. And here on the West Coast, when it comes to healing, "other things" often means "woo-woo stuff."

I wasn't sure if I'd like woo-woo stuff, but I had to admit that the catharsis of the grief retreat had been valuable. I was into making new mistakes, so when I saw on social media that an old childhood friend was hosting something called a "sound bath" at a yoga studio, I decided I would try it. It wasn't normally my thing, but whatever: Who knows what "my thing" is anymore?

At the yoga studio, Daniella sat at the front of the golden-yellow-walled studio on a pillow, surrounded by a half-dozen crystal bowls that were anywhere from a foot to two feet in width. Behind her was an enormous gong almost as tall as I was.

Along with thirty or so other people, I lay on my back on a yoga mat, and the lights were low, and Daniella started to play the bowls and sing.

The sound was completely immersive, and the tonal frequencies shifted between warm harmonies that vibrated through me and discordant tones that created an almost painful *WAH WAH* wobbly sound. Daniella described the discordant tones as "like a spaceship hovering just above the ground."

I lay on the mat, eyes closed, and let the waves roll over me. The hairs on my arms raised as the sounds wobbled through my tissue. My head filled with visions of holding a mortally wounded little girl. (Oh no, is this my inner child? This is happening . . .)

In the vision, I cradled this injured child in the crook of my left arm, her head lolling against my left breast. I used my right hand to wipe blood off her face, and looked up and thought, *I have to let go of my misery so that my arms are free to hold this child.*

In the yoga studio, the tears rolled down the sides of my cheeks and pooled in my ears. I was drowning in metaphors.

It might have felt like I was doing something new age, but chants and singing bowls used to restore health date back to ancient societies, from ancient Egypt to Australia's aboriginals, and sound therapy like today's sound baths are just the latest iteration of these time-honored practices.

Singing bowl therapy, specifically, dates back to twelfth century Tibet, and a 2016 study by Tamara L. Goldsby et al. showed that singing bowls help reduce stress, fatigue, and anger, which all contribute negatively to a patient's overall health. No one's totally sure why it works; the director of the Sound Healers Association in Boulder, Colorado, acknowledged that maybe it's just helpful in the same way that crying out when you stub your toe is—maybe because it releases endorphins, or maybe because it simply distracts you from the pain.

Whatever the cause, after the sound bath, I felt like I'd had a quick visit to the Not-Pain Motel. The monkeys inside my head (the ones that kept track of who I was, who reminded me constantly of all the ways that I was a disappointing failure who would die alone) were blessedly quiet.

Maybe it was the sweet sensation of doing something I didn't think I'd like, and loving it. Was that ego liberation? I felt unshackled from some aspect of myself that I'd always seen as "me" (the me that doesn't do new-age woo-woo shit, the me that was a pragmatic atheist), and things felt expansive.

Since I'd enjoyed the sound bath, I decided to keep going with my woo explorations. I booked a private session with Daniella to do something she called "energy work." As I confirmed the date and time, I realized that I wasn't fully sure what the session would involve. Despite being raised by hippies, I didn't actually know what "energy work" might mean.

My skepticism meant that I had low expectations of alternative treatments. I thought, *If nothing else, it will probably be relaxing, and I need more relaxation.* I still needed meds to sleep, and had to take a Xanax a couple times a month to stave off panic attacks.

But anything that promised a few more Not-Pain Motel minutes felt worth it. I knew I was vulnerable, and a sound bath seemed safer than getting spanked by a large stranger.

I decided to dip a toe deeper into the woo.

WHEN METALHEADS ARE MORE ENLIGHTENED THAN YOU

Later that week, heading out the door for a solo dinner with myself, I decided to grab a book to keep me company while I ate. My bedside self-dev stack was three stacks now, and I thumbed down until I got to a copy of Eckhart Tolle's *The Power of Now* that someone had given me.

This Oprah's Book Club pick felt like such a cliché that before I left the house, I put duct tape over the cover so no one at the bar would see just how stereotypically tragic I'd become. "Local woman used to be cool, now divorced and sitting alone at a bar reading best-selling pastel-covered spiritual book, news at eleven."

I sat by myself at the bar at Smith, ordered a burger and a masala mule, and cracked open the book.

By the time my burger arrived, I was misty-eyed over my duct-taped reading. My hands tingled and my brain was boggling, and I realized, holy shit, this book is everything I've been needing to read and WTF is wrong with me that I've avoided it for so long?

A metalhead dude a few empty seats down the bar made eye contact with me.

"I don't mean to interrupt," he said with surprising politeness for a guy with facial tattoos. "But is that *The Power of Now?*" Despite the duct tape on the cover, half the title still peeked out from the spine.

"Yeah," I said, embarrassed. "I can't believe I'm reading this, but it's surprisingly good."

"Dude, no shame," this guy with long hair and facial tattoos said. "Wait until you get to his next book, *A New Earth*. It's some next-level shit! Anyway, I'll let you get back to it—I just wanted to say fuck yeah, Eckhart Tolle!"

Apparently, my snarky judgments about how this book was too mainstream for me meant that I was years behind what metalhead dudes already knew.

You may have this experience, too; it's humbling to recognize how your prior judgments have held you back. You may find that stuff the old you dismissed as stupid or cliché ends up being your new favorite thing.

I'd been convinced that I was somehow too cool to find value in something I deemed mainstream, but loving *The Power of Now* was my official de-snowflakification. (Years later, the audiobook remains my go-to comfort listening.)

The upside of a shitshow killing your old self is the opportunity to find freedom from all the bullshit stories you've been telling yourself about who you are and what you do. You can do whatever the hell you want—including reading and loving the self-dev books you've avoided for years. As you slowly make peace with the loss of your former identities, you may find your life starting to feel expansive.

Neuroscientists Gabriele Flügge and Eberhard Fuchs found that trauma and stress can reorganize the brain and change the way it functions as an organ. In the same way that a negative impact on our emotions and thoughts can restructure the brain, trying new things (or even just trying new, more positive thought patterns!) can create new pathways between our neurons.

This means your brain is literally *physically* changing. At first it hurts like hell, then it shifts to just feeling awkward, and then (if you're paying attention!), it starts to feel good . . . like you've got more room inside yourself than you used to. Like even though your life has fallen down, you have a sense of freedom. This is the sensation of neuroplasticity, the pleasurable upside of learning and forming new synapses in your brain.

Psychologists have been dedicating more research in the past twenty years to this concept of post-traumatic growth, and the data is conclusive: folks who experience traumatic events will often experience aftereffects that are remarkably positive. In his book *The Leap*, psychologist Steve Taylor says that "in the long term, after the initial intense shock and stress have passed, many people report feeling more resilient and confident, and more appreciative about their lives."

You may not know who you are anymore . . . but sometimes, you might find yourself liking that feeling. Now you can be anyone you want!

FIND YOUR AFTERGLOW

As you feel your way through your own rehabilitation, remember that my guidance is less about the specifics and more about finding what appeals to you. Sound healing is a neat modality, but the value for me was less about sound healing itself and more about the experience of trying something that felt out of character, and being open to enjoying it.

If you've normally played things safe, now is the time to get weird with it! And if you've normally been weird, now's the time to consider how something you thought was mainstream may actually be super valuable for you. As the shitshow dust settles, this transitional time is the ideal playground for trying new things, freed from the shackles of what the old you allowed yourself to enjoy. Let's dig into this more . . .

◆ What previous identities have you had to let go of? Have you fully mourned them? How were your previous identities holding you back?

◆ Are you recognizing any post-traumatic growth in your life? What glimmers of afterglow are appearing on the horizon?

◆ What unexpected Not-Pain Motels are you finding? What things that you never ever imagined yourself benefiting from (and maybe even scoffed at) have revealed surprising comforts?

◆ Who in your life might be able to help you expand your horizons? Who do you know who might be able to take you to new places and be a buddy to you while you try new things?

If you're reading a self-dev book with the word *shitshow* on the cover, part of your old identity may be that you thought of yourself as iconoclastic or offbeat. For many of us, one of the identities that falls away is "uniquely special person." UGH! It's a grunt to realize we're all broken and united in our suffering . . . but there's an odd comfort in it, too. We're all in this together, sweet friend. You, me, and that metalhead dude at the bar.

Chapter 18

REIKI

WHEN RECOVERY IS A ROLLER COASTER

DANIELLA DID HER ENERGY-WORK SESSIONS OUT OF HER HOME IN WEST SEATTLE, SO I DROVE over on a rainy Friday morning for my scheduled appointment. She met me at the door of her bungalow, her long hair still blonde as ever and smile lines creasing around her blue eyes. It's alarming to see childhood friends aging. Sometimes I forget that getting older isn't a rare condition that I alone have contracted; it's the ultimate communicable disease, and it's killing us all.

We sat in her living room, and Daniella gave me a cup of tea and asked me how I was doing. I waved my hands around for half an hour, barfing out all the details: Blindsided! Heartbroken! Destroyed! Disoriented!

Daniella listened, nodding. The rain splattered against the living room's picture window. I ran out of words.

"Let's go downstairs," she said, standing up and taking my empty cup. I followed her through her kitchen and down the carpeted stairs that led to her basement studio, where she had me lie down on a massage table. I prepared to be . . . I don't know, probably relaxed? Maybe it'd just feel nice to be coddled for an hour?

Daniella started the session with me lying on the table, doing some breathing exercises and guided visualizations.

Hmm, I thought. *Since apparently now I am a person who sees visualizations at sound baths and reads* The Power of Now, *I guess I could try . . .*

Daniella guided me through visualizing roots coming up through my feet, up my legs, into my torso. She held her hands a bit over my skin and told me she was doing Reiki as she went.

By the time she got to my throat, I was shaking and wracked with . . . *what even IS this?* My skin tingled and my muscles pulsed. My temperature ran hot and then cold. My chest tightened and my throat constricted. My jaw locked.

"Your throat chakra is freaking out," Daniella said. "I think you probably have some screaming to do at some point. For now, just keep breathing."

I couldn't talk, so I just nodded and started crying and tried to keep breathing through my locked jaw. My face started tingling. What the hell?! The tears poured out of me. This was not at all relaxing! This felt more like a roller coaster than a spa treatment.

I was aware that while my internal experience was all white-knuckles, my body was actually just resting there on a table with tinkly music playing and geode crystals and heart-shaped rose quartz rocks lying around, and yet I was apparently very much Doing This Thing . . . or maybe this thing was doing me?! My skeptical mind and its thoughts spiraled away as the monkeys shouted at me, baffled and confused.

Through my clenched jaw, I whimpered and keened as Daniella sang over me for half an hour. My throbbing hands started trembling and rattling against my sides.

Finally, I gasped out to Daniella the most important thing I could think of to say: "I have to pee!"

Daniella stopped her singing, helped me sit up, held her hand on my back as I tried to stand from the massage table.

My knees buckled, and I looked at her with my eyes wide.

"You got this," she reassured me, and I wobbled my way along the wall and used the banister to pull myself up the stairs.

Sitting in the bathroom, I was stupefied. WTF! The treatment wasn't painful, but it was completely out of my control and the opposite of the relaxing placebo-effect new-age touchy-feely tinkly-music experience I'd expected.

I tenderly crept back down the stairs to the massage table and looked at Daniella, disoriented.

"What just happened?!" I asked.

"From my perspective, you discharged a lot of energy," she told me.

I started crying again, looking at my trembling hands in my lap. (What the HELL was going on with my hands? This is the same thing that happened with the opera singer! My mind ran through possibilities: *Hyperventilation? Vitamin deficiencies? Hormone fluctuations? Am I having a stroke?*)

"You need to go home and soak in a tub," Daniella said. "You sweated out a bunch of emotions, and you need to bathe it off."

Grateful again for someone telling me what to do, I told her I would, and wobbled my way out to the car.

After my hot bath that evening, I realized, "Huh, I'm tired," and I drifted into my first night of unmedicated sleep in months. I *slept!* All by myself! Not just that, but I slept for NINE HOURS.

GETTING A GOLD STAR IN GROWTH

The next week, in Atta's office, I recounted the unrelaxing energy work.

"I have no idea what happened at Daniella's," I told him. "I don't know what she did, or if it worked, or how it worked, or if I'm just such an exposed nerve that *anything* works, but holy shit. It was not what I expected, but it did something that felt profound, and then I slept really hard."

"Did you sleep all the way through the night?" Atta asked me.

"I woke up a couple times, but no nightmares or startles. When I woke up, I could feel a thrum in my hands, some kind of *something* that moved through me. I don't know what the feeling is, but it made me feel less lonely and afraid. I think I'm done with the sleep meds!"

"That's a major milestone," Atta said. "I know sometimes it feels like you're not getting anywhere, but I see you, and I'm tracking your progress . . . and that's big progress!"

Then he got out a sheet of gold star stickers, peeled off a single gold star, and stuck it to my hand. I felt like I'd won the Nobel.

Healing is not linear. You'll learn that seeing any new good feeling as "progress" in a traditional sense can be a recipe for misery when the next week (or the next day!) you find yourself feeling like shit again. You'll want to bemoan it as backsliding, but it's not.

When you view every new experience as a wave of resilience, you may start to notice how each subsequent wave feels subtly different. When you take the time to notice these differences, you'll slowly start to gain a sense of progress—not a line, but maybe a spiral, like a truly crazy roller coaster.

Your progress will loop around sometimes in ways that can make you feel on top of the world one day, vulnerable and terrified the next, and then by the end of the week you're just disoriented and confused. Certain loops might feel like backsliding, but if you can just notice which bits feel a little different than the last time around, you'll feel yourself spiraling forward.

FIND YOUR AFTERGLOW

If you want that gold star, you've got to notice when you're making progress. It's nice when someone like a therapist or friend can point out how far you've come in your afterglow, but ultimately it's up to each of us to be accountable for watching ourselves. Journaling can be helpful with this—it's nice to look back and see your progress.

◆ Celebrating each step of a journey is an important part of growth. What can you celebrate *today*? What's different today from last week? Last month?

◆ The next time you feel like you're backsliding (a great clue is hearing the voice inside your head say something like "Ugh, this *always* happens to me!"), see if you can take a breath and notice what's different this time around. It might be subtle, but see if you can find the differences. Be patient with yourself: putting your life back together takes time, and you'll loop around the same lessons until you're able to learn and apply new tools.

◆ Think about times in the past when you've felt a cathartic sense of relief and comfort after a stressful period— whether it was from crying, sweating, laughing until you peed yourself, whatever. Which healthy catharsis methods seem to work best for you? How can you get more of those in your life?

◆ What unexplainable moments have you experienced? Shock and grief can bend your mind in unexpected ways, some of which can feel fantastical even for the most pragmatic of us. (If you've read Joan Didion's *The Year of Magical Thinking*, you know what I mean.) What new beliefs have appeared in your life?

Take the time to celebrate your progress. Gold star stickers might feel silly, but after a few nauseating loops on the nonlinear recovery roller coaster, you deserve a tiny trophy. I'm proud of you!

Chapter 19

NESTING

WELCOME HOME TO YOUR DMZ

IN MY OLD LIFE, OUR FAMILY OF THREE SHARED AN 850-SQUARE-FOOT CONDOMINIUM ON THE top of Seattle's Capitol Hill. Our home was small compared to many American families', but it worked for us. That said, *all* spaces were shared spaces. There was gear stashed under the couch, toys tucked in cabinets, every bookshelf (and there were many) filled top to bottom. All spaces were everyone's.

Except one.

Two months before my marriage collapsed, I'd decided I would claim a corner of the bedroom. I'd buy a nice chair for myself. A *new* chair! Not something used off Craigslist, but exactly what I wanted: a sweet swiveling armchair that could be my little teatime spot.

In this chair, I could swivel one way to look out the window at the trees in front of the house, swivel another way to watch my geighbor and his husband walking their dog or see the sunrise over the Cascade mountains in the winter when the branches were bare. The chair would be a lovely light blue, with sloping arms and a high back.

"It'll be the Mama Chair," I'd told my then-husband. "The one special place in the house that's just for me!"

The chair had an eight-to-twelve-week fabrication timeline, so when I placed my order in September 2015, I thought of it as a Christmas gift for myself. Then at the start of November, quite suddenly, I went from sharing a small home with three people to living alone half the week.

Suddenly, the space that had always felt full (three people vying for the single bathroom, a child underfoot in the hallway, a husband doing handstands in the living room, the constant stuff-purging to fight the clutter) felt agonizingly empty. Half the week, I woke up alone in the dark, Seattle's winter sun not coming up until almost eight o'clock.

Through the first fall and winter of my shitshow, I tried to keep the house as unchanged as possible so my son could maintain a sense of familiar normalcy during his time with me. When he wasn't there, I sat alone on the old couch and added my tears to the old spit-up stains. I took over both closets in the bedroom, my clothes looking disoriented by the extra space, my sweaters flapping around like "What just happened?" The house felt mostly the same, but completely foreign. The monkeys in my mind sang that Joni Mitchell line on repeat: *The bed's too big, the frying pan's too wide.*

The Mama Chair didn't care about this change of plans. It showed up a month after my husband left, zero fucks given about the drastic domestic shift. The delivery guys brought it up the stairs, set it down in the bedroom, and asked me to sign on the dotted line.

The Mama Chair looked at me from its corner, across the gulf of my marriage's end. This chair was supposed to be the one little corner I had to myself in this home . . . but now the entire home was my corner, silent and dark and empty, like a scooped-out chest cavity.

I sat down in the blue chair and absent-mindedly rubbed my hand on my belly, tracing the scars beneath my shirt.

I swiveled and looked out the window. The branches outside were naked and dark against the perpetually overcast sky. The Mama Chair. This was supposed to be my maternal throne, the place where I could sip my tea, watch my little family go about its chaotic business, listen to the sounds of their bodies sleeping and eating and moving around me.

I started crying, like I did most days that year. The Mama Chair didn't care about this turn of events either. I grabbed a blanket and swaddled myself like a baby and cried until there was nothing left.

The tears having passed, I sat in the Mama Chair and looked out the window and realized I'd just created a new place in my home. One month after my shitshow began, the Mama Chair became the one place in my house that didn't hold any old memories. The rest of the house echoed with ghosts and demons, but the Mama Chair was just the Mama Chair. It knew only this time, this place, this new life.

CRYING ALTARS AND BREATHING ROOMS

Inspired, I decided I needed to create more new places in my home. I needed more places with no previous incarnation. So, what kind of little space did I need most? What activity did I do most these days? That winter day, the answer came quickly: crying. That's what I now did the most in this home.

Hi, my name is Ariel and my hobby is crying? It was a question, like everything else in my life.

I went to the hall closet, dug out an old steamer trunk that belonged to my grandma Becky. It's got memories in it—the corset I wore at my wedding, the baby clothes my son wore home from the hospital—and what do you know! It fit perfectly into a little nook-ish corner of the bedroom.

The trunk tucked into the corner, I assembled the first incarnation of my crying altar: a cheap spherical light from Ikea, a small confused ceramic monkey (one arm broken), some rocks. It wasn't much, but even in its sparseness, it embarrassed me (ugh, when did I get so woo?!). Yet again, I felt both ashamed and assured that I was doing the right thing.

My personality seared off by my shitshow, I was unable to be anyone resembling who I had been, so I made a new place for this skinless, faceless new self and cried some more. That winter day, I didn't know that later Studio Haaay would happen. I didn't know that later my home would be filled with dance and laughter.

At the crying altar, there was no later. There was only now, and when I built the altar, the now was engulfing pain. I didn't know that months later I'd practice my stripper sway next to the altar. I didn't know that months after that, the opera singer would confess that he had a similar altar in his hotel room. I didn't know, because I *couldn't* know.

I wish I'd been able to trust, but when I built the altar, all I knew was that my life was broken and I was terrified it would never be healed.

When Tavi came back to me after his days away that week, I introduced him to the crying altar and the new Mama Chair. He fiddled with the stones on the old trunk, assessed the little broken monkey, swiveled the chair.

"Will we both fit?" he asked me.

"Let's find out," I said, sitting down and pulling him into my lap. We spent half an hour before bedtime blissfully snuggling in the Mama Chair, swiveling toward the window to look at stars and clouds and smell each other's hair, making fresh memories in a new place in our old space.

I couldn't control or remove the pain that had happened in our home, but I had the agency to create new memories.

In Thich Nhat Hanh's book *Making Space: Creating a Home Meditation Practice*, he emphasizes the idea of returning "home" to yourself at the end of your day by having a special, dedicated space in your house to help put your mind in the right zone.

He explains, "The key to creating a home meditation practice is to create a space where the busyness stops. When we stop and bring our mind back to our body, we can pay full attention to all that is happening in the present moment."

Thich Nhat Hanh calls this space "a breathing room," and stresses that any home, no matter what size, can have a little corner dedicated to mindfulness. Establish boundaries around your breathing room: "There needs to be an agreement in advance that everyone respects the breathing area. Once you're in the breathing room or breathing corner, no one can shout at you anymore. You have immunity."

Even if you live alone, there's a value to a separate space with a perimeter you always respect; according to Nhat Hanh, it's the space that "facilitates coming home to yourself," and it needs to be separate—both physically and in your mind.

A few ideas for creating your own breathing room:

◆ Find a quiet spot in a room where you can either close a door for privacy or at least know that you're not in a high-traffic area.

◆ Get a dedicated pillow or blanket to keep there. Don't you dare use that pillow for anything else!

◆ If you want, decorate with talismans like a candle and matches, rocks, or a potted plant. Make it your own with whatever helps you feel focused and at ease.

If you want to go all out, of course you can set up an elaborate altar with seasonal items, sacred art, or whatever else you want! The key is just that everything in that space stays there, and is dedicated specifically to your breathing room.

Once you create a little space for yourself, make sure that you *hold* it. Don't sacrifice your space for anyone—even yourself. This means it's not a spot to pile unfolded laundry or mail waiting to be sorted. Your space is dedicated, and it's nonnegotiable. It's a DMZ.

DMZ typically stands for demilitarized zone: a nonnegotiable noncombative area. That works—your DMZ isn't a place for conflict either. But it also stands for Designated Me Zone, as of right now, anyway.

When you set a physical space like your DMZ and designate that it's yours alone, and you then *protect* that space, you're setting boundaries. This kind of boundary setting with yourself and others is the foundation of building self-worth. It's locking the door of a room of one's own behind you, and allowing yourself to focus only on you and your development. It's stabbing any monkeys in your brain that try to tell you this is selfish.

It's creating a place for your new you to find a home.

FIND YOUR AFTERGLOW

So many life implosions involve changes in living situations— either a big move, someone moving out, or someone moving in. Wherever you happen to be living these days, it's the place where you're going to be living through this transformation time. Let's see what it can tell us about you . . .

- ◆ If you're in a new living situation, what small changes could you make to help the space feel safe and cozy?

- ◆ If you're in a familiar home, what aspects of your space reflect your old self? How can you shift your space to feel like it reflects where you are now, and who you might be becoming? Go gently here—your life is jarring enough right now without a drastic remodel!

- ◆ Can you think of a spot in your home you could use to help you re-center yourself? How can you make a corner of your home conducive to your self-development? (This spot might be as small as a few inches of a windowsill!)

- ◆ Even if you have pain and loss associated with where you're living, what joys are hidden in your living situa-tion? What small gratitudes can you find?

The key here is small, gentle changes. Clearing off a shelf for a new plant, a meaningful book, and a small candle might be enough to give your home a sense of newness, and space for what's unfolding.

Chapter 20

VISUALIZING

CLEANSING RITUALS AND ROAD TRIPS

WHEN MY HUSBAND LEFT, HE DROVE AWAY IN THE VANTASY, OUR FAMILY'S BELOVED '86 VW Westfalia van. Almost six months later, as part of our division of assets, it returned home to me.

In the time the Vantasy had been away, I'd become increasingly superstitious and mystical-minded thanks to all my hallucinations and energy healings and crying altars. The Vantasy came back to me filthy, so I immediately took it to the car wash, but I still had a sense of it feeling unclean . . . not in a literal way, but in a woo-woo way.

Up at six one morning, I stretched and tried to feel what needed to be felt. Propping my left leg up on the barre, I rubbed my hands down my calf and it came to me: *The Vantasy needs to be cleansed! I must heal the van.*

I texted Janelle, another practitioner I was working with on My Healing Journey™, and asked her if she could perform a cleansing ritual.

You know, on the van.

Janelle does bodywork like Soma massage and craniosacral therapy, but she also does sound healing and sometimes calls in angels to help during her sessions; she's well versed in the woo, but I still thought she might find my idea a little too out there.

"My calf muscle told me to do it" didn't really help the whole idea feel more legit, but I was practicing making new mistakes and having agency! My identity had dissolved and I was trying to see what was underneath, and sometimes you just have to roll with the weirdness to keep things moving forward, y'know?

Luckily for me, Janelle was down with the idea.

"I understand," Janelle told me on the phone. "My mom had a stroke and brain surgery a few years ago, and it cracked my life open and got me to change my lifestyle choices, deepen my spiritual commitments, and pay close attention to nearly everything. I understand being sensitive about things like this."

The next week, we loaded four of Janelle's crystal singing bowls into the back of the Vantasy and caught a ferry out to Bainbridge Island, where my mom had agreed to let me do whatever it was I wanted to do out in the woods at Sacred Groves.

So, what does a van-cleansing ritual look like? It looks like a 1986 Westfalia parked in a dirt lot in the woods. It looks like Janelle's four crystal bowls set outside the van on the forest floor, with a cushion for her to sit on. It looks like a slightly unhinged fortysomething lady stretched out on the bed of the van, eyes closed and palms open.

It looks like Janelle making the bowls sing, and singing along with them, and talking me through meditative states where I floated up through my body into the forest canopy above. I could feel the metal of the van vibrating when the singing bowls went into discordant tones.

Interestingly, I didn't have much of a sense of my ex's presence in the van. It felt less about clearing him out and more just about setting my own intentions for going forward. It felt like getting a sense of closure on the old chapter and setting my sights on the horizon. I was trying to see where I was going.

I sat up after the session and thanked Janelle for humoring me. The endeavor felt silly, but somehow it had helped.

But really, ritualistic cleansing isn't all that silly. These rites are part of many cultures and date back millennia, from Christian baptism to Islamic *wudu* and *ghusl* and rituals of pagan and indigenous religions. It doesn't have to be ceremonial to have value and meaning—hell, spring cleaning is a type of ritualized cleansing! We do it as the winter thaws to give our homes and lives a sense of new beginning. If you clean with intention, even scrubbing the dang toilet can be a dynamic way to clear out the old shit and welcome the new. Life can be full of meaning if you want it to be.

Author Mary Mueller Shutan says that cleaning your house, though simple and boring, can be an important step to invite newness into your life: "Energy stagnates where there is stagnation—meaning if you have a pile of stuff, consider that to be a pile of internal stuckness within you."

Your external mess is your internal mess. This means that to clear out the mess of what happened, you gotta scrub the residue of your old self off the surfaces of your life. Then, you gotta get a new perspective to help you see where you're going.

SMALL ROAD TRIPS LEAD TO BIG AHAS

The first week of April, I hopped in the Vantasy's driver's seat with bad pop music on the stereo and spring sun in my eyes and the windows down and the air cold against my skin. From Seattle, I drove west for four hours of ferries, forested highways, gas-station food, and alpine lakes.

I arrived at the Washington coast community of La Push mid-afternoon, and parked at the trailhead of my favorite childhood beach. It's only a three-quarter-mile hike through the forest, and I cried the whole way . . . but it wasn't sad crying.

Thirty-five years of hiking this trail, and the trees grew and the stumps rotted and new trees grew out of them and it's all just rotting and growing and rotting and growing, and people come and they go, and it's all so fleeting, and fuck, man. *Loss! Time! Change! Life!*

Hikers passed me on the trail, and I'd smile like a normal human and then get back to crying once I'd gone around the next second-growth cedar tree.

I'll probably stop crying when I get to the beach, I thought heading down a bluff toward the sound of waves. I emerged onto the beach, and climbed over the enormous drift logs. I stepped onto the sand and the salty air hit me and I was crying even more.

The shifting sands! The Pacific! The tide! The moon! Evolution! It's all happening right now, holy shiiiit?! My emotional defenses were truly busted, and sometimes it felt like the entirety of the universe was coming at me all at once, sparkling and dense with potential.

It felt fucking great.

Life didn't feel like a punishment anymore. When did I stop feeling like this situation was *done* to me? When did I stop feeling like a victim? Instead, I realized with a jolt that I *liked* living my life like this, in solitude and turned up to eleven and burning so bright around the edges that it was a little overwhelming.

This wasn't a catastrophe, this was gratitude! This wasn't misery crying, this was happy crying!

I kept walking south down the beach, wind at my back, until I found a little spot at the very southernmost end of the sand where I could nestle down against the rocky bluffs to get out of the wind.

I was there for hours. I ate a snack and smoked a joint and took off my socks. I sunned the scars on my belly in the thin spring sunlight and read poetry and cried more. I meditated against the rocks and laughed to myself and made art in the sand while my hands tingled, and did some sit-ups because I could (not dead today!) and mused on where my life might be headed.

I choreographed a small dance routine to a song I sang out loud to myself about the life I was trying to usher in, filled with beloved people and doing good for the world and art and culture and mentorship and philanthropy. The song was part fantasy, part prayer, part visualization.

Here's the thing with visualizations: world-class athletes swear by the concept, and research shows that athletes who practice visualization perform better.

The difficult part of visualizing where your new life might go is remembering to keep a loose grasp on your goals. Yes, you need to be able to see where you want to go, but you don't want to get slammed with tunnel vision and be obsessive about them. One friend summed it up for me when he said his mantra was OTTO NATTO: Open to the Outcome, Not Attached to the Outcome. You might see outcomes you'd like, but you resist attaching to them.

During my road trip on the Washington coast, I might have just looked like a wild-eyed, tangle-haired, slightly stoned woman flailing alone on an empty patch of wet sand, but I was visualizing the life I wanted to create. I was getting down with the OTTO NATTO of it all, deeply present in the moment and open to all the possibilities. Remember those two-minute moments we talked about back in Chapter 9? Noticing those tiny moments that you can build a life out of? A getaway can be a longer version of that.

I was exactly where I needed to be . . . and so are you. Even if it feels awkward and in-between and unsettled, you're right where you need to be.

Once you've cleaned off the thickest gunk of your shitshow, things might feel strange and empty. Emptiness can be agonizing, and many of us experience it as a lack. (Something's missing!) But there's beauty in a blank slate. Sometimes all you need is a slight change of scenery to help you feel the wide-open opportunity of getting to choose where you want to go next.

FIND YOUR AFTERGLOW

Wiping off the grimy residue of your old life and visualizing the new life that's coming doesn't have to be about rituals or road trips. You can use whatever tools feel right, whether it's steel wool and vinegar or a long talk with an old friend who can help you get new perspectives.

◆ What in your life needs cleaning and clearing out? Look around your home. Where do you find clutter and un-attended piles? Do you have an ignored stack of stuff in your house or car that may correlate to an ignored pile of stuff internally? What five-minute step could you take today to clear that out?

◆ Visualization practice: If you had nothing holding you back or standing in your way, what would your ideal life feel like? Try to describe the sensations, with as many details as you can. What would it smell like? How would your mornings taste? What would your bedtime feel like against your skin?

◆ What OTTO NATTO outcomes come to mind for you? What would you love to happen in your life, and how can you stay unattached from *needing* it to happen?

◆ How are you exactly where you need to be right now? Even if it's excruciating, what are you learning that you've always wanted to learn?

As always, watch for any old stories that come up about why you supposedly can't do any of this. If you catch yourself thinking "But I'm a messy person" or "I tried visualizing before and it was dumb," then it's time to step back, take a breath, and recognize that your ego is trying to do its job to keep you safe, by keep-ing you trapped in old patterns. Shitty familiarity feels less scary than the discomfort of change, but give yourself full permission to make new mistakes. If not now, when everything's all ripped open, then when?

Chapter 21

VIOLENCE

FORGIVENESS AT THE FIRING RANGE

I DON'T ALWAYS KNOW HOW TO GET ANGRY. IN MY MARRIAGE, THERE WAS EXACTLY ONE time when I violently expressed anger: in a pregnant rage on a 104-degree day, I threw an empty soda can at my husband across the living room.

The can whiffled aimlessly through the air, the empty aluminum cylinder landing harmlessly on the floor a few feet away from where my pregnant self was walrusing on the couch. That was as angry as I got, even when bloated with a baby, blood boiling with hormones, miserable during a rare Seattle heat wave.

That soda can is the ultimate metaphor for my relationship with anger: empty, unfocused, not going very far, spiraling in a few aimless circles before falling hollow on the floor.

This anger is unbearable, my brain says. *Let's safely analyze something instead!*

As part of my shitshow, I recognized that I needed to constructively *deal* with anger when it came up, or else it might consume me.

Anger can't be pushed down, set aside, emptied, and gently tossed across the room. You can't sidestep it, can't analyze it away, can't talk it out and make it cerebral and beat it into submission with nonviolent communication words and namaste niceness.

For me, when I don't recognize and express anger, I feel it start to clot up my arteries, calcify in my bones, tangle my intestines, and metastasize in my cells. It doesn't do anyone any favors to deny it, shove it down, empty it out, deal with it quietly.

It also doesn't help me or anyone else to be violent toward people. I don't need to bring more harm into my life, or the lives of the people around me. If I act violently toward others, I'm accountable for their reactions—and that only hurts me.

Okay, so what to do with it? It's angry. How do I get it out?

While doing some reading about oxytocin (I needed all the natural mood enhancers I could get!), I stumbled across research about how oxytocin, dopamine, and serotonin could sometimes be released into the brain when shooting guns.

I hate guns. I am a good West Coast liberal, so of course I hate guns. They terrify me. Worse, they *horrify* me. In America, anger + guns = a really horrifically common combination, and the cause of an obscene amount of death. Guns scare me.

But I started to wonder if going to a firing range would help me work through several issues at once. Let's get that anger out! Let's get some dopamine and oxytocin into the system! Let's learn some gun safety so that maybe I could have one less thing to be scared about.

And hey, what do you know! Thanks to the rando roulette wheel that was Tinder, I'd met that gun-slinging nerd on a cross-country road trip. I figured, why not make an adventure?

"You're going to go shoot guns with some guy you met on Tinder?" one friend asked nervously. "That sounds like a mistake."

It was, but at least it was a new mistake.

My handgun training started in an Airbnb in Raleigh, North Carolina, with the gunslinger handing me his unloaded Glock handgun.

"Spend some time just touching it," he told me. "Get used to it as an object before anything else. Stick your fingers in it. Poke at it. Separate from what it does, just get to know it as an inanimate object."

Then he went to fetch something out of his Prius, leaving me alone with the gun.

I sat cross-legged on a kitchen counter and poked at the gun. Tears sprang to my eyes. It was heavy and deadly and awful. I prodded at the Glock, slid the metal over the plastic, saw which parts came off and how they fit back together.

"I think it's important for touchy-feely progressives to handle a gun," a Libertarian friend had told me. "It's good to see that it's essentially a Pez dispenser with a metal tube attached."

The gunslinger came back a few minutes later and spent an hour in the Airbnb teaching me how to hold the handgun, how never to put my finger on the trigger unless I'm shooting, how to shove the web of my thumb over the back, how to nestle my thumbs against each other on the side. I learned how to cock a Glock, pushing with my dominant hand instead of pulling with my weaker hand.

The gunslinger showed me how to stand to best absorb the impact of firing the gun, my brain conceptualizing the stance as a dancer's pose, with feet at nine and two o'clock, knees bent, leaning forward on my toes.

"It's all just choreography," I said to him, and he rolled his eyes and smirked.

THE MINDFULNESS OF SHOOTING A GUN

Neuroscientist Kevin Fleming explains that safely shooting a gun at a firing range can cause a sympathetic-parasympathetic nervous system cycle: the body's adrenaline peaks, and after it's all over, the body releases calming chemicals. This chemical response cycle is the same one that motivates thrill seekers to jump from planes.

After suffering a traumatic event, some people find taking risks more difficult. Their brains go into self-preservation mode and they don't want to try new things—especially not new things that scare them. Folks who've been through trauma have a pervasive unsafe feeling in their bodies, their past traumas showing up as a chronic internal discomfort. No wonder it can be difficult to put yourself in challenging situations for the sake of trying something new!

But pushing beyond that discomfort zone, you can remind yourself how good it feels to conquer something new and to survive something you never thought you'd be able to tolerate. It feels good to prove your self-doubt wrong. One way of thinking of it is resensitizing yourself, allowing yourself to get engaged and feel pleasure again. You get to remember that taking chances is part of what makes life worth living!

Shooting guns doesn't have to be all about high adrenaline and thrills, though. Buddhist monk Arthur Rosenfeld wrote about how he uses shooting guns as a mindfulness practice. Recalling a trip to the firing range, he wrote: "I raised the gun again, and engaged the silent mantra, 'there is no moment but this, there is no shot but this one.'"

Even if you don't achieve Zen-like aim, the sense of accomplishment of getting better at aiming at a target can help produce those feel-good chemicals, too.

After my safety training, the gunslinger and I drove to a local firing range. I signed a million waivers, and put on ear and eye protection. I walked through one door, let it close behind me, walked through another door, let that one close behind me.

The firing range was loud. *Really* loud. Even with the battery-powered supersonic silencing earmuffs I'd borrowed, the range was deafening.

"I can feel the sound in my body," I shouted at the gunslinger as we settled into a cubicle at the range.

"Give yourself some time to adjust," the gunslinger shouted back.

I blinked back startled tears and nodded. I took a belly breath and tried to stand tall and strong with both feet on the ground, stance wide. I faced it. I braced my newly discovered stomach muscles against the sound and let it ripple through me.

I tried working on the shooting stance I'd been taught. Legs at nine and two, knees unlocked, on my toes, I leaned into it. *It's all just choreography*, I reminded myself as the gunslinger handed me the loaded Glock.

My shoulders rolled forward, my arms extended straight out as I lifted the gun and fired.

I was startled by the shot, and my aim was terrible. My terror wavered a bit as my overachieving type-A honor student muscled her way to the front of my brain. *Your aim is an embarrassment, Stallings!*

"I can do better," I shouted at the gunslinger, and I was right. I spent fifteen minutes taking single shots, focusing on lining up the sights and improving my aim. I wasn't great, but I got better. The honor student was peeved at her B+ but stepped back a bit.

"Try firing two shots in a row," the gunslinger told me, then led me through other drills: Three shots in a row. One-handed. Left-handed.

Shifting the Glock from hand to hand, I contemplated anger. The people I felt wronged by. The rage. It was purely an academic exercise, though. I wasn't angry.

I looked at the orange paper target and didn't feel like I was getting anything out. I just wasn't angry—other than a little frustrated that I kept forgetting to take my finger off the trigger before I set the gun down, earning me a side-eye from the gunslinger. He was patient but extremely mansplainy.

After half an hour or so, I fetched a new paper target for myself. It was a bright pink human outline. I aimed for the heart while the gunslinger filled five magazines with bullets and lined them up in front of me.

With the new target six yards out, I tried firing in quick succession, running through the magazines one a minute, popping them out of the bottom of the handgun, reloading, and cocking it the way I'd been taught, with my right hand punching the handle forward as my left hand held the top secure.

As I squeezed the trigger quickly, absorbing the recoils into my arms and shoulders and core and widely set legs, my brain went into a blank state.

I took a breath, and these words ran through my head, without my choosing them:

I forgive myself.

I fired.

I forgive myself.

I fired again.

I forgive myself.

I squeezed the trigger faster.

I forgive myself. I forgive myself. I forgive myself.

Every shot kicked back into my arms, the impact beating the mantra into my body. I emptied a magazine of forgiveness, reloaded, cocked the gun, fired through another one. I aimed for the heart.

This wasn't what I was expecting. I went looking to gain insight into my own anger and rage, trying to find an outlet for my sense of wrongedness.

I forgive myself. Instead of anger, I stood there firing the shots into my own pink heart and every shot hammered the words into my muscles, until I was crying and started having trouble seeing the target. This was forgiveness at point-blank range.

I forgive myself.

Afterward, loading our gear back into the gunslinger's car, I leaned my head on the car door and cried more.

"Forgiving myself is hard," I rambled at the gunslinger, who probably wasn't expecting this much crying on a cross-country Tinder rendezvous but seemed to be rolling with the punches. It was all weird dates, all the time for me.

"It's hard to forgive myself for feeling so blind, for not seeing it before my life fell apart. I hate myself for the way I lived in a fantasy that I sold myself every morning and believed completely."

I got in the car and cried more, my arms still vibrating from the kickback of the handgun and my hands throbbing and tingling like they always seemed to during an intense experience. The gunslinger loaded the last of the safely locked gear into the trunk, got in the driver's seat, and looked at me.

He reached out his hand and I took it, feeling a strange new sensation. I felt . . . love? That was unexpected. Maybe it was just the firing-range dopamine? Therapy was everywhere after all.

I stopped crying. Exhaled.

I flew home a couple days later with bullet casings in my bag, arranging them with the rocks on my altar. The gunslinger and I tried dating for a few months after, but the relationship was mostly about trauma bonding and coercion and scissoring our emotional wounds. It was a new mistake, that's for dang sure.

If shooting guns isn't your new mistake of choice, you still might benefit from trying an emotional release that's physical, visceral, and possibly even a bit violent.

As with so many things, the concept is less about the specifics of what you do and more about your intent and finding something that feels like it fits. Basically, you just want emotionality + physicality + intent. Here are some ideas:

◆ Write down words or sentences about the emotions you want to release, violently tear the paper into confetti to symbolize it transforming into something new and different, and toss it in the air with abandon! The more theatrical the ripping and tossing, the better—just make sure you're okay with cleaning up the scraps when you're done!

◆ Get aggressive with weeding your garden, picturing the weeds as negative emotions and old patterns you're uprooting and discarding. Another version of this: chopping wood.

◆ Get loud! Laughing hard at a movie or screaming at a sporting event are some of the few socially acceptable ways to be extremely loud in public.

◈ Do some extremely vigorous exercise (the kind that makes you sweat and grunt—it must push you to the edge of your capacities) and visualize the emotions leaving your body through your beads of sweat. Bonus: the burn of your muscles working helps you concentrate on the present moment and not the screaming monkeys in your mind.

◈ Be creative. Beat a pillow with a tennis racket, throw water balloons at a brick wall, get plates at a garage sale specifically for breaking with a hammer—the key is just movement, healthy destruction, and your intent.

There's value in understanding danger, but it must be done with safety in mind. When you're dabbling in volatile qualities like anger and violence, it's important to give yourself a safe container. The emotions and energy need to get out, but it's important to wear your metaphorical ear protection and make sure you lock your symbolic weapons of choice in the trunk when you're done.

Stay safe out there, friends.

FIND YOUR AFTERGLOW

As psychoanalyst Carl Jung said, "Where your fear is, there is your task." Making the choice to intentionally and lovingly push yourself out of your comfort zone can help you get more familiar with the sensations of growth and unease. Life is going to repeatedly and violently throw you out of your comfort zone. Maybe if you make the choice to practice little discomfort exercises, it'll be less awful when life comes at you hard?

◈ What scares you? What gentle, loving steps could you take to practice facing your fear? How could overcoming that fear help you reclaim a sense of agency?

◆ What does anger feel like in your body? How do you express it? What new ways could you explore to get the sensations of anger out of your system?

◆ There's a lot of talk about forgiving other people, but how do you need to forgive *yourself*? In what ways was your shitshow a reflection of how you've abandoned, betrayed, or disappointed yourself? How can you work on repairing your relationship with yourself?

Pushing yourself out of your comfort zone is delicate and difficult, so go gentle on yourself. If you're taking risks and embracing discomfort, make sure you're also checking in regularly with people who love you or a counselor to make sure you're staying safe while you push your boundaries.

Chapter 22

TATTOOS

TORSCHLUSSPANIK AND BODY INK THERAPY

I SPENT MOST OF MY SOLO EVENINGS ROLLING AROUND ON THE FLOOR OF STUDIO HAAAY, feeling my way around the potency of my new life. After six months of practicing mindfulness daily, I'd gotten to a place where I could tolerate spending more of my time alone, conjuring my new life.

Sometimes I'd walk to Elliott Bay Book Company to browse the terrible covers of self-help titles to add to my stack. (Agonizingly, the wedding planning shelf was close enough that sometimes I'd catch the cover of my own first book winking at me from where I stood assessing the shitshow aisle.) I'd journal, dance with my reflection, breathe, scroll motivational inspo on my phone, and try to feel where my life might be going.

You can't make any of your future conjurings happen (OTTO NATTO!), but as you move through and out of the thick of upheaval, you may be recognizing that this unsettled time is also a remarkable opportunity.

During a massive life transition, everything feels liminal and confusing, like unrealized potential and unknown horizons. You feel like you're living in an in-between. Every day you eat ambiguity for breakfast. It can be agonizing (where the hell is this going? Why can't I be there already?!) and most of us want to rush through the discomfort as quickly as possible.

For me, the sensation of massive transition reminded me of something: I felt this way in my early twenties, during an era that set the stage for the next twenty years. I remembered being at raves in the mid-'90s and having moments of looking around and being like *"This is it.* This moment right here will never be here again, and I need to soak it all up because it won't be like this for long." I felt wide awake to the potential in my life.

In my early twenties, I'd woken up by eating ecstasy and dancing and reveling in my youth. In my early forties, I'd woken up by eating grief and dancing and reveling in the fact that I wasn't dead yet. Mostly, it just felt amazing to be *awake* again.

What if this shitshow isn't a curse but an opportunity, a fleeting moment of being ripped open and getting to choose how to sew yourself back together?

I developed a sense of urgency around using the moment as best as I could. I wanted to make the most of this shitshow—if not now, then when? I wanted to accept it fully, feel it completely, and swallow every last drop of it.

There's a word for this sensation of having a limited period for something, and it's one of those ominous German portmanteaus that combines words and gives them a whole added meaning: *Torschlusspanik.*

The literal translation is "gate-shut panic," but Torschlusspanik tastes like time running out. Literally, the term could be applied to East Berlin as the wall went up, but more metaphorically, it can refer to biological clocks ticking.

My shitshow had sliced me wide open, both literally and figuratively. First it sliced me open, pulled out my entrails, cut out the blown ovary, rinsed my half-empty abdomen three times with saline, flopped it all back in, and sewed it up. (Surgeons have such weird jobs.) Then it ended my marriage and ate several identities at once.

A year later, I was starting to understand that "this too shall pass." People told me it would, and my brain knew it was true even when my body couldn't comprehend it. But even after a year, the wound was still open, the tissue gristle glistening in the sun, and I understood I had this little window of unsettled time to make some conscious choices about what I wanted to do.

"Adulthood is about the process of maturation," Atta reminded me that week. "It's about making choices. It's about having the resources and mental capacity to have some agency in your world—however small!—and make choices about what you want to do."

"Ugh, but some of my decider muscles are so developed in certain ways that I don't even consciously know I'm making a decision," I whined. "It's like muscle memory takes over and I just default to the same thing I've always done," I said. "I want to be awake enough to know there's a decision on the table."

"If you're awake enough, you *do* get to make choices . . . but that means paying attention!" Atta said.

"Ugh, but I'm so distractible," I said. "Sometimes I just want to scroll and swipe and ignore it all."

"Just keep practicing at staying awake," Atta said. "Keep breathing."

As you're moving through a shitshow, you know the future is out there on the horizon waiting for you—but sometimes it can feel very, VERY far away. It's torturous to obsess about things you don't have. But what if you could bring some of the future's contentment here into your present moment?

Try this:

1. Picture an experience you would like to have in the future. Don't get lost in the details, but just take a moment to imagine a specific life goal.

2. Take a breath. Ground physically into where you are *right now*. Maybe feel the chair under your butt, or the book in your hands. Smell the room. Feel the air against your skin.

3. Now, imagine the sensations in your body if you achieved your goal. How would it *feel*? Would you have butterflies in your stomach? Would your chest puff up with pride? Would you feel like jumping up and down with excitement?

4. Close your eyes and spend a few moments imagining the sensations you want to feel in your future life. Feel the sun on your skin, the arms of a future lover around you, the smell of your future success. Take as long as you like!

5. Open your eyes.

Does anything feel different now? The idea here is that instead of being all up in your head in a state of wanting, craving, and future-casting, you can give your body a flood of good feelings right here in the present. Your nervous system is listening, and it doesn't talk in details; it communicates in sensations.

Now, what small action could you take *today* to experience one of those sensations you want more of in the future? How can you make the most today of this window of transitional time?

THE FORGOTTEN TRAMP STAMP

I had another idea about what I wanted to do to make the most of my transitional time.

After years of mostly forgetting about the tattoo on my lower back (because, well, I never saw it), spending more time naked around Tinderellas reminded me that it existed. I became convinced that there were body memories lying dormant in my skin, waiting to be woken up by new ink.

The tattoo was a doodle that my tattoo artist / drug dealer and I had worked on together when I lived in San Francisco in the mid-'90s. The ink was administered in my Lower Haight bedroom, on Waller Street. My artist/dealer spent five hours going over the lines, and when the pain got to be too much for me, we decided we'd finish up some other time. He died of a drug overdose a year later, and the tattoo was never completed.

So, the tramp stamp on my back was basically a half-done sketch from over twenty years ago. I have zero regrets about it, because my 1997 infant self made a vow that my current self totally agrees with: "Even if I don't like the tattoo design in a few years, I'll always respect who I was when I got it," I'd written in my journal. "This is a really important time in my life, and that won't change even if my tastes do."

Damn, 1997 Ariel! Maybe you weren't such an infant, because you were completely awake and keenly aware of what a pivotal life era you were in. Nothing's changed about how I feel about that. Sometimes you just know when you're in a *big fucking deal* time.

The sustained pain of receiving a tattoo can put people into a meditative trance, just like seated meditation can, or stuff like exercise, BDSM, or anything else that causes your body to be on high alert. Our minds respond by releasing endorphins to deal with the pain, and voilà: you have a therapeutic experience and permanent body art.

Beyond their physiological therapeutic value, tattoos can also be thought of as visualizations that you carry with you for always. Researcher December Maxwell interviewed survivors of sexual assault who got tattoos as a way to heal. Some survivors saw their tattoos as a way to reclaim their bodies for themselves. While Maxwell cautions that tattoos as therapy should accompany seeing a therapist, her research showed that many find therapeutic comfort in their ink.

Back in the '90s, my plan was that after I had my one kid (always just one), I would have the back tattoo wrap around my hips and stretch across my stomach, making a circle around my torso. But twenty years later, my stomach was a whole different creature . . . crisscrossed with scars and stories, stretched out from a breech pregnancy, flattened by anguish, strengthened by a year of physical training and daily dance practice. It'll just keep changing, too . . . but how? Bigger? Smaller? More scars? Who knows, but there will *definitely* be more gravity. I knew I wanted to finish the tattoo as a handshake between my present self, my past self, and all my future selves. We're all in this body together.

If you've considered a tattoo as part of your afterglow, embodiment coach Mackenzie Amara offers this guidance for those wanting to use getting inked as a consciousness-raising practice: "The process of deciding to get a tattoo itself can be an embodied one. The vision arises in your liminal, imaginative realm, sure, but after you see the image in your mind, drop into your body. Where does this drawing or symbol connect with your skin? What power can you feel emanating from that place?"

She points out that "like all pain, the extent to which we suffer while getting a tattoo is in direct proportion to how much we resist. The pain of the needle can fuel a deep trance with a surrendered stance."

Here's the guidance Mackenzie shared with me about how to have a mindful tattoo session:

◆ The first thing to do to keep yourself embodied during a tattoo session is breathe. Notice each straggly texture of your inhale, each tense push of your exhale. Notice it until it changes, and then keep noticing it.

◆ You'll want to grit your teeth or clench your fists, but don't. Try to keep your belly soft and full, with your attention scanning your entire body, not just being dragged down by the sensation of pain.

◆ When you find moments of relaxing in the session, hone in on the sensation of the needle on your skin—but titrate it, focusing on it only for brief moments at a time.

◆ Instead of focusing on the sensation of the needle on your skin, make it a practice to notice a sensation *other* than pain. See if you can detect a nuance of something more subtle than the gross sensation of pain.

◆ Whatever sensations are there during your tattoo session, keep surrendering to them fully, with soft breath and soft belly.

COMMEMORATIONS OF SURVIVAL

For my tattoo, I found a local artist recommended by a friend, and we worked together to create an ornamental design to honor my creative firstborn (a long-forgotten rave magazine called *Lotus*), as well as Thich Nhat Hanh's concept of "no mud, no lotus": "Most people are afraid of suffering. But suffering is a kind of mud to help the lotus flower of happiness grow. There can be no lotus flower without the mud."

I wasn't worried about the pain (HA HA, what's a buzzy little needle compared to a full-frontal life cataclysm!?), but I did warn the tattoo artist that I might get weird in the chair.

"I'm sure you've seen it all," I said. "It's not like I'm holding a séance . . ." But who knows. Maybe I was?

Lying on the table, under the needle, I did what I'd been practicing for a year: I breathed. I stayed present with the sensation. I tried to relax into it instead of resisting it. The needle burned across my stomach, tracing across my scars.

We're all here together, I thought, speaking to both my decades-ago former self and my decades-away future self.

Many sessions of needling later, all my selves (past and future selves, known and unknown selves) were adorned across the belly and over my hips. Did it hurt? It's all relative. Did it hurt as much as blowing an ovary during a wedding expo? No. Did it hurt as much as being cut open and scooped out and rinsed off and stapled shut? Ha. Did it hurt as much as my marriage ending? Nowhere close. That hurt more than anything I've ever known. But did it get a little hot and sliced-feeling by the end of each four-hour session as the endorphin high wore off? It did indeed.

I imagine the ink fading, my skin sagging. I imagine my transhuman grandchildren trying to pet it when they catch a glimpse of it under whatever space-age shirt I'm wearing to match my neural lace. I imagine my body dying and the ink still there.

When I dance in Studio Haaay, I watch the ink stretch over my hips with me. I dedicate the movement and the lines to the momentum that moves through me and keeps me alive. I trace the lines with my fingers, feel the ways they celebrate the scars that shape this body and this life. I wonder what future scars I'll endure. These tattoos are a commitment to myself, a wedding ring around my entire existence.

Commemorations of your progress can be a way to voice your commitment to yourself and celebrate your survival. This doesn't have to be a tattoo, of course, but it's nice to have something tangible to point at and remember, "See that? That's because I survived. That's a celebration of my resilience."

FIND YOUR AFTERGLOW

As you move through a transition, it can be challenging to keep going. Sometimes it's useful to remember it's a relatively small window of time (gate-shut panic!) and give yourself a little commemoration of how far you've come.

◆ Looking back, what other times in your life have felt similar to where you are now, in terms of growth, awareness, or change? What came out of those other transitions?

◆ How is this awful window letting in a breeze of opportunity? What might your shitshow be trying to teach you? What do you want to learn before the gate closes on this period in your life?

◆ What are your commitments to yourself? How can you commemorate them?

◆ If you were going to get an afterglow tattoo, what might it look like? Another way of thinking of this: If your afterglow had a logo, what would it be? Grab a pen and get doodling! Remember that no one ever has to see this—it's just for you.

◆ When you imagine looking back on this era of your life, what do you want to say you learned or accomplished or accepted? Imagine telling children a story about this time in several decades—what might the moral be?

However you choose to commemorate your journey, it's important to take the time to celebrate how far you've come. Even when your progress is nonlinear and going in loops and spirals that feel like backsliding, that means you're noticing! And if you're noticing, that means you're awake and fully doing this thing. Keep going!

Chapter 23

LISTENING

WHEN YOU GET QUIET, THE UNIVERSE SPEAKS

"HOW'S THE MEDITATION GOING?" MY AUNT ASKED ME AT THANKSGIVING, A YEAR AFTER MY life had fallen part.

"Great," I said. "It's really making a difference in my anxiety. I realized that I can't get rid of my anxiety, but do I have the ability to change my relationship to it. Mindfulness has been super useful!"

"I think you're going to get more spiritual as you get older," my aunt said.

"No, no," I protested. "Meditation isn't really spiritual for me. It's more of a mental health thing."

"Oh, okay," my aunt said, clearly unconvinced.

Afterward, I realized I was a liar. For sociological reasons, I wasn't into organized religion, and a youth spent with hippie ceremonies shoved down my throat meant that I didn't feel comfortable with spirituality as a performative practice. I felt that if you needed to be *seen* as spiritual to *feel* spiritual, you probably weren't.

I mean, validation-seeking is great. I LOVE VALIDATION! It's just that it's a slippery slope to tangle up your validation-seeking with your spirituality. In my experience, those who understand the most about the value of inward spiritual practices tend to say the least . . . and yes, I'm squirming in hypocritical discomfort typing these words.

But my aunt had seen through my defensive posturing. I'd invested lots of time into developing my personal spiritual practice. I was indeed getting more spiritual as I got older, and my spirituality mostly boiled down to *listening*.

Every day I got up and I listened to my body while I stretched. (What hurts today? What's a joy today? What's there to be grateful for today?) Every day I sat down and closed my eyes and focused on my breath and got very quiet and listened. (What are the monkeys screaming about today? What sensations went by when I got still?)

It turns out, when you listen more, you notice more. It turns out, when you start listening, the universe starts talking to you. You just have to get quiet and patient enough to listen. (For a loud, impatient woman, this is a lifelong challenge.)

As life soldiered on, it started feeling like everyone I knew was descending into their own shitshow, or was desperately trying to avoid one. I watched my geighbor take a huge leap with buying a new home, and then a week later get laid off from his job of fourteen years. One dear friend's father committed suicide by cop, while another friend navigated multiple late-term miscarriages. I watched several marriages collapse, and then there were the folks dealing with divorce, a child's autism spectrum diagnosis, and their own emerging chronic health conditions. Sometimes life felt like a game of shitshow bingo.

Everyone seemed to be having health issues or major relationship problems or fertility issues or a mental health flare-up or losing a parent or having a friend die violently. I started spending a lot of time delivering meals, sitting with friends on the floor while they sobbed in my arms, washing grief-stricken beloveds' faces with a warm washcloth when they were so depressed they couldn't get out of bed for days at a time. The geopolitical climate didn't help. Everyone struggled.

I tried to talk less and listen more.

Riding the bus home from therapy one afternoon, headphones on, I was quietly integrating that week's batch of lessons. I was chewing over vulnerability, and how softness is a superpower, and how people who are repulsed by insecurity are often battling their own insecurities, and blah blah blah. I wasn't crying or discombobulated—just contemplative.

A block from my stop, I started gathering my things and the well-dressed black woman in her fifties sitting opposite me leaned across the aisle and put her hand on my arm.

I slipped off my headphones and smiled at her.

"I was just talking to God," she said. "He wanted me to tell you something."

"Oh?" I said. This kind of thing would have bothered me a couple years ago (are you trying to convert me? Leave me alone!), but now I just tilted my head and tried to listen to her with my whole self.

"God wanted me to tell you that He loves you," she said. "And He's there for you, when you need Him."

"Thank you," I said. As the bus pulled to a stop, I stood up, touched my hand to her arm, and said again, "Thank you. I really needed to hear that today."

The monkeys in my head were quiet, because they were listening.

The next day, on our way home from school, Tavi and I got into a conversation about genies.

"If a genie says you can make a wish, the only thing you can't wish for is more wishes," Tavi said, and then followed up, "but genies aren't real."

My little literalist. He's not big into fantastical thinking, that guy. I didn't used to be either.

"True," I said. "*Literally* speaking, you're probably not going to pick up an oil lamp and rub it and have a magical spirit come out to grant your wishes. But *figuratively* speaking, I think we all encounter people who come into our lives to help."

Then I told him the story of the woman on the bus.

"Now, you know me," I said. "Do I believe in the Christian God?"

"No," Tavi said.

"Do I think there's some dude with a beard in the clouds who called that lady on the bus? 'Hey, Carol. What's up? It's me, God!'"

Tavi laughed, and I kept doing my God voice, holding an invisible GodPhone to my ear.

"'Carol, do you see that confused-looking white lady across the aisle over there? Can you relay a message to her? Yeah, girl. I'll hold. It's cool.'"

I put my imaginary phone down.

"I totally do not believe that happened in a literal way," I told him. "I don't believe in that particular vision of God. BUT! Did I appreciate that someone on a bus gave me some encouragement? I did!"

"So," I concluded (because I could tell I was losing my first grader's attention and I might be losing yours as well), "while I don't believe in genies, I do believe in people helping each other out. And while I don't believe in the Christian God, I do appreciate when people share their sense of faith, because I'm working on finding my own kind of faith."

A study by the Pew Research Center in 2017 suggests that I'm not the only one working on my own kind of faith. Pew found that 27 percent of US citizens refer to themselves as "spiritual but not religious."

Professor of politics, philosophy, and religion at Lancaster University in England, Linda Woodhead hypothesizes that the reason for this is that identifying as spiritual is a stepping-stone from being religious to being nonreligious. But that's not necessarily the case, as there are a growing number of people who were never religious but found themselves becoming more spiritual sometimes after a period of overwhelming emotional turmoil.

What's up with that? One possible answer is that becoming more self-reflective can put us more in tune with a sense of the divine—however we conceptualize what that means. In Katherine

Ozment's *Grace Without God: The Search for Meaning, Purpose, and Belonging in a Secular Age*, she writes, "Christians believe that it is God who grants us grace, but I believe we create it for ourselves, through persistence, awareness, and clear-eyed reflection." She explains that for her, grace is all around when we are open to life and the world—with or without a deity.

Once I surrendered to the sensation that the universe was talking to me all the time, the messages started coming in more often. When I could get myself more quiet, more often, I heard more.

The books around my home became talismanic messages that called out to me when I needed them . . .

It's OK That You're Not OK, author Megan Devine reminded me from the stack in the living room, and I thought, *Yeah, it is. Thanks.*

Come as You Are, author Emily Nagoski instructed from my bedside, and I thought, *Okay, I will.*

Pema Chödrön's *Taking the Leap* smiled at me from the kitchen counter, and I thought, *Good idea.*

You Are a Badass. A New Earth. No Mud, No Lotus. The reminders were everywhere. *Go the Fuck to Sleep*, Adam Mansbach reminded me at night, the book a gifted leftover from my son's early years. The universe gets snarky sometimes.

I also started wearing words on my body as physical affirmations. I bought a chunky crystal on a thick chain with the words *NOSCE TE IPSUM* hammered into the raw brass. When I walked around my neighborhood, I could feel the weight of the metal and stone hammering itself into my chest: *Know thyself, know thyself, know thyself.* It was a form of spellcasting, and my body moving through the world was my cauldron.

After a year of Tinder, I'd decided to switch dating apps. With Tinder, you can only get messages from people you've matched with, but on OkCupid, *anyone* can message you. I found this totally overwhelming, especially when god messaged me.

Your [*sic*] beautiful. Your profile screams 'I'll stab you in your sleep!!!, lol.' You don't need to try so hard. What you are is good enough. Trust me.

I was working on trying to observe how my body handled emotional input, and this message gave me a distinct jolt of anxiety through my chest that then radiated out my arms. Not because god was snarky (although that, too), but because it felt true. Maybe I *didn't* need to try so hard. Maybe I *was* good enough. Maybe I *did* need more trust.

This was something I heard over and over again from pretty much everyone . . . my friends, my therapist, colleagues, randos on the internet: *Ariel, it's a lot. Ariel, you try too hard. Ariel, what if you handled it all with a lighter grip? Ariel, you can't control it. Ariel, stop forcing it. Ariel, stop trying so hard.*

When a message comes in from every possible unrelated source, it's pretty clear that it's time to listen.

WHEN ALL MUSIC IS GOSPEL MUSIC

Then I started hearing all song lyrics as a timeless conversation between me and the universe.

Under the twinkly lights of Studio Haaay, I'd put on my headphones and move while I listened to certain songs over and over again, and I'd imagine myself living inside the songs. When you're truly immersed in a song, moving to it, letting it move you, sometimes it feels like you're folding the fabric of time and space and communing with yourself through time within the song.

Here's how it works: The you listening to the song now is visiting with the you listening to the song later, and you're both hanging out with the you who was has listened to the same song in the past, maybe many years ago. There are infinite yous, communing together inside infinite moments, all brought together in this one song! If you can get inside the music and the moment, then you can travel through time to visit your other selves existing inside the same music in other moments.

Listening to music in this way turned every love song into gospel for me. A cheezy song crooning "I love you" that used to trigger my loneliness suddenly shifted to a devotional to the universe.

Every heartbroken track whining "You haven't called me!" became a lament to my own spiritual struggles and challenges with feeling connected to my practice.

I mostly listen to indie pop, and the joy and pain of pop songs is that they get stuck in your head because they're engineered to be full of earworms. That can be irritating, but if you pick music with positive messages and then fill the songs with meaning, you can use the looping earworminess to your advantage. You can use music as a catchy affirmation, using the repetition to train yourself to think new thoughts and heal.

Early on, I listened to Rihanna's "Sex with Me" on repeat for months, singing loudly to myself as I tried to rebuild my self-esteem, desperately trying to believe that sex with me really would be amazing someday when I was having sex again. (I told the gunslinger about this and he rolled his eyes at me and said, "That's an inauspicious origin story for a wonderslut." Whatever, bro. Shut up and enjoy the ride.)

I listened to Sia's "Reaper" endlessly (Don't come for me today / I'm feeling good / I'mma savor it), Ariana Grande's "Be Alright" (But the hard times are golden / 'Cause they all lead to better days), a song called "Every Every" by an indie artist named MOONZz (You see me in a different way / My love for you is every day / Count my blessings and I sing your praise / You're my every every everything). Through this lens, even mindless pop music became a mindfulness practice. It's just me and the divine, bending the fabric of space and time through this pop pablum.

As with many of the out-there things I tried during my recovery process, there was some logic behind the wackiness. Music therapy is totally a thing: it's a form of therapy practiced by a credentialed professional where patients listen to and make music as treatment for conditions ranging from PTSD to Parkinson's disease.

Dr. Elizabeth Stegemöller at Iowa State University studies music therapy and neural control, and wrote in a 2014 study that music therapy is "a powerful tool to enhance neuroplasticity in the brain." The music therapy field formally started after World War I, when it became popular for musicians to play for war veterans suffering from trauma.

Dr. Stegemöller argues that principles of neuroplasticity explain why music therapy is effective: enjoyable music activates dopamine production, and pairing music with movement, breathing, or vocalizations can help strengthen neuronal connections in different brain areas. So yeah: music, dancing, and singing can help you feel better because they're actually rewiring your brain. You can use music as a neurological trigger, reminding yourself to move toward your afterglow.

Just be thoughtful about the songs you put on shuffle: the lyrics you sing on repeat in the car might be shaping your new existence!

FIND YOUR AFTERGLOW

You might listen for messages from strangers on buses, bad pop music lyrics, or dating app messages from randos, but most of us going through this kind of thing get a *lot* of unsolicited input about what we should do and where we should go next. You don't have to take everyone's advice, but it's wise to listen and watch for patterns in what you hear from others. And then it's even more important to get quiet and listen to *yourself*.

- ◆ What methods work best for you to get quiet and listen to yourself? For some of us it's movement to music or a seated meditation practice, but for other folks it's knitting, gardening, running. What practices help you?

- ◆ How do you use the words around you to talk to yourself? What messages do you see in your daily life? What patterns appear?

- ◆ What rituals (secular or religious) have been the most meaningful in your life? Remember that a ritual doesn't have to mean incense and candles—a simple morning routine is a ritual of sorts, as is a regular afternoon cup of something warm. Where do you find meaning in doing the same things, in the same order, at the same times of day? What makes them meaningful?

◆ What's your response to unsolicited advice? What can you learn about yourself by observing your reactions? What advice pisses you off, stresses you out, or depresses you? What clues can you get about your own values from your reactions?

Listening is a lifelong practice and can be extra challenging for those of us who deal with anxiety. We'll talk more about listening and trusting your intuition in Chapter 29, but for now just focus on observing *how* you listen. Have you ever closed your eyes and tried listening through your skin?

Chapter 24

SPIRITUAL AWAKENING

BEING IN A POLY RELATIONSHIP WITH THE DIVINE

WHILE TALKING TO ONE FRIEND ABOUT HER STRUGGLING MARRIAGE, SHE SAID, "MAYBE I just need more sex in my life . . . it's cool that so many people are exploring forms of polyamory, but that's not me and that's not my marriage."

Why do so many shitshows somehow involve sex? Or maybe my friends just talk to me about their sex lives a lot because they know I am absolutely DTFTAF: Down to Fucking Talk About Fucking.

"You can totally have tons of kinky, transformative sex, though," I said. "Even if your husband isn't interested and you're monogamous, you can still try a sacred jack-off!"

My friend laughed. "Did you make this up?"

And I was all, "Pssht. No!" I am not the first to have this practice.

A sacred jack-off is just about bringing conscious intent into your masturbatory activities. Pleasure can be a reliable, safe access point to the divine, and when you're suffering and struggling, you need all the reliable, safe access points you can get.

We talked about masturbation way back in Chapter 3, but this is different. This isn't palliative to ease your stress or help you sleep . . . it's a bit more sacred. It's about using your own pleasure as a divine communication method.

Here's how to try it:

- **Set your intention.** Like almost everything in life (career goals, saving money, changing your diet, New Moon manifestations), it's all about setting your intent. This is not just a normal jack-off, NO MA'AM. This is going to be something special. For some people, this could mean doing a whole elaborate self-care ritual (bath, candles, lotion, blah blah blah), but for those of us with busy schedules, it's more like making sure you have uninterrupted time/space, taking one quick breath (WE ARE FUCKING OURSELVES RIGHT NOW YES), and just asking yourself a question: What am I hoping to get from this?

- **Fuck yourself the way you want to be fucked.** Whatever your favorite fantasy is about the way you'd like someone else to *bring it*, try bringing it to yourself. Want it rough? Slap yourself around. Want it sweet? Whisper the sweetest nothings while you caress yourself with oils. Want more of a sense of surrender? Push yourself past your own comfort zones and go with it. Want boundary pushing? Establish your own safe word, and then do shit to yourself that pushes you right up to your own edge. Moral of the story: we're all just expressions of the divine anyway, so be your own dream lover.

- **Get weird with it.** Chances are decent that you know best how to get yourself off in the most efficient way possible. Favorite toy, favorite porn, favorite pillow, *whatever*—you know how to do it, but that efficiency might get a little dull. Now, of course getting a new toy is always a fun way to spice things up (I invested in a rose quartz dildo and it was a great excuse to get extra woo-woo with my wanking), but novelty is NOT just about new stuff. Getting weird with it is completely free: Bend yourself over a chair. Position yourself in front of a mirror in an unexpected way. Stretch yourself out on the kitchen counter. Use more fingers! Less fingers! Stick fingers in places you don't normally explore! Flop yourself upside down on the stairs! Use your nondominant hand (oh my, who is this clumsy stranger with their hand down your pants?). Stretch your legs in unusual ways and fuck yourself until they start shaking! Just GET WEIRDER WITH IT.

◆ **Speak in tongues.** Give yourself permission to babble, especially if you come. We all know orgasms can provide physical catharsis, but if you give yourself permission to open your mouth and see what comes out when you come, sometimes shit gets really, REALLY interesting. Laughing, crying, shouting, whispering—the words that pour out contain secrets and truths that you might not expect or have access to in more buttoned-up mental states. Let yourself come unhinged. Shake! Scream! Fall off the bed! GO THERE. All the way.

Then maybe jot down some notes and get on with your day.

I was super into my sacred jack-off practice because it was part of how I celebrated what had become the most important relationship in my life: I'd started dating god.

Now, I'm talking about "god" lowercase nondenominational, so maybe this turn of events is a little less surprising than if the story here was "Offbeat Bride lady raised by hippies becomes a nun," but still. The first year after my life fell down, I had to surrender to my mortality and the loss of my marriage. The second year, I had to surrender my concept of what my primary relationship would look like.

Basically, once I settled into my afterglow, it became clear that my primary relationship was with my spiritual practice.

Esther Perel, famed marriage and family therapist and author, has spoken extensively about how the American expectations of marriage have changed so much in the past century: "Relationship expectations are at an all-time high," she said in an interview with NPR. "We want everything that we expected in traditional marriage in terms of companionship and economic support and family life and social status; and then we also want what the romantic marriage brought us, which was a sense of belonging and connection and intimacy and a best friend and a trusted confidant and a passionate lover. And then we now also want self-fulfillment in our relationships and we want to find a 'soul mate,' a word that for most of history was reserved to God."

It makes sense: we moved out of the era of marriages as arranged business relationships into an era of marriage as a romantic expression, and that happened along the same cultural timeline as the secularization of America, and so is it really any wonder that my old self was an apathetic agnostic who worshipped at the altar of my marriage?

When a friend asked me in the summer of 2015 what I was most afraid of in the world, all I could think of was "my marriage ending." My marriage was my foundation. It was everything: home, work, social, psychological, financial, sexual, romantic, and spiritual (in that as much as I had faith in anything, I had faith in my marriage). I mean, my life was rich and full of other stuff, too—but my marriage was the foundation on which *everything* was built.

This is totally normal, of course, but it helps explain why for some of us, when our marriages end we go through an existential devastation so profound that our nervous systems can't keep up. I know I'm not the only person to have had a traumatic response to divorce, but it was so embarrassing to deal with physical PTSD symptoms for a year. (*Aww, little bb is so sheltered! So few coping mechanisms! So weak!*)

Stumbling through my recovery process, I assembled bits and pieces of practice and comfort into systems to help me feel sane and safe and grounded. I combined some attachment theory with some mindfulness, and trained myself to emotionally anchor myself to a different kind of relationship: my relationship with my spiritual practice.

You know who's always there for me? My meditation cushion.

You know who always texts me back right away? My morning dance practice.

You know who fucks me great and holds me afterward? My sacred jack-off sessions.

You know who I can always count on? The momentum of the universe breathing through my lungs.

You know what else is guaranteed? MY OWN DEATH!

Like any good relationship, I find little ways to touch base and stay in touch, by sitting quietly for a few minutes a day, but also through dance, walking, happy crying, sex, in-the-moment awareness, parenting, and wherever else I can be conscious enough to be aware of where I actually am and what's actually happening.

Do I sound like a born-again, without the religious stuff? It's confusing for me, too. But I finally understood that the throbbing in my hands was the sensation of the universal momentum that flows through everything. It's in me all the time. It's *been* in me all the time. It's the molecules and chemistry and DNA that make up everything everywhere. It's the movement that keeps me alive. That panic attack? That was my soul knocking. That experience with the opera singer? That wasn't a sexual awakening—it was part of a *spiritual* awakening.

Another way of phrasing this shift is that I'm as polyamorous as ever, but my primary relationship is with god.

I don't go to church, but I do lap dances for god in my living room.

WE'RE ALL ONE: SCIENCE AND NONDUALITY

One perspective on this belief system is that it's just an awareness of "nonduality," the philosophy that everything on the planet (hell, everything in the universe!) is interconnected.

There are lots of different ways of understanding the concept, but for many nondualistic thinkers, "we're all one" isn't about some all-seeing magical deity or new-age vibe. Nondualism can be a more practical understanding that we're made from the same stuff—science-y stuff like atoms, molecules, chemicals.

Basically, nonduality is just about the interconnectedness of all life, which folks access through all sorts of hard sciences like mathematics, chemistry, physics, ecology, and more. When you get into nonduality, it starts becoming clear that a spiritual awakening can be a thoroughly nonreligious, secular experience.

This stuff is way out of the scope of this book, but if you identify as an atheist, just know that recognizing and being amazed by the interconnectedness of all things is NOT just for the woo-woo among us. Or as Canadian author and philosopher Carrie Jenkins told me, "There are myriad different routes to the conclusion that everything is connected to everything else. . . . Of course, that's exactly what you'd expect if it's true!"

Awakening to nonduality and developing a personal relationship with the divine doesn't necessarily mean you don't seek connection with people, though. Personally, I'm an extrovert and love connection. But the shift did change the way I *relate* to the people in my life. They don't need to be my everything . . . or even my *most* things.

There's a reduction of pressure, because now I anchor to my relationship with the present *moment*, instead of my relationship with the present *person*. This gives me some compassion for my relationship face-plants—how could people not be terribly disappointed by each other? Humans are all disappointing and unreliable compared to the energy moving through the universe! (Again, who always calls me back? My ability to be fully present at any moment!)

There's also an elevation in standards. When I don't need someone to fill an existential gap, I'm clearer-headed about what situations and people are the best for me to mix with, and what my motivations might be when something dark feels compelling.

Look, I understand that this is getting a little ephemeral. I understand I may be losing some of you, and I'm sorry! I don't mean to make this sound like I'm now floating in some celestial spirit bubble of transcendent woo; most of my life is still motivated by human connection, and my favorite moments are still intimate ones where I get to be intensely physically present with my favorite humans. (Fucking, is what I'm saying.)

The difference for me is that now I understand not to get attached to the specific situation; the key for my sanity is awareness of and sharing presence in the moment with my favorite people. I understand now that specific situations (who's there with me, what we're doing together) are just different access points to finding the same sense of presence. We're all just slices of god in this nondualistic pie.

If I'm paying attention, wherever I go, I can feel the universe moving through me, and feel it moving through other people. I can feel it in you, here with me right now! I LOVE THAT FEELING!

I take a breath and feel it in my hands, feel it against my skin, see it in the trees outside my window. Feeling the universe in everything makes it easier for me not to get as anxiously attached to specific people or situations. People arrive in my life, and if I'm really present in the moment, it feels divine. People depart from my life, and if I'm really present in *that* moment it can feel divine, too. Okay, fine, I'm definitely getting woo, but maybe you feel me?

This stuff is almost impossible to verbalize, and I know I'm failing. I resolve again to talk less and listen more. I know I'll fail at that, too, but all I can do is keep noticing and trying again. That's what sucking practice looks like: you notice, surrender, accept, try again.

"When I talk to my friends who have kids your age," my dad told me, "everyone's struggling."

And he's right. Not just us aging Gen Xer fortysomethings wobbling through our midlife transitions (or desperately avoiding them), not just our boomer parents advancing into an insecure seniorhood, but our younger millennial siblings who are just starting to see how deep the cracks go, and then our even younger "cool friends," the irate and horrified twentysomethings crushed by student loans and chronic anxiety and systemic racism.

Who am I kidding: it's the whole culture. We're all just freaking out. These are culturally difficult times, and we're all strung out on the dopamine of the news cycle and our screens. It's the whole planet! These are cataclysmic, climactically difficult times for all of us. We are in it with the Anthropocene extinction wave.

Sometimes the only thing that helps is wiggling your toes and feeling the inside of your skin and remembering that we're all gonna die. Once you surrender to that truth, it feels easier to enjoy the breath in your lungs today.

One thing's for sure: it will never be like this again, thank fucking god / fucking tragic. Everything's changing, all the time.

All there is to do is look up from the screens, take a breath, and find the awareness of being alive in this present moment, in all its heart-wrenching, beautiful, horrific, amazing glory.

You're exactly where you need to be right now.

FIND YOUR AFTERGLOW

However you make sense of it, everything on this planet is in relationship with everything else. Hopefully even the most atheistic of us can recognize that the building blocks of life are all interconnected by chemistry and molecules and star stuff. Let's dig in more . . .

◆ What ways of connection feel the most nourishing for you? (Intellectual connection? Platonic connection? Sexual connection?) How could you get more of your favorite flavors of connection in relationship with *yourself*?

◆ If you don't see yourself as a spiritual person, what aspects of your recovery have felt unexplainable? How do you work with those unknowns? How do you contextualize any moments of magical thinking?

◆ How do your relationships with people interplay with any spiritual practices you may have? When do you find yourself neglecting your spiritual work?

It's painful getting woken up by a shitshow, but it's nice to be awake. Secular mindfulness remains the best tool for waking up. Remember that secular mindfulness isn't necessarily about anything woo—it's just about *noticing*.

part four

ONWARD

INTEGRATING THE AFTERGLOW

Chapter 25

EXISTENTIALISM

LIFE IS EMPTY AND MEANINGLESS— AND AWESOME!

DURING THE WORST OF MY SHITSHOW, UNFILLED TIME FILLED ME WITH TERROR. THE EMPTY minutes would stretch into hours. The hours felt like they stretched into days.

Emptiness was always difficult for me, but when there was a family and a marriage and a bustling home to fill the days and distract me from the gnawing meaninglessness, I managed to keep my terror at bay. Time alone felt like a gift—a few minutes to myself!—instead of a confusing, disorienting float through the dark vacuum of space.

When the anxiety of empty space got to be too much, I had a time-honored coping method, first developed in college while facing down finals: I would schedule every minute of the day, breaking it into fifteen-minute increments, and methodically grind through it. Scheduling and working became my favorite safety net. I was good at sticking to my plans, because sticking to a plan made me feel like I was getting stuff done and therefore of worth. If I could control every fifteen-minute increment, and schedule those increments carefully to avoid empty moments in which to wonder what I was doing next or who I was, I could pretend I was in control of my life. (Aww, RIP to my illusion of control. Adorable!)

This method of controlling time to cope with anxiety serves some of us well, often for decades. It can make you an excellent student, reliable employee, and efficient parent. In terms of "ways to deal with stress," compulsive productivity can seem like a pretty functional one.

But like any Band-Aid that covers the superficial scratch instead of the root injury, harnessing anxiety this way is unsustainable. A few decades into adulthood, I looked around and saw the ways in which my overscheduling was a functional anxiety-management method with a high cost in terms of flexibility, freedom, health, and joy.

Overfocusing on structure and control to manage anxiety boxes you in, making you a slave to your lists. You end up spackling layers of anxiety on top of each other—schedules! deadlines! calendars!—all to avoid the root injury, the core wound.

. . . Which seems to be this: sometimes being human is uncomfortable. There, I said it.

Should I say it again? Should I shout it?

BEING HUMAN IS UNCOMFORTABLE.

We all have different compensatory ways of dealing with this discomfort, and while some of us try to cope by overscheduling and overworking (me!), others of us try to cope by avoiding our responsibilities altogether. Instead of going anxious and manic with your discomfort (this to-do list will save me!), maybe you go depressive and avoidant with your discomfort (not looking at this to-do list will save me!).

Dr. Piers Steel, professor of motivational psychology at the University of Calgary, says that procrastination is a form of self-harm—not just average laziness. People procrastinate for the same psychological reasons they engage in many other forms of self-harm: seeking the illusion of control over a situation against which they feel powerless. Essentially, overworking and procrastination are both attempts to gain control over an uncontrollable situation—we're all trying to feel in charge, just in opposite-looking ways.

Dr. Fuschia Sirois and Dr. Tim Pychyl, professors of psychology at the University of Sheffield and Carleton University, respectively, say that procrastination happens when you can't manage the negative associations with a given task. Basically, doing that thing has a shitty feeling associated with it, and since that shitty feeling is intolerable, you avoid doing the thing that needs doing to avoid the shittiness.

"Procrastination is an emotion regulation problem, not a time management problem," they explained. Procrastination is about being hyper-focused on "the immediate urgency of managing negative moods" rather than completing tasks.

Whichever way you go, balming uncomfortable emotions with work-arounds and avoidance isn't sustainable. Instead, you must make the agonizing effort to just sit with your most uncomfortable moments. It sounds awful (and it IS awful!), but the effort of hanging out with discomfort is ultimately easier than avoiding it through your dysfunctional work-around of choice.

I'll say it again: being human is uncomfortable. The more you can surrender to that reality, and the less energy you spend finding elaborate ways to avoid the discomfort . . . the less you'll suffer. No one can make things *not* suck, but the games we play to avoid the sucking make our lives suck much, much more.

When my life fell apart, my ambient human discomfort ballooned into a panic so intense that it was physically excruciating. Suddenly, scheduling every minute of my day didn't work anymore. Suddenly, I realized . . . did scheduling *ever* really work? When it comes to avoiding your root misery, every work-around has an expiration date.

What if, instead of avoiding anxiety and fear and discomfort with elaborate multitiered calendars and double-pronged plans (or numbing out, or trying to spackle over it with distractions, or trying to overanalyze it, or whatever your favorite coping mechanism is), *we just let ourselves be uncomfortable for a minute?*

You can run from it, you can schedule around it, you can build whole empires as a way to avoid the reality of the discomfort, but the discomfort will still be there. Even when I built my publishing business, the Offbeat Empire, I still felt uncomfortable. I put a lot of effort and intent into building and creating and cultivating . . . but when the motivation was to avoid discomfort, then of course the results didn't get me any closer to contentment or peace because, duh, the root pain was still there.

Truly, this is a life's work, sitting with the discomforts of being human.

A mindfulness practice is the best tool you've got. You can't stop your brain from doing its particular thing, but at least mindfulness helps you step back and watch from a safe distance.

When you watch for long enough, sometimes you can even see that you could make different choices, instead of just defaulting to the same old mechanisms that your personality tells you are the only way to cope with the discomfort.

At one a.m. on a summer night, I woke up to Tavi crawling into bed with me, clutching his stuffed monkey.

"I can't sleep," he said, curling up in front of me.

"What's going on in your head?" I asked. "Are you feeling scared or sad or nervous?"

"Nervous," he said. "But I'm not sure about what."

"Oh man," I said, squeezing him close. "I hear you on that. I feel like that a lot."

Even as I was starting to bask in my afterglow, I could feel the return of my old familiar friend, Floating Anxiety. It drifted around in my peripheral vision, catching my eye just enough to distract me. It avoided being looked at directly, like all good ego tricks. They're called blind spots for a reason: they're difficult to catch, because your mind doesn't want you to see what it's up to behind that curtain.

Catastrophe had burned off the hardened edges of my personality, but as things settled back down, I could feel the ol' girl re-forming. *Stallings, let's worry about something,* the monkeys whispered from the darkness, bruised and bandaged but ready to get back to doing their job. *If we worry hard enough, then we can DO SOMETHING and feel better.* High-functioning anxiety is a grunt, yo.

Back in bed on that July night, all there was to do was snuggle Tavi close.

"I know that nervous feeling," I said. "But I gotchoo. You're safe. Can you picture all that nervous feeling dribbling down your legs, into your feet, and dripping out your toes? I'm here for you."

I took a breath and felt Tavi twitch to sleep in front of me as I thought, *If the clusterfuck of the past few years burned off the outer defenses of my ego, the new me must continue to dismantle it. I will not pass this anxiety down to my son as a legacy.*

I see you, anxiety. I see you, personality. You're not me. You're just the scaffolding I've built around the existential pain of being human.

MOVING AWAY FROM ANXIETY'S FOSSIL FUELS

"I feel like the crisis has passed, but my stupid floating anxiety is coming back," I told Atta that week. "I'm doing my mindfulness practices, and sometimes they help me feel calmer, which is amazing! But then in that calm, I catch myself thinking, wait, if I get rid of the anxiety, *how am I supposed to get anything done?!*"

Atta laughed. "Yeah, I know that game. It's the fuel you've used for a long time, isn't it?"

"My whole life!" I said. "My whole career! My whole marriage! Anxiety is the fuel that kept me moving, kept me chasing, kept me trying to prove myself, kept me always trying to be better . . ."

"Yeah, but that's the old you," Atta said. "Anxiety is an old fuel from a prehistoric time." His eyes got brighter as he tasted a good metaphor. "Anxiety was your fossil fuel!"

"Anxiety as fossil fuel?" I laughed. "That makes perfect sense—it's totally unsustainable."

"Pollutes the environment," Atta riffed.

"Gunks up the entire engine and all the gears," I said.

"It's extremely expensive," Atta said, and I could tell we were both into this metaphor. "And it causes wars!"

"Anxiety is the crude, dark sludge made from the decomposing bodies of my ancestors!" I shouted, fully invested. "I need to switch to a renewable resource. I need to convert my entire system to a more sustainable fuel!"

"Love," Atta offered.

"Love," I agreed, and started happy crying.

What would our lives look like if we made choices to move toward a sense of abiding internal love instead of moving away from external discomforts?

What if we could finally make peace with the meaningless emptiness and find that it's not empty at all? What if it's awesome, and it's been awesome all along?

FIND YOUR AFTERGLOW

Since a shitshow tends to strip your identity and push your coping mechanisms past capacity, it's a great time to learn about the tricks your ego plays when it's defending itself. Really, that's all your personality is: a defense mechanism. It's not "you."

The more you understand egoic defense tricks, the more compassion you gain for yourself and others. We're all hurting and just trying our best to deal! If you're into this stuff, you may want to read up on the Enneagram, a typology system that gained popularity in the 1970s.

◆ What coping strategies and defense mechanisms used to serve you really well but have caught up with you in ways that might be holding you back? Some favorites: perfectionism, helping others, achieving, feeling special, intellectualizing, being loyal, distraction, controlling others, or opting out.

◆ A crisis enforces drastic life changes, but then as we emerge, sometimes old aspects of our former selves reappear and don't feel like they fit anymore. What aspects of yourself are you ready to let go of because you no longer need them?

◆ What do you feel like your core wound is? What's the bad feeling that you're always trying to avoid? Common wounds include feeling horribly flawed, unlovable, worthless, insignificant, incompetent, unsafe, bored, vulnerable, or invisible. How does understanding that we all wrestle with these core wounds affect how you see the people in your life?

And can we talk about time for a minute? If you've read this book and thought, *Cool story, bro, but I don't have time to do all this shit!*, reconsider how you think about time. When you're mindlessly moving through your life, it is easy to feel like you don't have any time.

Culturally, we love to talk about how we're all so busy (How are you doing? BUSY!) but let's be accountable: *we have plenty of time*. How many hours a day do you spend scrolling on your phone or watching TV? How do you spend your downtime—and how do you feel afterward?

You will find that you have time for what you choose to make time for. As you rebuild your life, be extremely aware of how you're spending your time, especially your downtime. Don't talk about how you don't have enough time, and make the effort to notice the abundance of time in your life. As you talk about time differently, you may notice how your concept of time changes.

You're creating a new life for yourself. Make using your time *consciously* a part of that new life.

Chapter 26

SELF-RELIANCE

AFTERGLOW ACCOUNTABILITY

THE MORE TIME I SPENT WITH THE EMPTINESS, THE MORE I SETTLED INTO BEING RESPONSI-ble for how I dealt with it.

See, here's the thing: in the context of my previous lives (first as a child, and then as a spouse), if there was a bad feeling, I would look outward for someone to help me fix the bad feeling. I used my beloveds as emotional windbreakers and security blankets.

To put it in less kind language: if I felt bad, somehow it was someone else's responsibility.

If something hurt, like many of us, I would look around for someone to help me manage the discomfort. If they couldn't (or wouldn't) help me, then I would get frustrated, disappointed, or impatient.

The first step of my self-reliance process was making my well-being no longer the responsibility of a spouse. Since I felt surprised by my marriage ending, that first step was out of my hands. The pain of the split was so excruciating that my brain just flipped into trauma mode, which effectively hacked off the emotional arm and cauterized the wound. I couldn't really do much but move on as quickly as I could as an emotional amputee. The abruptness was rough on my nervous system, but there's no arguing that it got 'er done quickly.

The second step of the self-reliance process was making NO ONE BUT ME responsible for my moods. So basically, first I gave up on my marriage as a primary source of comfort, and then I gave up on *other humans* being a source of comfort. That sounds awful (I gave up on humanity!), but afterglow accountability actually feels amazing and makes me love humanity more than I did before.

A big part of the process is reparenting. Tiny children (all baby mammals, really!) are dependent on their caregivers to be responsible for them, and inevitably part of childhood is being disappointed when a caregiver fails to attend to your needs in some way. (Not necessarily because of bad parenting but just because . . . *human.*)

Afterglow accountability means releasing the need to blame others for failing you, and instead making the effort to stop failing *yourself.* This means stuff like not getting impatient or irritated with yourself when emotions you don't like come up—like feeling clingy or whiny or needy or sad.

Instead of abandoning yourself in your needy baby mammalian moments, try taking extra-good care of yourself instead. It's on YOU to show up for yourself in the ways that you wish others did. No one else! That's true emotional accountability.

When I was single (which was most of my shitshow), I learned that the times when I was the most desperate for attention and communication from others were the times when I most needed to show up for myself.

The sensation of desperately needing to connect to others was actually an intense cue to connect with myself. The more I pushed the need away or put it on other people, the more I was injuring myself, telling myself I was too this, too that, too unworthy. The more embarrassing and shameful the neediness felt, the more acute was the need for me to take care of myself.

Basically, the calls were coming from inside the house. When I most wanted attention from others was when I most needed to STFU, put my phone down, and take care of myself.

This is all easy enough to say (stop holding others responsible for your discomfort! start parenting yourself!), but the ways it plays out don't feel cute or empowered. Crying at home alone for a couple years doesn't really feel like you're getting anywhere . . . but when you compare it to the years (decades!) you can spend avoiding discomfort by blaming other people for your emotions, those years of crying alone on the floor feel totally worth it.

Afterglow accountability is about bravely confronting discomfort so that you can learn how to sit with it. Those of us who've wrestled with codependence or anxious attachment, lean into those discomforts ALONE so that we can learn how to manage them without trying to control other people.

Because let's be honest: while controlling other people might feel good for a minute ("I told them to do a thing, and they did a thing, and now I feel like I'm in charge!"), it ultimately just externalizes all your good feelings on being able to get people to deliver them.

(UGH! Why did I play this game for so long? "My happiness is reliant on other people accommodating my needs"? What a shaky-ass, terrifying place to be! "My sense of well-being is completely dependent on some other human doing what I tell them to do"?! Yikes.)

Humans are flawed and fundamentally unreliable, not because we're malicious but just because . . . *we're human*. Not that we shouldn't deeply love and trust each other, but having your whole sense of security dependent on your ability to manipulate other people's behavior is a recipe for suffering.

WHAT AFTERGLOW ACCOUNTABILITY LOOKS LIKE WHEN YOU'RE PARTNERED

Self-reliance makes sense when you're single, but as I stumbled into my first significant relationship a few years after my marriage ended, I called on myself over and over again to completely release any control over my partner.

That doesn't mean I excused behavior that was unacceptable to me (I got ninety-nine problems, but boundaries ain't one), but it meant that I alone was accountable for my reactions.

I alone was responsible for figuring out what I needed, and doing it for myself.

I chose not to spend my time negotiating, trying to convince anyone to change their behavior to help me avoid discomforts that were ultimately my responsibility.

Oddly, this doesn't translate into not trusting people—it's the opposite. Because I'm accountable for my own emotional and spiritual needs, I'm able to trust people more because I'm not afraid of them taking my equanimity away from me. It's a paradox, but somehow it works.

When you focus your time on reparenting and learning how to care for your emotional needs, you're in a way better, more whole place to be present in relationship with others, because you're not begging them to accommodate your reactions, trying to control their behavior to dance around your discomforts, or seeking validation from them that you need to build internally.

I now recognize just how much of my marriage (many marriages? *most* marriages?) was about tossing a ball of blame and responsibility back and forth. "I feel bad—YOU DID THIS!" "Hey, it's not my fault you feel bad!" "But this discomfort can't be mine to deal with—here, take it! If you don't take it, I will sit around for hours tonight crying! Don't make me sit around for hours tonight crying!"

Here's my painful truth: I should have sat around for hours crying. I wish I hadn't spent so many years avoiding the tears.

Maturation is painful and rips you open at times.

Tending your wounds can hurt.

Growth comes with loss.

We're all gonna die.

You're dying right now, and you probably need to grieve, and it should be a privilege and honor to hold you as you wail, to witness it with love.

Nothing needs fixing.

It's nobody's fault.

I wish I'd understood that sooner. Feeling uncomfortable isn't bad. Crying for hours isn't necessarily someone's fault. It's natural and healthy and the only way through it is to really do it and stop making it someone else's responsibility.

When you release blame (and it's hard—REALLY HARD), your reward is a surge of power. You can't control what happened, but you have the agency to move forward with intention.

Things hurt. Stop building elaborate defensive scaffolding to make them hurt less. Just sit in the hurt and eventually the hurting shifts, or maybe you shift? I'm unclear on the specifics, but somehow staying present with the pain transmutes it.

Somehow, when you can stop blaming others and avoiding discomfort and you start just sitting with it, holding yourself accountable for your reactions, loving yourself despite your suffering, the emptiness becomes spaciousness and the hurt stops being as painful.

When you stop blaming others and focus on attending to your injuries, you'll feel yourself come into a stronger space of self-reliance.

What happened to you isn't your fault, but it's your responsibility to choose how to heal. I believe in you.

Once you can accept and integrate the loss, you start to find the capacity to send your newfound strength outward. It's like a drop of water going into an ocean, sending out ripples.

FIND YOUR AFTERGLOW

If the early days of a shitshow are all about chewing over the details of your on-ramp, the afterglow is about letting all those stories go and focusing on accountability for how you're moving forward. Your shitshow happened and it sucked . . . but you have the agency to make your afterglow *whatever you want*. You just have to focus on taking care of yourself instead of wasting energy tossing blame balls back and forth with other people.

◆ Where in your life do you most want to blame others? What happens if you allow that culpability to be there while also focusing your mind on where you can be accountable for moving forward?

◆ Can you think of any examples in your life when your choice not to take care of yourself ended up hurting the people around you? How is caring for yourself part of being a good friend, lover, family member, or citizen?

◆ What can you do today, this week, this month, to show compassion toward yourself and take care of your own emotions without blaming others?

◆ And again, watch for your mind's patterns. What stories come up about why you shouldn't have to be accountable? Lots of us find our victim narratives oddly comforting, but when you release blame, you gain power. You can't change what happened, but you get to choose where to go.

When we talk about afterglow accountability, we're NOT talking about doing it all on your own and being a lone wolf. Using isolation as a defense mechanism means you're trying to keep yourself safe by pushing others away—that's not accountability because you're still making your well-being about other people, just in the other direction. Some of us are grabby, some of us are shove-y—the key to accountability is just sitting with what is, without grabbing or shoving.

Chapter 27

COMMUNITY

EYE CONTACT IN SEATTLE

I WANTED TO FEEL MY AFTERGLOW RIPPLES GO OUT A LITTLE FURTHER, SO I STARTED STARing at my neighbors.

Seattleites are terrible with eye contact. So, *so* incredibly bad. It's an aspect of the Seattle Freeze, my city's notoriously passive-aggressive, polite, reserved nature that we've honed into performance art.

We're willing to engage in polite banter, but then we will shut you down if you want anything more than that. One theory is that, as a city, we're too passive to get ourselves out of awkward conversations (we just aren't great at saying "Fuck off, leave me alone"), so we'd rather just avoid getting too far into them.

We won't look at you when we cross paths with you on the sidewalk, but we're happy to give you directions if you ask. We'll smile and wave you off, and then put our earbuds back in and lower our eyes and ignore each other again. We're so, *so* nice, but so, *so* distant.

In the darkest of my shitshow days, I would float down Capitol Hill's streets not needing to blink because I was in a state of almost constant tearing. My social filters were blown, and when I passed people on the street, I would impolitely stare, unblinking, at their faces. I saw a sea of polite urban human suffering. Once I started noticing, it was overwhelming just how many people were shattered.

I'd see them standing in line at Trader Joe's, glazed eyes staring politely into space, and my nose would fill with the heavy smell of loss. Someone's mother just died. Someone just got evicted. Someone just got sued for something they didn't do. Someone is so overwhelmed by the news cycle that they can't sleep through the nightmares of political demagogues and images of polar bears swimming through melting arctic oceans. Someone is on the brink of losing their job and knows it.

Seattle is a prosperous city in a first-world country, and globally speaking, we're a privileged lot. We don't live in a war zone and so many of our lives are relatively good . . . but once I better understood just how pain scars people's faces, I could see everyone's cheeks pockmarked with it. Everyone's been through (or is going through, or is about to go through) a shitshow.

It felt like I was drowning, one nostril above the ocean of grief.

In an emotional moment of nostril-drowning desperation, I decided I would take on a new side project: I would compliment people on the street as much as I possibly could. The founder and owner of my coworking office greets coworkers with a compliment pretty much every day, and it always feels . . . well, *nice!*

The reality is that when you take the two seconds to notice something (that's all you're really doing) and then speak it with a smile, you usually get a smile in return.

A smile! You just made someone feel seen and appreciated.

It's such a simple, mundane thing to take an interest in the people around you and show them appreciation. It's a gratitude practice on a neighborhood level. It felt ridiculous when I first started doing it, but those early shitshow days were so gray and colorless and devoid of pleasure that I'd take any quick hit I could get off that Not-Pain Motel bong.

A neighbor smiling because I complimented their coat? Sharing pleasantries with my playground parent cohort? One less jolt of cortisol in my bloodstream? A shitshow can feel so physically painful, and if exchanging a smile can give you two minutes of physical relief from the icy fires of your own misery? Totally worth it.

Let's pause to remember how many of the sensations of a life crisis are influenced by the chemicals in your body. The short-term stress-release chemicals—serotonin and oxytocin—have a relative called cortisol that the body relies on when our stress is longer-lasting, like when you're dealing with an existential implosion.

Cortisol is the body's stress hormone, and it's produced in the adrenal gland. It regulates sleep, energy, blood pressure, and how your body processes carbs, proteins, and fats. Cortisol is an important tool our bodies use when we're in the thick of it, but if it stays around too long, it can exacerbate your challenges.

A study from the University of Freiburg, Germany, showed that even moderately high levels of increased cortisol sustained for too long can cause sleep disruptions, weight gain, and brain fog, and impair the immune system. These symptoms can then add to your stress, spinning up a vicious cycle.

Reducing levels of cortisol overproduction involves reducing stress in your life—ha ha, no shit, right? The most effective ways to reduce cortisol overproduction include the basics we've talked about all through this book: regulating sleep, getting habitual about relaxation (stretching, breathing exercises), and regular moderate exercise.

But here's another strategy: a study called "It's Not What You Think, It's How You Relate to It" showed that even just *describing* stress in a mindful way was linked to lower cortisol levels.

Let's try this:

◆ Put into words exactly what is making you feel stressed right now. There's nothing too big or too small for this list. Get it all out of your brain and onto paper, or speak it out loud.

◆ Take a belly breath. Can you accept that these stress-ors just *are*? Separate from story making, whether they *should* be, what your life might be like if these things weren't happening, what if you just focus on accepting that, yep, this is what it is. It won't always be this way (everything is temporary, thank fucking god / fucking tragic), but this is what it is right now. Don't fight it. Surrender to it, like it's a huge opera singer spanking your ass. Things just ARE.

◆ Take another breath into your belly and shift your focus to compassion and self-mercy. Acknowledge that all these things feel stressful for a reason! Your feelings are valid and appropriate. (Don't go stabbing yourself with that second arrow, telling yourself you "shouldn't" be stressed. It's appropriate to feel stressed when your life feels catastrophic.)

◆ Now take three breaths and jump around or flap your arms, HARD, to get things moving out. Then grab a drink of water.

You may have just busted some cortisol . . . but at the very least you've got a bit more oxygen in your brain and are better hydrated, so you win.

GETTING A SOLID ROI ON YOUR COMPLIMENTS

In my daily neighborhood gratitude practice, I tried to start small with my compliments.

"Love those boots," I told a lady at the bus stop, and she gave a politely tight grimace.

Huh, I thought. *That was a low ROI on that particular compliment, but it still felt nice there for a moment.* If a polite grimace gave me a 6 on the 1–10 warmheartedness meter, then maybe I could feel better if I could compliment better.

These are important compliment metrics, folks! I wanted to project-manage the shit out of my depression! And yes, this is totally my ego up to its old tricks of strategizing pain management, but oh well. We can't always be perfect.

I knew that complimenting someone's physical appearance was low-hanging fruit—people don't necessarily have a sense of ownership over whatever aspect you're complimenting them on. Your friend with the gorgeous eyes might feel a bit squirmy when you gush about them because, really, it's just about genetics; thanks but whatever.

Instead, you'll get a better ROI from complimenting them on the choice they actively made in selecting a top in that shade because it brings out their eyes. Your friend feels like you've noticed something more specific, and you're complimenting their decisions—not just their genes.

I learned that these genuine compliments, ones that took careful attention and thoughtfulness, had a way better ROI. It was easy enough to practice. I worked my way up from complimenting shoes, slowly getting up to complimenting necklaces and people's hair. As I got bolder, I added campy hand gestures to my compliment repertoire.

"I'm loving everything that's happening here," I said, walking past a fabulously nonbinary person in a body-conscious gold jumpsuit and coordinated vest. I splayed my fingers and waved my arm like a grand old dame, from sky to sidewalk. ". . . Everything!" I crowed over my shoulder, speed-walking on in my orthopedic Adidas high tops. Grand old dame likes everything that's happening here, people! *Everything!* I barely looked back to see what the reaction was, but I'm pretty sure I at least got a smile.

I got more creative and enthusiastic with my compliments. And you know what? The more I did that, the more joy got bounced back. It was thrilling. It was also truly terrifying for a Seattleite. It was vulnerable and brazen at the same time. Making eye contact and speaking to a stranger, out here on the passive streets of Seattle?! Unheard of! I loved it.

COMPLIMENTING OTHERS IS SELF-SERVING (AND THAT'S OKAY)

Walking down the street in Raleigh on my way to dinner after my trip to the firing range, I pointed at a woman's earrings as she walked by. They were enormous raw-brass hoops, and they glowed against her dark skin.

"Those earrings are beyond phenomenal," I called out to her, not slowing down as we passed each other.

"Thank you!" she shouted over her shoulder back at me, laughing. There was no need to get into a whole conversation or take time out of anyone's day—you can just drop a quick compliment and keep on moving!

"Why bother doing that when you'll never see her again?" the gunslinger snarked. "What motivates making the effort?"

"It's not just about her," I said. "It's partially a selfish act. I mean, if you're doing it right, complimenting someone makes *two* people happy—them and me. Complimenting her earrings took me two seconds and made me feel warm and fuzzy for a minute. And those brass hoops were great. Now I want some brass hoops . . ."

Complimenting others enhances our own well-being. Raj Raghunathan, PhD, author of *If You're So Smart, Why Aren't You Happy?*, explained that one of the reasons complimenting others makes you feel better is that it helps you perceive yourself as a generous, bighearted person, which in turn increases your self-esteem.

In contrast, tearing people down with criticism or snark might make you feel superior in the short term, but Raghunathan says that negging others makes you view yourself poorly. These "downward comparisons" have an echo-chamber effect, in that they make others feel negative, which can lead them to criticize *you*. This then can lead to you being more likely to attract critical, unforgiving people. That's a shittiness spiral, which is the last thing you need in your new life.

But complimenting others isn't a completely selfish act. Dr. Alex Lickerman, coauthor of *The Ten Worlds: The New Psychology of Happiness*, tried smiling at and positively engaging with service workers he saw regularly, and discovered that their demeanor seemed to change overall. He observed that workers who'd been reserved or even sullen began to engage more positively and happily with other customers (although Lickerman noted that there was an initial period of feeling like he was weirding out service workers when he was friendly with them).

People who receive compliments are also more likely to give them, just like those who receive criticism are more likely to be critical. So you can think of your compliments as a way of paying it forward and spreading positivity beyond yourself. Again with the ripples!

To be fair, all the complimenting can feel ridiculous at times. Other people work with cancer patients in Uganda while I compliment people in line with me at Ada's Technical Books? On the scale of contributing something of value to the world, my compliments felt small and piddly because they *were* small and piddly.

But I felt like if I turned up my high beams often enough, I could directly transfer a small bit of support to a fellow human. It was a tiny transfer, but if I could just do it enough times, in enough mediums, on enough streets, in enough cities, on enough screens, in enough books . . . if I could just spread enough bits of support, maybe the bits could add up to something more substantial.

Compliments are a very small daily practice, but it's a good practice. It keeps the energy moving ever outward.

FIND YOUR AFTERGLOW

When things feel overwhelmingly big, it's helpful to go very, very small. You want to heal the world? Start with healing yourself. You want to help the world? Start by helping one other person today in a small way.

◆ How does eye contact make you feel? If it makes you feel exposed, vulnerable, or scared, how could you find ways to stay with that discomfort just a moment longer the next time you encounter it? What might shift?

◆ Reflect on some compliments you've received and how they've made you feel. Then, reflect on some compliments you've given and how *they've* made you feel. When might you have opportunities to compliment others?

◆ Where in your life have you felt the pull of the negative spiral, where complaining begot more complaining, where criticism led to more criticism? Given that we can't change others' behaviors, what shifts could you make to get on an upward spiral? How could you give out more of what you wish to receive?

Thinking small about the changes in your life can also help you focus on sustainability. Practicing mindfulness with a five-minute seated meditation every day, most days, is waaaaay more valuable than meditating once for twenty awful minutes, deciding it's too hard, and never doing it again. Dancing around your living room every morning for five minutes for a full month is way more valuable than doing it once for an hour and never again. Remember, you're trying to build a life out of two-minute moments. Think sustainable. Think small. Think gradual. But keep going.

Chapter 28

EPIGENETICS

REUNITING DEAD GRANDMOTHERS

IT ALL STARTED WHEN A BRUNETTE I WAS DATING DIDN'T TEXT ME BACK.

See, here's the thing with the afterglow life: it's equal measures liberating, silly, and profound. When your life splits open and you take it as an invitation to start mucking around in your psyche and your soul, not only does YOUR messy stuff come to the surface, but if you prod enough, you start to uncover messes that aren't even yours.

If you commit to experiencing all the afterglow grist in your personal development mill, you may eventually bump into multigenerational wounds and the trauma of your ancestors. Sometimes a crisis can unlock genetic predispositions that your heritage set you up with, and then surprise! You get to do the healing that your grandparents didn't have the awareness, resources, or capacity to address.

This might seem ethereal or highfalutin or woo-woo. (Oh, ancestral healing! Oh, multigenerational wounds! How precious!) But there's science behind it, and when it's playing out in your life, it doesn't feel especially precious. It doesn't look like sparkly times at an altar or waving some incense around . . . for me, a profound moment looked like pacing around my home *a-fucking-gain*, freaking out over an unanswered text.

On that particular day a couple years into my shitshow, I was waiting to hear back from a choreographer about our date that night. Several of my texts had gone unanswered, and I was starting to feel the anxiety circling.

Why does this always happen to me? Why do I always feel like I'm chasing people and begging for their attention? Why does everyone always reject me? Why am I always abandoned? Why am I so unworthy?! Why will I die alone?!

Whoa. Hold on. You know that when the monkeys start screaming about how "this always happens," your brain is up to some bullshit. That's a clue that you're looping on an internal script, a story that only you can rewrite.

I stopped, took a breath. I tried to feel my feet on the floor. Tried to recognize that my ego was telling me its very favorite story (aww, it's the rejection bus, *beep beep!*) and waving at me to get on board. I took another breath. *In this moment, there's a lot of attachment anxiety in the system.* I tried to watch the bus go by.

I'd been preparing for this kind of thing. I knew what I needed to do.

The month before, a book had shouted at me from Atta's shelf: *It Didn't Start with You* by Mark Wolynn. I noticed because I was trying to listen more.

"That's what it feels like sometimes," I said, pointing at the book. "Like this needy, clingy, anxious behavior comes out of me but it doesn't make any sense and isn't even mine."

"I haven't had a chance to read this yet," Atta said, pulling the receipt out from between the uncreased pages of the book. "Do you want to borrow it first?"

"Yes," I said, greedily taking it out of his hands.

Mark Wolynn's book deals with the concept of epigenetics, an emerging field of study that bridges biology, neuroscience, and psychiatry. Epigeneticists study how DNA transmits information to best prepare you for the life you're about to live based on the environment you're born into.

While phrases like "multigenerational family dynamics" might seem new age, epigenetics attempts to take the concept into the realm of hard science. Researcher and professor of psychiatry and neuroscience Rachel Yehuda posits that genetic changes prepare us biologically to manage the crises and traumas that we may deal with based on what our parents and grandparents experienced.

From an epigenetic perspective, you're born with a unique biological skill set to help you navigate your life. This is awesome, because this environmental resilience helps each of us roll with stressful situations that show up. But the adaptations can also be a burden, since the coping tools your grandparents needed may not be relevant to your life, but may still show up for you—especially when triggered by a traumatic event.

Lots of us like to blame our parents for our problems, but *It Didn't Start with You* suggests looking for fractures further back in your lineage. Through the lens of epigenetics, you can consider where you may have inherited challenges from your grandparents, or ancestors even further back. Wolynn suggests thinking back on extended family members you felt most connected to, whom you felt a unique bond with. In my life, all the arrows pointed to my paternal grandmother, Grandma Becky.

I'm an only child, and my father is also an only child. His mother, my grandma Becky, was herself an only child. My son is also an only child, and we like to joke that with these four generations, the Stallings family tree is really more of a family stick.

Despite living several states away, I was always close with Grandma Becky, and we were weekly pen pals from the time I could write until she died in my midtwenties. She was born and raised in Tennessee, a southern belle who suffered through a series of losses: first her mother abruptly dying when she was four, then her husband abruptly dying in her midthirties. Widowed with a small child, she then married a physically abusive man.

Grandma Becky did the best she could, getting a teaching degree and escaping her abusive husband. She settled into a long career as a fifth-grade teacher, eventually married a third time, and enjoyed a quiet retirement watching *The Price Is Right*, reading *Reader's Digest*, and keeping in touch with her nerdy, wordy only granddaughter who sent long letters every other week.

A few years before she died in her late eighties, she told me and my father, "I made my worst mistakes because I was so afraid of being alone."

Somehow, I knew that the abandonment fear that I couldn't shake, the worthlessness that stuck to me even when I was winning, the self-esteem issues that had followed me around despite all the love in my life, they went back to my grandma Becky.

. . . And I'd be damned if I was going to pass them on to my son, so I called my father. "Dad," I said. "Don't I remember you saying that you have some boxes of leftover stuff from when Grandma Becky died?"

He did, and so we spent a couple days sorting through beautiful photos of my grandmother in her younger years as a finger-waved, wide-eyed, pixie-faced debutante. We flipped through my grandmother's baby book, made by an auntie after my great-grandmother had died.

The baby book included a newspaper clipping about Grandma Becky's second birthday party, with thirty children in attendance and descriptions of lavish buffets and ice cream sundaes. Her father owned Humboldt, Tennessee's biggest sporting goods store, and her mother was a piano composer who did quite well for herself. The baby book also included handwritten stories of how my grandmother would sit on her mother's lap while she composed, and that little Becky's favorite song was called "Just a Baby's Prayer at Twilight."

My great-grandmother died when Grandma Becky was four, taken down in thirty-six hours by the 1918 flu pandemic. My grandmother went from being the most spoiled kid in town to being a heartbroken little girl with a distant, grieving father.

With my father, I had cried over my grandmother's baby book, feeling a preschooler's horror of suddenly losing her mother, knowing that a child would be convinced that somehow it was her fault. I made a note of the song my great-grandmother had played for my grandmother as a child. I wasn't sure why it mattered yet, but I searched the web for the song, found a scratchy version on YouTube, and bookmarked it.

Back at my house a month later, pacing and panicking over unanswered texts, I tried to get my shit together so I could take care of myself and my grandmother.

I turned off my phone and put it away. My brain was screaming at me that I should send another text message, but I understood that this panic wasn't going to be solved by that brunette. Anxiety tells me to desperately claw outward for relief, but I was trying to learn to just be quiet and look inward.

I cued up "Just a Baby's Prayer at Twilight," the song that my great-grandmother had played on the piano for my grandmother. I put it on repeat. Then I swaddled myself in a blanket, curled tightly into a ball, and cried, listening to old-timey music.

I tried to stay with the terrible feeling in my body—loss, abandonment, fear, worthlessness. The feeling told me that if I felt alone, it was absolutely my fault. The feeling said that if someone wasn't there for me, it was because I was to blame. I cried more. The song started over.

What if these were my grandmother's feelings, expressing through me? Trapped in my body in layers of flesh and tissue and one hundred years and three generations, unlocked by my shit-show, what if these feelings were a four-year-old's emotions from unexpectedly losing her mother? What if these feelings weren't about an unanswered text . . . but my grandmother's unanswered grief?

I closed my eyes and tried to speak softly to my grandmother, this sobbing preschooler inside of me.

"It wasn't your fault," I reassured her. "She didn't want to leave you. She would have done anything to stay with you."

The song started playing again. In that moment, I was a woman in my forties swaddled in a blanket sobbing over my great-grandmother's death (but also an unanswered text?). As always, it was a little shameful (*This is my life now? When did I become this person!?*), but I was learning to stay with the discomfort.

A vision of DNA strands settled in behind my eyes. In that moment, I understood how my grandmother and her mother were both inside me, entwined in the genetics of my body. I saw the spirals of my own DNA, the pieces coiled around each other, and imagined my great-grandmother and my grandmother reunited within me.

We can do this together, I thought to myself, and to them. *We can heal this.*

I imagined the strands hugging each other, felt the broken bond of a mother and child reconnecting, tried to stay out of the way and just be the container for the reunion. It didn't start with me, and it wasn't really about me. I fell asleep tangled in visions of the spiraled DNA, embodying the reunion of energies that had been separated too soon.

I woke up an hour later still swaddled, face crusted, and feeling more whole. Unanswered texts no longer mattered.

THE COLLECTIVE UNCONSCIOUS

It might have felt new to me, but I'm far from the only one to use personal healing in this way. As L'Erin Alta, a mystic and medicine woman from Oakland, explained to me, "My healing is inextricably connected to that of my ancestors, elders, the earth and those yet to come. By taking time and making space to center my own healing, I honor those of my lineage who didn't have the time, energy, opportunity or know-how to do it themselves. I draw on their wisdom, tools, and medicine as a means to heal myself, and subsequently the collective. By healing myself, I am also healing centuries of compounded traumas so that future generations don't have to."

Epigenetics is just one take on the concept of "it didn't start with you." The idea of the collective unconscious, notably defined by psychoanalyst Carl Jung, is a way of looking at how parts of our deep unconscious has been inherited. According to Jung, the collective unconscious (sometimes called the objective psyche) is responsible for instincts, beliefs, and stuff like spirituality, sexual behavior, and phobias.

Good ol' Eckhart Tolle (beloved by Oprah and metalheads at the bar!) addresses a similar concept, which he calls "the pain-body." He describes it as "the accumulation of old emotional pain that almost all people carry. . . . There is also a collective human pain-body containing the pain suffered by countless human beings throughout history."

Jung's and Tolle's theories are regarded to be more symbolic than scientific, but new studies of gut bacteria might lend credence to a scientific collective unconscious. The genes in gut bacteria (which number more than the genes in our bodies!) may produce neuroactive compounds that could regulate human behavior. These might be, in essence, the collective unconscious. Basically, you're sad because the bacteria are sad. It's okay.

Symbolically, the idea of collective unconscious can be applied to cultural behaviors, too. One example is the concept of *han*—essentially a form of grief and resentment—in Korean culture. *Han*'s origins stem from the Japanese occupation of Korea. Sandra So Hee Chi Kim explains in her article "Korean *Han* and the Postcolonial Afterlives of 'The Beauty of Sorrow,'" "The insistence on the uniqueness of *han* to the Korean people has a biologistic element to it—if one is Korean, one is born with *han* and cannot escape it."

Epigenetics, biology, physiology, psychology, culture, and symbolism intertwine through grief, so it makes sense to acknowledge all of them as you wind through your afterglow process.

I'm certainly not suggesting that my great-grandmother's death is anything on the scale of the horrors that much of epigenetics research focuses on. But as researcher Rachel Yehuda says, "What we look for, when we study the impact of a trauma, is how big the event is compared to what usually goes on for a person . . . this overwhelming change is what resets and recalibrates multiple biologic systems in an enduring way."

A trauma response is a trauma response, and the reality is that everyone's family is overflowing with them—horrific abuses, mental illness, child abandonment, violent deaths, on and on. You can likely think of at least a half-dozen traumas in your immediate family. Bodies and nervous systems do the best they can to manage the input effectively, and part of that management is your nervous system unlocking your genetic predispositions.

It's important to understand how a shitshow can unleash not just your own immediate reaction, but also trigger some epigenetic reaction. It's like the worst kind of achievement unlocked.

These weak spots can bring up a lot of shame (what kind of feeble creature am I, clutching my phone hyperventilating because someone didn't text me back?!), but try this: take a belly breath, feel your feet on the ground, and remind yourself that you're working with the genes and stories you inherited. For me, I had to understand that the epigenetic babies inside me are understandably sensitive to losing people. We've lost a lot of people.

Ultimately, each embarrassing trigger and shameful pain can become an invitation to send some love and healing on up the lineage, for all those in your family who didn't have the resources or the ability to manage the pain.

Reframing personal challenges as part of a larger system of multigenerational care can make it easier to have compassion for how difficult a situation feels. For me, when I stopped shouting at myself inside my own head for being an overwrought needy disaster (*Stop whining, Stallings!*) and shifted instead to seeing how I was acting out the pain of my grandmother, I was able to feel more compassion. Compassion both for myself, and for all of us who are stumbling along, trying to do our best to heal ourselves and our families and our communities and our worlds.

The next time you find yourself triggered ("This always happens to me!" is your best clue), stop looking outside for a solution or an answer or someone to blame. Don't send that text message.

Go internal. Hold yourself afterglow accountable. Attend to the hurts. Grieve the losses, even if they weren't yours. Stay with your discomforts, loving them like upset children.

Wrap your pain in a blanket, play it music, and allow it to be felt. Comfort it, in the name of all your ancestors who didn't have the time or capacity to feel it, and all those in the future who hopefully will have a lighter burden.

It might feel silly in the moment, but it's important to send those afterglow ripples out even further, through time, back into the lineage.

FIND YOUR AFTERGLOW

Hoo-doggies, we are *in it* now, aren't we? If your loss feels bigger than you at times, that's because it might be. Remember all that talk of nonduality a few chapters back? We're all just individual expressions of these larger systems, and the most immediate systems are our family lines.

◆ What are the stories of tragedy and loss in your family? What traumas have your parents, grandparents, and ancestors survived? When you think of them, how do these stories feel in your body? How might you give some time to these unattended sorrows? How might you move them out of your body?

◆ What triggers do you have in your life where a small input like an unanswered text causes a disproportionate reaction? Where might those feelings really be coming from? How can you address the root feelings more directly?

◆ How might the ways that you're working to be accountable and attend to your own hurts have an impact on your interactions with others? When you stop externalizing your pain and start taking ownership for tending to it, how does it change your relationships with friends, family members, or partners?

Epigenetics is a relatively new and evolving field, and if this stuff piques your interest, it's a great rabbit hole to go down. The more you understand about how your unhealed family issues have affected you, the more you can do to hopefully prevent inflicting *your* issues on others.

Chapter 29

SERVICE

HEAL IT FORWARD

I COULD FEEL MY RIPPLES CONTINUING EVER OUTWARD . . . FROM MY CENTER OF AFTERGLOW accountability, out of my home into my neighborhood, out through my family and back to my ancestors. The expansiveness felt intoxicating, so on the anniversary of my marriage ending, I decided to celebrate. It was one of Tavi's weekends with his dad, so why not?

It started with a lovely Friday night lady-dinner with Ashlee, and I was super excited to tell her about a thing I had been grinding on for months: how to tell the difference between intuition and anxiety.

"I think I finally got it!" I shouted, my mouth full of burger at the bar of Smith, the taxidermized animal heads on the wall unfazed by me waving my arms around yet again. "Intuition is when your body *just knows*, and anxiety is just your head *thinking* it knows when it totally doesn't."

Ashlee nodded as she took a sip of her wine. She was quiet tonight.

"My body knows things, but my brain really has no idea," I continued, waving my burger at her. "Now I'm understanding that if I get a *physical* intuitive hit, I need to listen. If it's just a mental loop, I can note it and let it pass by."

"Sounds like a great new tool for that never-ending loss training," Ashlee teased.

"I'm sorry I'm talking so much," I said, stopping myself and trying to listen with my whole body. "What's up for you this week?"

"I think I'm moving out of the house," Ashlee said, eyes filling with tears. "We've been trying for so long, but I think the marriage is just over."

"Oh no," I said, reaching across the table to hold her hand. It just keeps happening.

We went back to my house and talked for hours. This might not sound like a way to celebrate, but after a shitshow, things get tangled up . . . the joy and the loss aren't opposites anymore. It's all just life, and it just keeps on happening.

You may find yourself in the arms of a wonderful new lover, feeling heartbreak. The neighborhood cemetery may become your happiest place. And even in the pain of a friend's marriage collapsing, you may feel the beauty of their growth. Ashlee was one of my strongest, stiffest-upper-lip lady friends, and it was an honor to hold her while she cried, and help her carry some of the burden as she groped her way through the darkness.

INTUITIVE TECHNOLOGY

In his classic self-defense book *The Gift of Fear*, security specialist Gavin de Becker posits that intuition has gotten a bad rap. Intuition, he says, is just "knowing without knowing why."

We often dismiss our intuition because we think conscious thought is somehow superior. We think of intuition as mystical or magical, when in actuality it's our brains working so quietly and efficiently to notice things (body language, turns of phrase, things feeling *off*) that we don't even consciously recognize that we've noticed them. In the absence of knowing *why* you know certain things, you sometimes dismiss your own knowing.

"Intuition is usually looked upon by us thoughtful Western beings with contempt," de Becker explains. "It is often described as emotional, unreasonable, or inexplicable. . . . If intuition is used by a woman to explain some choice she made or a concern she can't let go of, men roll their eyes and write it off."

My intuition speaks to me through my body—I'll have physical responses like butterflies in my stomach, tingling in my legs, or my arm hair standing up. These sensations often tell me more about what's *actually* happening than my brain does, because my mind is usually too busy storytelling to notice. Some people call this kind of physical intuitive sensation "clairsentience," but it's just one of many different ways we have of knowing what we know, without knowing how we know it.

The Saturday of my shitshow-iversary weekend, I spent the day completely alone and enraptured by it. Tea! Journaling! Meditations! Dancing! Sweating! Smoking weed! Walking under an umbrella and paying attention to how my feet felt on the ground! Long showers with scalding water! More writing! Conjuring! Contemplating clairsentience, interpersonal dynamics, strength, and vulnerability! Just my new-usual Saturday things.

This was the type of day that used to feel like the worst kind of punishment. Now a wide-open Saturday (where literally the only thing on my calendar was "7 pm: Floss") felt like a delight! It was the rainy-day in-home staycation version of my trip out to the coast. These days of sacred solitude had become my favorites.

The next day of my shitshow-iversary, I spent the morning grocery shopping, first at Trader Joe's and then at the Capitol Hill farmers market. On my way to the farmers market, who should walk down the opposite side of the street from me but . . . MY SON! And his father! A few months earlier, this would have sent a jolt of adrenaline and fight-or-flight panic through my nervous system.

Instead I was just like, "Oh, hey, guys! How's it going? Tavi, I see happy chocolate all over your face, so lemme guess, were you at the bakery? Yeah, I'm headed to the farmers market. Okay, see you later!"

It was no big deal.

I internally high-fived myself for the milestone. Atta wasn't around, so as I walked down the street, I mimed peeling a little gold star sticker and sticking it on my hand. I gave myself a nod. GOOD JOB.

AIN'T NO PARTY LIKE A SHITSHOW PARTY!

We're a few years now into the trend of marking divorces and separations with a kind of reverse bachelor/bachelorette-party-type celebration. Delineating a specific end and celebrating a fresh start can be a loving way to move into your new normal.

Marriage and family therapist Renee Beck explains, "To really bring closure, as humans, we go back and look at what happened. Marriage is initiated with a very special energy. For a relationship that started that way to end without any formal marking is sad, and can make it really difficult."

Any major transition could benefit from this mind frame, though. Isn't it worth honoring the feelings you had when a door opened and acknowledging the emotions now that it's closed? Isn't it worth taking the time to recognize *all* the big transitions?

As for me, I decided to have a little happy-hour house rewarming party. It wasn't anything fancy: I invited over about twenty friends and neighbors for some hot toddies from the kitchen stove, joints on the balcony for those who wanted, and a snack spread of protein and produce. My excuse for the house rewarming was celebrating a year since my home had its, uh, *drastic shift* . . . it was sort of the unspoken theme of the evening: celebrating making it through a year, with some of the folks who helped me do it.

Friends rolled through for a hot toddy and a stretch at the barre. My endless piles of self-development books were on every table, shelf, and the back of the toilet, and provided no shortage of cocktail conversation.

"Oh, that one? It's about how you can hack your neurotransmitters to battle depression. This one? It's about how you can manage your attachment disorders so that your family-of-origin wounds don't chase you into toxic adult relationships. Oh, and that Jett Psaris one is all about the hidden blessings of a midlife crisis! 'A part of us has to die to transform; and a part of us dies if we don't. Which part will prevail?' Man, that's good shit!"

I seemed to have lost all capacity for small talk, and cocktail convo included stuff like, "Oh jeez, I totally hear you on feeling so stressed out all the time! I wonder, are there any ways that you've benefited from being stressed so now it's a pattern? Like, you keep yourself stressed to keep yourself moving?" Friends didn't always appreciate my probing questions ("Can I just drink my hot toddy without you analyzing me!?"), and I resolved for the thousandth time to listen more, talk less . . . once you acclimate to digging deeper, sometimes it's hard to put the shovel down!

Spirits were high, but we were all struggling and doing the best we could to let the struggle buses go by. I wasn't the only one who'd started a meditation practice, because it was late 2016 and everyone was terrified of the state of the country and the planet . . . not to mention our crumbling lives, decomposing bodies, and interpersonal tragedies.

"I'm so terrible at meditating," my friend Nicky told me in the kitchen, holding her hot toddy.

"ME TOO!" I squealed. "How do *you* suck at meditation?"

"I sit there and think, 'Oh, look at me, I'm so spiritual! I'm doing so well!'" Nicky said, mocking herself with a silly voice.

"That's the opposite of what you're supposed to do. That's not meditation!"

"Ooh, fascinating," I said. "So your brain goes to pride and sanctimonious righteousness! What an interesting thing. My brain doesn't go there—instead it's like, 'God, you're so distractible! You're terrible at this! Why can't you just settle down?' It sounds like you suck as much as me, which means as long as you keep doing it and keep observing how much you suck at it, YOU'RE DOING IT RIGHT!"

Eventually, after a few too many hot toddies, I gathered everyone in the living room.

"I just want to thank all of you who've supported me as I've struggled through this past year," I said, getting teary again, which everyone was used to. But a damp thank-you didn't feel like enough. These were the people who'd healed me, who'd read me poetry and held my hand while I sobbed in bed, these were people who'd delivered groceries for me when I could barely walk.

"I don't know how to say thank you enough, so maybe I'll do this new-age stripper move that Inga taught me as a demonstration of my appreciation . . ."

And I did. I danced my thank-yous. But lap dances for my friends were never going to be enough. My afterglow ripples kept expanding, and I kept expanding with them.

Then I read this passage, in adrienne maree brown's book *Pleasure Activism*:

BUILD COMMUNITIES OF CARE

Shift from individual transactions for self-care to collective transformation. Be in community with healers in our lives. Healers, we must make sure our gifts are available and accessible to those growing and changing our communities. Be in family with each other—offer the love and care we can, receive the love and care we need. Share your car or meals with a healer in exchange for Reiki sessions. Facilitate a healing group in exchange for massages. Clean a healer's home as barter for a ritual to move through grief. Pay healing forward—buy sessions for friends. Let our lives be a practice ground where we're learning to generate the abundance of love and care we, as a species, are longing for.

. . . Commit to developing an unflappable devotion to yourself as part of an abundant, loving whole. Make a commitment with five people to be more honest with each other, heal together, change together, and become a community of care that can grow to hold us all.

I underlined "Pay healing forward" twice, heavily.

Now, this—THIS is what I'm talking about! Yes to being accountable and then sending my ripples out into my neighborhood and back into my family line and out into my immediate circle of friends—these were all good and loving ways to spread the healing. But this concept of healing it forward? THAT'S what I wanted my new life to be about.

I'm not alone in feeling an afterglow pull to service. Once you make it through a shitshow, you may want to spread your healing outward, in part as a way to amplify it.

A study by Stephen G. Post from Case Western Reserve University showed that being altruistic and compassionate for others correlates with a sense of well-being, health, and happiness. (Kinda like the opposite of the symptoms of adjustment disorder, yeah?) Studies have consistently shown that those who volunteer have lower instances of depression, and that spending money on others predicts an increase in happiness over spending it on yourself.

Another study, this one by Soyoung Q. Park et al. at the University of Lübeck, Germany, showed that there is an actual neural link between happiness and generosity. Using fMRI studies, the research team showed that donating money to charities boots up the same parts of the brain that correspond to rewards or sex. It even showed that just the *intention* of being generous can stimulate neural change and increase happiness.

My therapy budget was redirected again. Honestly, I didn't need much therapy anymore—I could do myself just fine with some old-timey music and a blanket and imaginary gold stickers, you know?

As a good West Coast progressive who already had monthly donations going to Planned Parenthood and the ACLU and National Bail Out, it wasn't like I wasn't putting my money into philanthropy, but I knew I could do better. I mean, sure I'm just a middle-class self-employed single mom, but I could *still* do better. I could heal it forward more.

I called my moms out at Sacred Groves to set up an ongoing scholarship for their grief retreats, so that I could pay the way for someone without the resources to attend.

I contacted each of the healers who'd helped me and offered to pay for a session for them to see *their* favorite healers.

I reached out to my favorite young queer artists, offering them the gift of free massage therapy or talk therapy, or hair removal during their gender transition, or whatever modality worked for them. "I know how much creation comes from hurt," I said. "I want to support you in feeling healthy as a way to support you making more art!"

I organized a fundraiser for a nonprofit clinic for sex workers— because if I learned anything from getting Reiki spanked by an opera singer who had no idea WTF he was doing, it's that when it comes to therapeutic BDSM, you're waaaaay wiser to go for pros before bros—and those pros deserve access to health care and social services.

I started Venmo-ing money monthly to folks working in the social justice activist trenches, sending money to the people of color doing the backbreaking emotional labor of trying to educate white women like myself about how we benefit from systemic racism and complicitly support white supremacy. Now those folks are doing the *work*, and it was my honor to be able to contribute to their therapeutic budgets, or self-care facials, or whatever made them feel strong. It's all therapy.

Wait, is writing about this a form of virtue signaling? On the one hand, I don't care—if my sharing inspires you to do something similar, spreading your own ripples and creating your own communities of care, then I'll risk looking like an asshole. On the other hand, I also resolve to talk less, heal it forward more.

Even years into your afterglow, you'll keep seeing the tricks your ego plays on you, keep rediscovering the ways you still need to surrender, keep finding ever more ways to stay humble and release control and find faith and trust . . .

. . . But you'll also notice when you feel solid enough that you're able to heal it forward. Moving through this new life, it's clear that the only way we're going to get anywhere in our friendships, in our partnerships, in our families, in our communities, in our struggling countries, and on this ever-warming planet, is by healing internally first and then rippling that healing outward.

This book is one more ripple.

FIND YOUR AFTERGLOW

And so now you know that these probing Find Your Afterglow questions aren't just something I do in this book, they're something that I do in my daily life . . . sometimes much to the irritation of my ever-patient friends. I can't help it: I have questions, and I want to know more about how people grow through holding themselves accountable! I ask because I want to learn more about how we can all grow more together!

- ◆ How does YOUR intuition show up? Do you feel it in your body, see things in your mind, or hear things?

- ◆ Reflect on blessings in disguise from your past, or those of people you know. How did it look in the thick of your shitshow, and how do things look now?

- ◆ How could you "heal it forward" in your own life? What does building a community of care look like in your world? Remember, think small and accessible for now. What small steps could you take today to spread a ripple outward? Consider how a step today might be the first of a long journey.

One more thing: as you move out of your shitshow and fully into your afterglow, you may find yourself having a hint of grief at the loss of your shitshow. At first, healing feels awful, but as you sink into it, it can become a centerpiece of your life . . . so much so that, when you're settling back down, you might feel a little disoriented (again!). Let that identity go, too—you had your shitshow. You don't need to stay there. You can have closure and move forward.

Chapter 30

CLOSURE

SET SOME SHIT ON FIRE

WE'VE ALMOST REACHED THE END, SWEET FRIEND. BEFORE WE DO, THOUGH, JUST FOR A minute let's go back to a New Year's Eve I spent out on Bainbridge Island, at my mom's house.

"Maybe you should have a bonfire to burn away your tough year," my mom had suggested, and I found myself nodding instead of rolling my eyes. Sure, a bonfire ceremony. Maybe that would help. I didn't know anymore. What the hell, right?

I sang my son to sleep in his *My Little Pony* pajamas and tucked him in under the Goodwill comforter in the roundhouse guest room. I pulled on my heavy coat and walked with a flashlight through the forest to the meadow clearing on my mom's property. I was headed for the fire circle.

I squatted down next to the firepit and crumpled newspapers and laid the kindling, which proved to be dry and burned bright once lit. I settled back on my haunches, pulled out paper and a Sharpie that my mother had given me, and started writing words on each scrap.

On the first piece of paper, I wrote out OVARY.

"That shit exploded," I said out loud to the dark trees that circled the meadow. "But we had a good run, ovary. We had a solid thirty-nine years together. Thank you for your years of ovulation and bringing me my son. I love you. I'm sorry. Goodbye."

Then I tossed the OVARY slip of paper into the bonfire, where it curled up and blackened. That ovary had given me more than my son, actually—its explosion had woken me to my own mortality, an awareness that would become the motivation I needed to finally start paying attention to my body. My awareness of death had given me a better life.

I pulled out the next piece of paper, uncapped the Sharpie again, and wrote in all caps: INNOCENCE OF YOUTH.

"I went from a healthy, married thirtysomething to a frightened fortysomething in a blink. Bye, innocence of youth! I'm glad I enjoyed you as long as I did, but here I am now: older and better prepared for shit."

INNOCENCE OF YOUTH fell into the bonfire, becoming quick ash. I watched the fire burn and imagined my life as a mountain. What a sweet ascent I'd had up the slope of the first half of my life! I stood at midlife, enjoying the vista, and imagined myself gleefully sledding down the second half toward death. I was learning that losing youth is the price of admission for gaining wisdom.

I wrote phrases like SHARED PLOTLINE that might make sense only to a writer going through a divorce, and ones that make sense to anyone, like BLIND TRUST. I tossed BLIND TRUST on the fire and watched it turn to ash. I was learning about a new level of eyes-wide-open trust that went way beyond that lost partnership, way beyond the concept of marriage, way beyond humans. I was learning about faith.

I scribbled out ABANDONMENT STORY.

"I have to let this one go, too—sure, my husband left, but so many people have stepped in to show me that I'm not alone." I was learning that my abandonment story was an old family script repeated through generations that I'd internalized and kept whispering quietly to myself, like the worst bedtime story. I was learning how to heal things up the lineage.

I was learning.

By this point, the bonfire was tall and roaring, the flames fueled by all the emotions being released. Exhilarated and terrified, I got to the last piece of paper and wrote on it, pressing so hard that the Sharpie ink soaked through the paper and onto my pants: MY FORMER LIFE.

I tossed MY FORMER LIFE on top of the fire, which crackled its accompaniment as the flames climbed high into the cold gray Pacific Northwest sky.

It blazed, and my heart ached and glowed—broken, but also cracked open. Something new and remarkable was shining from the embers of my worst year ever.

CLEANSE IT WITH FIRE

Fire rituals go back millennia and are pretty much ubiquitous worldwide, from Sanskrit *homa* and Aztec New Fire ceremonies to Beltane bonfires and Burning Man. Many of these rituals focus on themes of sacrifice, devotion, and offerings, and having a personal fire ritual can be a great way to transition from your shitshow into your afterglow, helping you tap into the sensation of transformation that humans have harnessed for millennia. Think of it as a cross-cultural, nondenominational form of historical healing.

If you don't have access to a bonfire, a small flame can give you a sense of purification and empowerment. Even just a single candle can symbolize letting go of the past. As the candle burns down and melts, your connections to the past and your previous life can rise and move on in the smoke. You can tailor a closure fire ritual to be as woo-woo or matter-of-fact as you want—if you're not into the spiritual aspect, just think of it as an exercise in burning away your old life.

All you need is a fireproof receptacle (which could be as small as a glass tealight holder), some paper, and a pen. If you can do this outside, great, but inside works too as long as you've got a safe spot. Duh alert: make sure to practice fire safety while you burn things, and never ever leave flames unattended.

Then, try this:

◆ Take a piece of paper and write down something that represents your shitshow.

◆ Speak the phrase out loud, and then set the piece of paper aflame.

◆ Say goodbye.

◆ Focus your attention on the flames, and on feeling any sensations that arise in your body.

◆ Repeat the process with other phrases that capture your shitshow.

◆ After you've burned your last word, let the ashes cool, staying focused on how your body feels.

◆ After the ashes have cooled, you can toss them into the wind, bury them, or scatter them, all while saying one more goodbye and reflecting on all that you're learning.

BURNING AND LEARNING

Seriously, I *know* it burns, but you're learning so much! If you want to glean everything you can from your shitshow, you have to fully experience the friction between that burn of what you've lost (*feel all the feels!*) and the sweet release of feeling wide open to the unknown joy of what's to come (*heal all the heals!*).

That singe of loss is real, though. I mean, your old life may not have been perfect, but it was *yours* and you probably felt like you knew it. You knew its shapes and you knew its drawbacks. Even the crappy parts were familiar, like an old security blanket. Your coping mechanisms may have been threadbare, but they worked . . . until they didn't. That loss is real.

But the release and liberation of opening to your new life is *also* real! When you commit to really finding that afterglow, you can weave a new life that crackles and sparks with awareness and gratitude. Holy shit, you're not dead today! You're learning things! You're becoming a new person right now in this moment, even when it hurts! (. . . *Especially* when it hurts?) You are doing the damn thing!

This doesn't change the fact that the loss is still a loss. I know the monkeys might whisper that you're alone, that no one understands, that your road is steeper than anyone else's, that you're on your own. But please, please hear this: *you are not alone.* I'm right here with you, feeling you here with me close in these words, feeling my way along with you, cheering you on.

Your new life is already there for you, just waiting for you to live. Your afterglow is blazing inside you right fucking now! If you get quiet enough, you can feel it moving in you. If you can just stay awake enough to actually notice those two-minute moments of not-pain, you'll start to feel it.

You'll feel it when you notice the breath moving in and out of your lungs. You'll feel it in the drop of pee that sneaks out during an unexpected belly laugh. You'll feel it in that little burst of energy after you make a choice about how to move forward, and then do it. That's agency! That's momentum! It's happening!

You'll feel your afterglow when a raw conversation with some new person gives you a zap of insight and shifts your perspective. You might feel it when you're out on a weirdest date ever, or when you're at home alone writhing on your bedroom floor. The afterglow feels like joy, it feels like relief (who needed that old life?), it feels like expansiveness and horizons leaning forward. It feels like being blindsided by the thing you were the most afraid of and somehow still being alive . . . more than alive. Awake!

If you can be brave enough to make new mistakes, you can create this new life. If you can hold yourself accountable for attending to and loving all those pieces of yourself you've been ignoring and avoiding for years, you'll find that wide-open freedom feeling of new selfhood. This new afterglow version of you is *way* beyond anything your old self in your old life could have imagined.

Seriously, I know a shitshow sucks, but I am so, *so* excited about what's coming for you . . . a new life that can be filled with depth and joy and maybe the whiff of a survivor's high. You're going to make it!

How do I know you can do it? *Because you're already doing it!* Right now in this moment, if you're here with me, facing your unknowns and finding just the tiniest seed of trust that somehow your life could be starting to glow? You're fucking doing it! Even when it's uncomfortable (*especially* when it's uncomfortable), you're moving forward into your new life.

I can't wait to see how you glow.

DISMANTLED AND WIDE AWAKE

I WAS IN PORTLAND, STANDING IN A WAREHOUSE FILLED WITH INFLATABLE BOUNCY CASTLES and slides, surrounded by dozens of first graders screaming with glee.

"If you're like me," my former brother-in-law said, "your weeks are pretty similar; they just sort of slide by." (Our kids are still cousins, and we're still pals.)

"Oh yeah, they totally used to be like that," I said. "I had all my systems in place, and the weeks were smooth and time slipped by . . . but now life doesn't slide like that."

Surrounded by black lights and exhausted parents chasing shrieking children, it wasn't the time or place to get into it, but I wanted to shout wild-eyed at the entire party: "WAKE UP, EVERYONE! DON'T LET YOUR LIVES SLIDE BY!"

Back in my old life, I appreciated what I had. I remember an early dawn moment when I lay in bed and realized I could hear all the warm creatures in the house breathing while they slept: the loving spouse next to me, the tiny dog snoring at the foot of the bed, the toddler a few feet away in his walk-in closet bedroom. I remember sighing and thinking, *Everything is in its place, and everything is right.*

Everyone was sleeping contentedly.

My eyes might have been open, but I was also sleeping contentedly.

Now the loving spouse is gone, the tiny dog is dead, and the toddler is a big kid who wants to talk about tardigrades and long division.

Sometimes it's difficult not to be overwhelmed by the losses, and tense in fear over which beloved will be taken away next in the never-ending loss training of being human.

All you can do is be awake and hug the whole beautiful broken world close and appreciate what it is, while it is.

BALLS-DEEP IN SELF-DEV

I'm still deep in it with my self-development, but life has quieted down. I swapped my panic attacks for a daily mindfulness practice, Tinder for Insight Timer, my missing tooth for a titanium implant, and my mornings of existential dread for dawns of lap dancing for the divine. I traded in #vanlife for a midlife-crisis Miata from 1999. I traded in all the Tinderellas for a sci-fi writer with a high EQ.

But even in my afterglow calm, sometimes I'm still skittish and hypervigilant, my old scars aching. My ego gets up to its old tricks, desperately mentalizing to try to avoid discomfort.

"I love you," my boyfriend told me as we sat on his roof, basking in a San Francisco sunset.

"I love you too," I said. ". . . But I don't think it's actually ME that you love, it's just the slice of the divine in me that resonates with the slice of the divine in you, but actually you own the love you're feeling!" My mind spooled up and my nervous system leaned in. I HAVE A STRATEGY HERE!

My breathing got faster. "I can't ever take that love away from you, not ever—even if I got hit by a bus or we stopped spending time together! The love you're feeling is your own love within yourself! It's not mine!! It's not about me!!!"

"Please don't micromanage my experience of falling in love with you," my boyfriend said with a placid smile, squeezing my hand. "I'm in my late forties. At this point in my life, I think I know what I'm feeling."

"Oh," I said, tearing up with relief, my anxiety draining out of me like I'd let go of a balloon that then deflated loudly through the air, farting itself over the edge of the roof. "That makes sense. Sorry for freaking out."

I don't know that you ever fully forget the psychedelic haze of acute loss, and sometimes when I hear people I love talk about life sliding by, I get all spittle-mouthed and frantic and want to plead with them, *Open your eyes up wide and enjoy this while you can because it's temporary and fleeting and beautiful, but you must be awake enough to notice!*

That's all I can do. That's all any of us can do, really: just notice. *Holy shit! I'm not dead right now! I'm at peace! That week was so smooth that it went like clockwork.*

The clockwork of life should not have to break for us to notice time passing. I truly want to believe that you can wake up and understand how it's all so precious and fleeting, *without* a shitshow . . . but it took the most profound suffering I've ever experienced to wake me up, so what do I know? Sometimes it has to hurt so much that the pain of growth is less than the pain of staying the same.

Now I don't want to go back. I make the conscious daily decision to try to stay awake, even when life feels tedious or unbearable. I try to stay conscious enough that I can recognize the fleetingness of it all.

I remember that pre-shitshow sensation of weeks just sliding by, and I remember that it felt comfortable. Everything was in its place. All systems were go. I was happy . . . but there was also a sense of rigidity and fear. I wanted to stay happy, so could I make it stay this way. How could I lock things down? How could I ensure nothing ever changed, so the bad feelings would never happen?

Now I don't believe in happiness. I believe in peace. I believe in contentment. I believe that what we call "happiness" is just when you're in a state of peace and contentment, and your brain decides "This is good, I want it to stay like this," which is a setup for more misery. I understand now that what I used to call "happiness" was a dangerous game that led to suffering, because NOTHING stays the same.

All you can do is appreciate the peace when you've got it and make the most of the unrest when it arrives. Life burns you down sometimes and then you get to choose how to rebuild. Sometimes rebuilding involves even more dismantling.

In the years since my shitshow, I've ended up hospitalized several times, my intestines obstructed from tangles of traumatized scar tissue from prior surgeries. In the hospital, I lie quietly for hours and count my breaths as the air moves past the tube down my throat. I remind myself, "We're all gonna die, and if today's the day, at least I was awake while I was here." In the mornings, I stand next to the hospital bed and do my morning movement practice, very small and very slow. I dismantle myself even more.

Loss training never stops. That one era, that one shitshow. What's coming next year? The death of a friend? The collapse of a business? The illness of a family member? Then what are the losses for the coming decades? We know this much is guaranteed: Children grow up. Parents die. You die. *Loss training!*

It's all just practice: this breath of loss, this breath of growth, this breath of peace. Each breath is one step closer to death, and one more chance to be right here in your life, right here with me in these words, finding our afterglow together.

Onward, sweet friends.

ACKNOWLEDGMENTS

Let's start here: epic gratitude to Caroline Diezyn, my *Sh!tshow* research associate and collaborator. Caroline worked with me closely to structure this book and find the evidence-based research to help me sound less unhinged. This work would not exist without Caroline's contributions.

Second, gratitude to my editor Laura Mazer at Seal Press for believing in me when I desperately needed it. Also, genuine gratitude to all the literary agents in New York who couldn't quite see how this book would work—your thoughtful feedback helped me shape the material into something better.

Gratitude to all my former Offbeat Empire staffers for their self-directed sausage-making skills, keeping the factory churning while I worked through my shitshow grief and disorientation. These folks were so much more than coworkers, supporting me through some of my darkest moments. Gratitude also to my Lovesick Inc. colleagues who traveled with me for two months during the Lovesick Expo tour when I was at my absolute messiest.

Gratitude to the Offbeat Empire's readers and advertisers, who have patiently educated me in the trenches of language and culture and biz dev, and empowered me to support my family doing the work I love. Extra-special love to the tenacious readers who've been with me in these tangled, dense words for decades. Thank you for sheepishly introducing yourselves on random street corners and forgiving me when I impulsively hug y'all without asking first! (I'm working on my toxic masculinity.)

Gratitude to the friends who sat by my bed and held my hand and read me poetry when I was mute with grief . . . who then, once my voice came back, patiently listened to my endless, eternal, looping verbal processing. Gratitude to my Capitol Hill neighbors for being kind to me when I was puking in alleyways, and the entire city of Seattle for being disproportionately packed with healers, weirdos, and woo-woo. Gratitude to all the lovers, with an extra shout-out for the grief-stricken opera singer, the trauma-addicted gunslinger, and the teeny-tiny ob-gyn. Gratitude for Ms. C for showing me the ropes.

Gratitude to my endlessly loving parents, David and Therese, for making me the way I am (for better and for worse!). These two remarkable humans acted as pillars of support through my shit-show, and I am so grateful for their guidance, insight, friendship, and willingness to stay present with me at my worst. Gratitude in advance to my son Octavian Orion, who will read this someday and inevitably roll his eyes and be like, GAWD, MOM. Gratitude to his father for being a dedicated co-parent.

Gratitude for all my therapists and teachers, especially Atta Dawahare and Jett Psaris. Gratitude to Michael, the godslice who loves me across many multiverses not despite my complexities but because of them.

But most of all, the deepest gratitude to the momentum that moves through me, that moves through you, too. Shout-out to the universe for bringing these pieces of itself (You! Me! Us!) together in this moment to share these words. When I close my eyes, I can feel all of us here together, and it feels divine. Thank you.

SH!TSHOW READING LIST

These books were my favorite comforts and inspirations, and I can personally vouch for each one. Obviously, everyone has different on-ramps, so some of these may be less relevant to where you're at, but I truly believe that most folks can gain something from each of these titles.

GRIEF & LOSS

It's OK That You're Not OK: Meeting Grief and Loss in a Culture That Doesn't Understand by Megan Devine. The best modern take on grief. Megan pulls no punches and goes for the gut.

Unattended Sorrow: Recovering from Loss and Reviving the Heart by Stephen Levine. A more poetic take on loss from a respected educator and author focused on death and dying.

Taking the Leap: Freeing Ourselves from Old Habits and Fears by Pema Chödrön. This is a Western Buddhist take on loss and transitions, and Pema's book *When Things Fall Apart: Heart Advice for Difficult Times* is also worth reading.

PSYCHOLOGY & TRAUMA

Rock Steady: Brilliant Advice from My Bipolar Life by Ellen Forney. This graphic novel is theoretically written for folks dealing with bipolar disorder, but is full of actionable coping strategies for all of us dealing with overwhelming moods. The information is easy to understand, even when you're mid-crisis and can barely focus your eyes!

The Mindful Way Through Depression: Freeing Yourself from Chronic Unhappiness by Mark Williams, John Teasdale, Zindel Segal, and Jon Kabat-Zinn. Page 42 changed my life. Not sure what else to say.

The Upward Spiral: Using Neuroscience to Reverse the Course of Depression, One Small Change at a Time by Alex Korb. A super-practical book full of a neuroscientist's advice for how to use the same spiral of brain functions that pull you into depression, to get you back out of it.

The Body Keeps the Score: Brain, Mind, and Body in the Healing of Trauma by Bessel van der Kolk. A little dense if you're still in the thick of it, but great research. One note: the author has dealt with some #metoo accusations, so supporting his work can feel frustrating.

SPIRITUALITY

The Power of Now: A Guide to Spiritual Enlightenment and *A New Earth: Awakening to Your Life's Purpose* by Eckhart Tolle. Dudes, I know these are Oprah's Book Club picks and everyone has already told you to read them and maybe you want to duct-tape the covers because they make you feel so cliché, but really and truly, these books change lives.

How to Wake Up: A Buddhist-Inspired Guide to Navigating Joy and Sorrow by Toni Bernhard. A nice inroad for understanding Buddhist teachings from the author who wrote *How to Be Sick: A*

Buddhist-Inspired Guide for the Chronically Ill and Their Caregivers, about applying Buddhist concepts to chronic illness.

The Leap: The Psychology of Spiritual Awakening (An Eckhart Tolle Edition) by Steve Taylor. Not everyone's shitshow includes a spiritual awakening, but if yours does, this book will help you understand WTF is happening to you and why you feel so disoriented.

RELATIONSHIPS & SEX

Attached: The New Science of Adult Attachment and How It Can Help You Find—and Keep—Love by Amir Levine and Rachel S. F. Heller. Accessible, easy read for those who want to understand more about how attachment issues play out in adult relationships. It's most useful for those who skew anxious, but everyone can benefit.

Undefended Love by Jett Psaris. Let's talk about radical emotional accountability in relationships—WHOA.

How to Be an Adult in Relationships: The Five Keys to Mindful Loving by David Richo. This book posits that adult relationships should only provide about 25 percent of your emotional needs, which kinda blew my mind and then put it back together.

Come as You Are: The Surprising New Science That Will Transform Your Sex Life by Emily Nagoski. Heavily researched but easy-reading book about female sexuality, trauma, and intimacy.

AGING & MATURATION

Broken Open: How Difficult Times Can Help Us Grow by Elizabeth Lesser. Comforting personal perspectives on how your brokenness is appropriate and valuable, from the founder of the Omega Institute.

Hidden Blessings: Midlife Crisis as a Spiritual Awakening by Jett Psaris. What if your midlife crisis isn't the worst thing that ever happened to you but the most amazing opportunity to grow? Best for readers over forty.

ALGORITHMIC ORACLES:
MY FAVORITE INSTAGRAM ACCOUNTS FOR SELF-DEVELOPMENT

Each of these accounts acted as a digital divination tool for me. By the time you read this, who knows which of them will be active or whether Instagram will still be a thing, etc., so I'm including each person's name in addition to their current handle so you can hopefully track them down:

Psychologist Dr. Nicole LaPera @the.holistic.psychologist

Author Amit Pagedar @findingawareness

Astrologer Chani Nicholas @chaninicholas

Spiritual teacher Maryam Hasnaa @maryamhasnaa

Artist and author Yumi Sakugawa @yumisakugawa

REFERENCES
AND CITATIONS

Asbrand, Julia, et al. "Repeated Stress Leads to Enhanced Cortisol Stress Response in Child Social Anxiety Disorder but This Effect Can Be Prevented with CBT." *Psychoneuroendocrinology* 109 (July 24, 2019): 104352. www.ncbi.nlm.nih.gov/pubmed/31386987.

Bowlby, John. "The Bowlby-Ainsworth Attachment Theory." *Behavioral and Brain Sciences* 2, no. 4 (December 1979): 637–638. https://doi.org/10.1017/S0140525X00064955.

Brooks, Katherine. "An Illustrated Guide to the Seven Simple Ways You Can Practice Peace." *HuffPost*, November 4, 2015. www.huffingtonpost.ca/entry/there-is-no-right-way-to-meditate_n_56 3a2928e4b0411d306f00dd.

brown, adrienne maree. *Emergent Strategy: Shaping Change, Changing Worlds*. AK Press, 2017.

brown, adrienne maree. *Pleasure Activism: The Politics of Feeling Good*. AK Press, 2019.

Chödrön, Pema. *Taking the Leap: Freeing Ourselves from Old Habits and Fears*. Boulder, CO: Shambhala, 2019.

Daubenmier, Jennifer, et al. "It's Not What You Think, It's How You Relate to It: Dispositional Mindfulness Moderates the Relationship between Psychological Distress and the Cortisol Awakening Response." *Psychoneuroendocrinology* 48 (October 2014): 11–18. https://doi.org/10.1016/j.psyneuen.2014.05.012.

de Becker, Gavin. *The Gift of Fear: Survival Signals That Protect Us from Violence.* New York: Bloomsbury, 2000.

Devine, Megan. *It's OK That You're Not OK: Meeting Grief and Loss in a Culture That Doesn't Understand.* Boulder, CO: Sounds True, 2017.

Doyle, Glennon. Momastery website. https://momastery.com/blog /about-glennon/.

Durso, Geoffrey R. O., et al. "Over-the-Counter Relief from Pains and Pleasures Alike: Acetaminophen Blunts Evaluation Sensitivity to Both Negative and Positive Stimuli." *Psychological Science* 26, no. 6 (April 2015): 750–758. https://doi.org/10.1177 /0956797615570366.

Forney, Ellen. *Rock Steady: Brilliant Advice from My Bipolar Life.* Seattle: Fantagraphics, 2018.

Fuchs, Eberhard, and Gabriele Flügge. "Chronic Stress and Depression." In *The Handbook of Stress: Neuropsychological Effects on the Brain,* edited by Cheryl D. Conrad, 463–479. Oxford, UK: Blackwell Publishing, 2011. https://doi.org/10.1017/S0140525X00064955.

Gaynor, Mitchell L. *The Healing Power of Sound: Recovery from Life-Threatening Illness Using Sound, Voice, and Music.* Boston: Shambhala, 2002.

Gill, Bhali. "New to Visualization? Here Are 5 Steps to Get You Started."*Forbes,* June 22, 2017. www.forbes.com/sites/bhaligill/2017 /06/22/new-to-visualization-here-are-5-steps-to-get-you-started /#2abce5546e3f.

Goldsby, Tamara L., et al. "Effects of Singing Bowl Sound Meditation on Mood, Tension, and Well-being: An Observational Study." *Journal of Evidence-Based Complementary & Alternative Medicine* 22, no. 3 (2017): 401–406. https://doi.org/10.1177/2156587216668109.

Gross, Terry. "As Marriage Standards Change, A Therapist Recommends 'Rethinking Infidelity.'" NPR, December 13, 2017. www.npr.org/2017/12/13/570131890/as-marriage-standards -change-a-therapist-recommends-rethinking-infidelity.

Heelas, Paul, et al. *The Spiritual Revolution: Why Religion Is Giving Way to Spirituality.* Oxford, UK: Blackwell, 2018.

Hendriksen, Ellen. *How to Be Yourself: Quiet Your Inner Critic and Rise Above Social Anxiety.* New York: St. Martin's Griffin, 2019.

Korb, Alex. *The Upward Spiral: Using Neuroscience to Reverse the Course of Depression, One Small Change at a Time.* Oakland, CA: New Harbinger, 2015.

Kotler, Steven. "Addicted to Bang: The Neuroscience of the Gun." *Forbes,* December 18, 2012. www.forbes.com/sites/stevenkotler /2012/12/18/addicted-to-bang-the-neuroscience-of-the-gun /#32967d227eed.

LePera, Nicole. Nicole LePera website. www.nicolelepera.com.

Lesser, Elizabeth. *Broken Open: How Difficult Times Can Help Us Grow.* London: Ebury Digital, 2010.

Levine, Amir, and Rachel Heller. *Attached: Identify Your Attachment Style and Find Your Perfect Match.* New York: Rodale, 2011.

Levine, Stephen. *Unattended Sorrow: Recovering from Loss and Reviving the Heart.* Rhinebeck, NY: Monkfish, 2019.

Lickerman, Alex, and Ash ElDifrawi. *The Ten Worlds: The New Psychology of Happiness.* Deerfield Beach, FL: Health Communications, 2018.

Lipka, Michael, and Claire Gecewicz. "More Americans Now Say They're Spiritual but Not Religious." Pew Research Center, September 6, 2017. http://pewrsr.ch/2xP0Y8w.

Maxwell, December, et al. "Cathartic Ink: A Qualitative Examination of Tattoo Motivations for Survivors of Sexual Trauma." *Deviant Behavior*, (September 2019): 1–18. https://doi.org/10.1080 /01639625.2019.1565524.

Nagoski, Emily. *Come as You Are: The Surprising New Science That Will Transform Your Sex Life.* New York: Simon & Schuster, 2015.

Ozment, Katherine. *Grace Without God: The Search for Meaning, Purpose, and Belonging in a Secular Age.* New York: Harper Perennial, 2017.

Post, Stephen G. "Altruism, Happiness, and Health: It's Good to Be Good." *International Journal of Behavioral Medicine* 12, no. 2 (June 2005): 66–77. https://doi.org/10.1207/s15327558ijbm1202_4/

Psaris, Jett, and Marlena S. Lyons. *Undefended Love.* Oakland, CA: New Harbinger, 2000.

Psaris, Jett. *Hidden Blessings: Midlife Crisis as a Spiritual Awakening.* Oakland, CA: Sacred River, 2017.

Pychyl, Timothy A., and Fuschia M. Sirois. "Procrastination, Emotion Regulation, and Well-Being." In *Procrastination, Health, and Well-Being,* 163–188. London: Academic Press, 2016. https://doi .org/10.1016/B978-0-12-802862-9.00008-6.

"Rachel Yehuda—How Trauma and Resilience Cross Generations." The On Being Project, November 9, 2017. https://onbeing .org/programs/rachel-yehuda-how-trauma-and-resilience-cross -generations-nov2017/.

Raghunathan, Raj. *If You're So Smart, Why Aren't You Happy?* New York: Penguin, 2018.

Richo, David. *How to Be an Adult in Love: Letting Love in Safely and Showing It Recklessly*. Boston: Shambhala, 2013.

Romano, Tricia. "The Many Faces of Grief." The Crying Game. https://triciaromano.substack.com/p/the-many-faces-of-grief.

Rosenfeld, Arthur. "Taking Aim at Mindfulness." *HuffPost*, June 2, 2016, www.huffpost.com/entry/taking-aim-at-mindfulness_b _7498764.

Rumi, Jalal al-Din. *The Essential Rumi*. Translated by Coleman Barks. San Francisco: Harper, 1996.

Sagarin, Brad. "Never Tried BDSM? Go On, It's Good for You." *Guardian*, February 9, 2015, www.theguardian.com/commentis free/2015/feb/09/bdsm-good-for-you-fifty-shades-of-grey -relationship.

Shutan, Mary Mueller. *Managing Psychic Abilities: A Real World Guide for the Highly Sensitive Person*. Forres, UK: Findhorn, 2016.

Silverman, Stephen. "Keanu Reeves: 'I Want to Get Married.'" *People*, June 6, 2006. https://people.com/celebrity/keanu-reeves -i-want-to-get-married/.

Steel, Piers. "The Nature of Procrastination: A Meta-Analytic and Theoretical Review of Quintessential Self-Regulatory Failure." *Psychological Bulletin* 133, no. 1 (January 2007): 65–94. doi:10.1037/0033-2909.133.1.65.

Stegemöller, Elizabeth L., et al. "Experiences of Persons with Parkinson's Disease Engaged in Therapeutic Singing." *Journal of Music Therapy* 54, no. 4 (Winter 2017): 405–431. https://doi.org /10.1093/jmt/thx012.

Taylor, Steve. *The Leap: The Psychology of Spiritual Awakening*. London: Hay House, 2017.

Thich Nhat Hanh. *Making Space: Creating a Home Meditation Practice*. Berkeley, CA: Parallax Press, 2012.

Tolle, Eckhart. *A New Earth: Awakening to Your Life's Purpose*. New York: Penguin, 2016.

Tolle, Eckhart. *The Power of Now: A Guide to Spiritual Enlightenment*. Sydney: Hachette, 2018.

van der Kolk, Bessel. *The Body Keeps the Score: Brain, Mind, and Body in the Healing of Trauma*. New York: Penguin, 2015.

Wallace, David Foster. *Infinite Jest*. Boston: Little, Brown, 1996.

Wexler, Toni. *How to Wake Up: A Buddhist-Inspired Guide to Navigating Joy and Sorrow*. Somerville, MA: Wisdom, 2013.

Williams, Anna. "Scientists Discover Neural Link Between Generosity and Happiness." Northwestern University Feinberg School of Medicine News Center, August 1, 2017. http://news.feinberg.north western.edu/2017/08/scientists-discover-neural-link-between -generosity-and-happiness.

Williams, Mark, et al. *The Mindful Way Through Depression: Freeing Yourself from Chronic Unhappiness*. New York: Guilford, 2007.

Williams, Zoe. "Out of the Traps." *Guardian*, June 11, 2005. www .theguardian.com/film/2005/jun/11/features.weekend.

Wolynn, Mark. *It Didn't Start with You: How Inherited Family Trauma Shapes Who We Are and How to End the Cycle*. New York: Penguin, 2017.

JENNY JIMENEZ

Author of the three editions of *Offbeat Bride* and the art book *PROS BEFORE BROS*, **Ariel Meadow Stallings** likes to poke at the soft places of overlap between culture, identity, relationships, and self-development.

She got her start in the mid-'90s editing a rave magazine, graduated the Columbia Publishing Course in 2001, and then spent most of the '00s as a corporate copywriter for the *Seattle Times*, Microsoft, and Amazon.

Since 2009, Ariel's focused her time on her bootstrapped digital media company, the Offbeat Empire LLC. Her work has reached about fifty million people through her web and social media properties like *offbeatbride.com* and *offbeathome.com*. Ariel's projects and writing have been featured by dozens of publications and media outlets including the *New York Times*, the *Guardian*, and *The Today Show*.

Ariel divides her time between Seattle and San Francisco, and if she's not writing or reading with her son, chances are good that she's dancing, on a long walk, or happy crying. You can find her online and introduce yourself at *findyourafterglow.com*.